Fundamentals of Property Tax Collection Law in North Carolina

Christopher B. McLaughlin

2011

Reflects all major legislative changes to the Machinery Act and related statutes through June 2011

The School of Government at the University of North Carolina at Chapel Hill works to improve the lives of North Carolinians by engaging in practical scholarship that helps public officials and citizens understand and improve state and local government. Established in 1931 as the Institute of Government, the School provides educational, advisory, and research services for state and local governments. The School of Government is also home to a nationally ranked graduate program in public administration and specialized centers focused on information technology, environmental finance, and civic education for youth.

As the largest university-based local government training, advisory, and research organization in the United States, the School of Government offers up to 200 courses, seminars, and specialized conferences for more than 12,000 public officials each year. In addition, faculty members annually publish approximately fifty books, book chapters, bulletins, and other reference works related to state and local government. Each day that the General Assembly is in session, the School produces the *Daily Bulletin*, which reports on the day's activities for members of the legislature and others who need to follow the course of legislation.

Michael R. Smith, Dean
Thomas H. Thornburg, Senior Associate Dean
Frayda S. Bluestein, Associate Dean for Faculty Development
Todd A. Nicolet, Associate Dean for Operations
Ann Cary Simpson, Associate Dean for Development
Bradley G. Volk, Associate Dean for Administration

FACULTY

Gregory S. Allison
David N. Ammons
Ann M. Anderson
A. Fleming Bell, II
Maureen M. Berner
Mark F. Botts
Michael Crowell
Shea Riggsbee Denning
James C. Drennan
Richard D. Ducker
Joseph S. Ferrell
Alyson A. Grine
Norma Houston
Cheryl Daniels Howell
Jeffrey A. Hughes

Willow S. Jacobson
Robert P. Joyce
Kenneth L. Joyner
Diane M. Juffras
Dona G. Lewandowski
James M. Markham
Janet Mason
Christopher B. McLaughlin
Laurie L. Mesibov
Kara A. Millonzi
Jill D. Moore
Jonathan Q. Morgan
Ricardo S. Morse
C. Tyler Mulligan
David W. Owens

William C. Rivenbark
Dale J. Roenigk
John Rubin
Jessica Smith
Karl W. Smith
Carl W. Stenberg III
John B. Stephens
Charles Szypszak
Shannon H. Tufts
Vaughn Upshaw
Aimee N. Wall
Jeffrey B. Welty
Richard B. Whisnant
Gordon P. Whitaker

© 2011
School of Government
The University of North Carolina at Chapel Hill

Printed in the United States of America

24 23 22 21 20   6 7 8 9 10

ISBN 978-1-56011-681-3

Contents

Preface

This book updates and replaces William A. Campbell's seminal work, *Property Tax Collection in North Carolina*, the most recent edition of which was published more than a decade ago. Professor Campbell's enduring scholarship served as both a foundation and an inspiration for this book.

Several chapters included herein were previously published as School of Government *Property Tax Bulletins*. While those bulletins will remain available free of charge on the School of Government's website, their content has been updated and expanded for publication in book format. This book reflects all major legislative changes to the Machinery Act and related statutes through June 2011.

Christopher B. McLaughlin
June 2011

Acknowledgments

I am indebted to my School of Government faculty colleagues Shea Denning, Ken Joyner, and Kara Millonzi for generously sharing their tax and finance wisdom and for never losing their patience with my incessant questions. My friends at the North Carolina Department of Revenue's Local Government Division, especially David Baker and Lee Harris, were always available to discuss particularly knotty tax problems. Without their input, this book would have suffered greatly.

I also owe thanks to the hundreds of dedicated local government tax professionals across North Carolina with whom I have had the pleasure of working and from whom I have learned much over the past three years. I am continually impressed by the dedication of these local government officials to the property tax profession, in particular Valerie Curry, Neal Dixon, Lorie Domnas, Stan Duncan, Pat Goddard, Jo Roberson, David Reid, Pete Rodda, Kim Simpson, and the many other talented leaders of the North Carolina Tax Collectors Association and the North Carolina Assessing Officers Association.

Most importantly, I thank my wife, Lynn Leubuscher, for her love and friendship.

Chapter 1

Property Tax Collection Administration

This chapter discusses the key legal issues involved in property tax collection administration, including appointment of the tax collector, public record requirements, and settlement.

1. What is the Machinery Act?

The collection of property tax statutes found in Subchapter II of Chapter 105 of the North Carolina General Statutes (hereinafter G.S.) is commonly referred to as the Machinery Act because it is intended "to provide the machinery for the listing, appraisal, and assessment of property and the levy and collection of taxes on property by counties and municipalities."[1] Every two years, the North Carolina Department of Revenue issues a new print version of the Machinery Act, annotated with references to court cases interpreting the statutes.[2] The most up-to-date version of the Machinery Act can be found on the webpages of the North Carolina General Assembly at www.ncga.state.nc.us/gascripts/statutes/Statutes.asp, which allows for easy searching by statute number or key words.

2. Who appoints the tax collector?

The governing board, meaning the county commissioners or city/town council, unless there are local bills or charter provisions to the contrary. Several municipalities have received authorization through their charters

---

1. G.S. 105-272.

2. The next version is scheduled to be printed after the close of the 2011 legislative session.

for the tax collector to be appointed by the town/city manager rather than the governing board.[3] Until recently some counties elected their tax collectors, but all one hundred counties now fill that position by appointment.[4]

Tax collectors must be appointed for a specific term of one or more years to be determined by the governing board.[5] Although the Machinery Act does not mandate any specific length of term, two- or four-year terms are most common across the state. The board also has the authority to set the tax collector's compensation, which can be based on salary or commissions or a combination of both.[6]

The Machinery Act requires municipalities to appoint tax collectors, meaning that even those municipalities that rely on counties to collect their property taxes should still appoint a tax collector.[7] The appointed individual is often the county tax collector but also could be a municipal employee who is ordered by the governing board to delegate his or her property tax collection duties to the county and retains collection authority only for other taxes, such as occupancy taxes or privilege license taxes.

3. Who may serve as tax collector?

The basic requirement to serve as tax collector is not very restrictive: the candidate must simply be "a person of character and integrity whose experience in business and collection work is satisfactory to the governing board."[8]

---

3. See, e.g., Charter of the Town of Tarboro, 1995 N.C. Sess. Laws ch. 73, and Charter of the City of Elizabeth City, S.L. 2001-227.

4. Avery County was the last remaining county to elect its tax collector. As the result of a recent local bill, Avery County will appoint individuals to that position after the elected tax collector's current term ends in 2012. S.L. 2009-75.

5. G.S. 105-349(a).

6. G.S. 105-349(d). Commissions for tax collectors are increasingly rare. If paid, they must be deducted from the taxes collected before they are turned over to the local government's general fund. The commissions cannot be added to the taxes owed by taxpayers. For example, assume a collector is paid a commission of 1 percent on all taxes collected. If a $100 tax bill is paid in full, the collector would keep 1 percent and the local government would get $99. The taxpayer could not be required to pay an additional 1 percent on top of the $100 taxes owed to satisfy the commission payment.

7. G.S. 105-349 uses the term "shall appoint," not "may appoint," meaning the appointment of a tax collector is not optional for a local government that levies property taxes.

8. G.S. 105-349(b).

Unlike county tax assessors, tax collectors are not subject to any educational requirements.[9] The North Carolina Tax Collectors' Association administers a certification process for collectors, which is highly recommended for collectors and sometimes required by governing boards.[10] At present, however, certification is not required by the Machinery Act.

The individual appointed as tax collector cannot begin work without a bond "conditioned upon his [or her] honesty and faithful performance."[11] This bond essentially is an insurance policy for the local government against losses caused by the tax collector's negligent or fraudulent conduct. It must cover all taxes charged to the tax collector for collection, both current year taxes and prior year taxes, although the specific dollar amount of the bond may be determined by the governing board.[12] A tax collector must obtain an individual bond even if the local government already has in place a "blanket" performance bond for all of its employees. Normally the premium for this individual bond is paid by the local government rather than by the employee.

The office of tax collector is one of the few that may be held simultaneously with another appointed or elected public position. In general, the North Carolina Constitution prohibits dual-office holding.[13] However, the Machinery Act exempts the tax collector position from this prohibition and permits a tax collector to hold one other elected or appointed position.[14] Combined with an identical exemption for county tax assessors,[15] this exemption allows for the increasingly popular practice of appointing

---

9. G.S. 105-294(b) requires assessors to possess a high school diploma or five years of related employment experience and to pass four specific tax courses and a comprehensive exam conducted by the N.C. Department of Revenue. Once certified by the Department of Revenue, assessors are subject to a continuing education requirement. G.S. 105-294(d).

10. The certification requirements are available at www.nctca.org/content/getting-certified. In general, the process requires two years of experience, four initial tax courses, and annual continuing education.

11. G.S. 105-349(c). It is a criminal offense for a board member to vote to deliver the tax receipts for collection to a tax collector who has not obtained the required bond. G.S. 105-352(d)(1).

12. G.S. 105-352(b)(4).

13. N.C. Const. art. VI, § 9.

14. G.S. 105-349(e).

15. G.S. 105-296(f) authorizes dual-office holding by assessors.

one individual as both county tax collector and assessor in a joint position called "tax administrator" or "tax director."[16]

The dual-office-holding authority for tax collectors is subject to two limitations. First, a tax collector may not serve on that local government's governing board. Second, a tax collector may not also serve as that local government's finance officer unless the North Carolina Local Government Commission determines that sufficient internal controls exist to prevent improper handling of public funds.[17]

4. Must the local government appoint a deputy tax collector?

No. This position is entirely optional. The local government *may* appoint one or more deputy tax collectors, each of whom must be bonded and may be granted the same authority a tax collector has to employ enforced collection remedies.[18] Some tax offices have individuals who hold the title of deputy tax collector but have not been formally appointed to the position. This approach is acceptable so long as all involved realize that these individuals are not authorized to sign notices of attachment or to levy upon personal property. Only a duly appointed tax collector or deputy tax collector may exercise that collection authority.

5. Is the tax collector required to take an oath?

Yes, as are deputy tax collectors. It is the same oath required by the North Carolina Constitution for all elected and appointed officials with the additional affirmation that the tax collector "will not allow my actions as tax col-

---

16. The joint position of tax administrator may create concerns if a county also collects taxes for its municipalities and those municipalities each appoint the county tax collector as the municipal tax collector. That situation would result in the tax administrator holding three (or more) appointed offices, in violation of the Machinery Act and the N.C. Constitution. The solution seems to be for municipalities to appoint their own tax collectors with limited authority even if they contract with the county for tax collection.

17. G.S. 105-349(e) uses the terms "treasurer or chief accounting officer," but at both the county and municipal levels those positions are more commonly conflated as "finance officer."

18. G.S. 105-349(f).

lector to be influenced by personal or political friendships or obligations."[19] Failure to take the oath is grounds for removal and/or a $500 fine.[20]

6. How may a tax collector be removed from office?

A tax collector may be removed from office in the middle of a term only by the governing board and only for "good cause" after the opportunity for a hearing before the board.[21] The Machinery Act does not define the term "good cause," but similar statutory provisions covering other appointed officials elsewhere in the General Statutes suggest that adequate grounds for removal include inefficiency, neglect of duties, misconduct in office, violation of state conflict of interest laws, violation of written policies adopted by the governing board, and commission of a felony or other crime involving "moral turpitude."[22] These grounds mirror the general consensus from other states that use similar language in their removal statutes. In the words of one respected authority, "good cause" is generally viewed as requiring a ground that "specifically relates to and affects the administration of the office and must be restricted to something of a substantial nature directly affecting the rights and interests of the public."[23]

7. What happens if the tax collector leaves office before the end of the term?

Regardless of whether the tax collector quits or is removed for cause, the governing board must either appoint a qualified individual to serve as tax collector for the remainder of the term[24] or make "temporary arrangements"

---

19. G.S. 105-349(g) and N.C. Const. art. VI, § 7.

20. G.S. 128-5.

21. G.S. 105-349(a). No hearing is required if the tax collector is removed for failing to obtain the required bond or make a settlement for the prior tax year as required under G.S. 105-352(b) for the board to deliver the new tax receipts for collection.

22. G.S. 130A-35(g) (grounds for removing county board of health members) and G.S. 160A-553 (grounds for removing members of municipal parking authority).

23. 63C Am. Jur. 2d *Public Officers and Employees* § 181 (2009).

24. G.S. 105-349(a).

Figure 1A. Form for Order of Collection Required by the Machinery Act

State of North Carolina
County (or City or Town) of ____
To the Tax Collector of the County (or City or Town) of _________________________________:

You are hereby authorized, empowered, and commanded to collect the taxes set forth in the
tax records filed in the office of _________________ and in the tax receipts herewith delivered
to you, in the amounts and from the taxpayers likewise therein set forth. Such taxes are hereby
declared to be a first lien upon all real property of the respective taxpayers in the County (or City
or Town) of _________________ , and this order shall be a full and sufficient authority to direct,
require, and enable you to levy on and sell any real or personal property of such taxpayers, for
and on account thereof, in accordance with law.

Witness my hand and official seal, this _____ day of _________________ , _________

_____________________________________ (Seal)
Chairman, Board of Commissioners of
_____________________________________ County
(Mayor, City (or Town) of _________________)
Attest:

____
Clerk of Board of Commissioners of _________________________ County
(Clerk of the City (or Town) of _____________________________________)

---

for the collection of taxes.[25] These temporary arrangements could be the
appointment of an interim tax collector or reliance on an appointed deputy
tax collector until a replacement tax collector is appointed. Either way, the
individual given temporary responsibility for tax collection must be bonded
to the same extent as a tax collector. Before a new collector begins his or her
duties, either the departing tax collector or the finance officer must make a
settlement for all taxes that were charged to the departing tax collector for
collection.[26] See Question 11 below for more about the settlement process.

---

25. G.S. 105-373(e). See also G.S. 105-352(c), which mandates the appointment
of a "special collector" if the tax collector has not satisfied the bonding and prior-
year settlement requirements by the time the governing board is ready to deliver the
current year's tax receipts for collection. The cost of the special collector's bond and
compensation may be deducted from the compensation of the tax collector.

26. G.S. 105-373(d).

8. When is the tax collector authorized to collect taxes?

If a local government intends to levy property taxes for a given fiscal year, the governing body must adopt a budget ordinance including those taxes by July 1.[27] Once the tax rate is set, the local government can produce tax receipts for all taxable property in the jurisdiction. The tax receipts are the records that list all of the relevant taxation details, including each property's assessed value, the applicable tax rate (or rates for property subject to special district taxes), and the total amount of taxes owed on each property.[28] The receipts are created based on information provided by the assessor and his or her staff.

After the tax receipts are created but no later than September 1, the governing board must adopt an order charging the tax collector with the obligation to collect the taxes included in those receipts.[29] This "order of collection" has the same effect as a court judgment against the jurisdiction's taxpayers, meaning tax collectors may use collection remedies against personal property, such as attachment and garnishment, and levy without additional involvement by the courts.[30] The Machinery Act requires that the order of collection be in a form similar to that presented in Figure 1A.[31]

After the governing board adopts the order of collection, the tax collector becomes obligated to "employ all lawful means" to collect the taxes covered by the order.[32]

Payments received before the tax receipts are delivered by the board to the tax collector are considered "prepayments."[33] Tax offices need not accept prepayments until the budget estimate has been filed with the clerk of the

---

27. G.S. 159-13(c).

28. See G.S. 105-320 for a complete list of the items that must be included on tax receipts.

29. G.S. 105-321(b) (order of collection); G.S. 105-352(a) (September 1 deadline).

30. See G.S. 105-366 (remedies against personal property generally), G.S. 105-367 (levy and sale of tangible personal property), and G.S. 105-368 (attachment and garnishment of intangible personal property, such as bank accounts and wages). Foreclosure, the collection remedy aimed at real property, requires a court order before the real property can be sold to satisfy outstanding taxes. G.S. 105-374 (mortgage-style foreclosure) and G.S. 105-375 (in rem foreclosures).

31. G.S. 105-321(b).

32. G.S. 105-350(1).

33. G.S. 105-359(a).

governing board, which should occur by June 1.[34] After that point, the tax office must accept prepayments despite the fact that the final tax rate has not yet been set or the collector charged with the taxes for the coming year. For more on how to calculate and account for prepayments, see Question 8 of Chapter 3.

9. What tax records are subject to disclosure under public records law?

The subject of public records law can fill an entire book.[35] For the purposes of this chapter, the most important rule for tax collectors to remember is that all records and information compiled by the state and local governments are "property of the people."[36] Public records broadly defined are all documentary materials, regardless of physical form or characteristics, made or received in connection with the lawful transaction of public business by any state or local agency.[37] This includes paper documents, photographs, e-mails, voicemail recordings, and computer files.

Public records must be made available for inspection and copying unless a statute specifically exempts a record from the disclosure requirements.[38] In other words, the default rule is that all government records are open for inspection and copying unless the government can point to a statute that provides otherwise.

There are three important categories of local tax information that state law makes confidential and exempt from disclosure. They are:

1. records that show income or gross receipts, such as circuit breaker or elderly and disabled homestead exclusion applications;[39]

---

34. G.S. 159-11(b) (filing of annual budget estimate).

35. For a detailed examination of this topic, see David M. Lawrence, *Public Records Law for North Carolina Local Governments*, 2d ed. (Chapel Hill: UNC School of Government, 2009).

36. G.S. 132-1(b).

37. G.S. 132-1(a).

38. G.S. 132-1(b).

39. G.S. 153A-98 (counties); G.S. 160A-168 (municipalities). Records containing income information are not public records and therefore not subject to disclosure requirements. As a result, a government is permitted but not required to disclose these records after redacting (eliminating) the income information.

2. inventory lists, statements of assets and liabilities, and similar information submitted by taxpayers during the listing and appraisal process;[40] and

3. Social Security numbers and other "personal identifying information," such as bank account numbers and drivers license numbers.[41]

Otherwise, tax records generally are considered public records and cannot be withheld from disclosure simply because a taxpayer—or perhaps even a member of the governing board—would prefer to keep certain information private. Tax values, tax payments records, and even photographs of residences made for appraisal purposes are all subject to public disclosure.

As county tax office websites proliferate, complaints from taxpayers about public access via the Internet continue to grow. Because counties are under no obligation to make their tax records available via the Web, those counties that maintain websites could choose to limit the information available on those sites. Any public records excluded from the website would still need to be available in person from the tax office, however. And the website should clearly indicate what types of records are excluded so that users are not misled into thinking that the website contains the entire universe of public county tax records.

A government must provide copies of nonconfidential public records for "free or minimal cost."[42] As a result, a government normally may charge only the actual cost of the copy, not any overhead costs associated with responding to the request. For example, if the response to a public record request requires a government to produce copies of 100 pages of records, the government may charge the requester the actual cost of those 100 copies. Presumably that actual cost would be a few cents per page. The government could not charge the requester for the time spent by an employee making those copies or for the electricity used making the copies or for a portion of the lease payment on the copying machine that made the copies.

If the response to a public records request would require "extensive use of information technology or extensive clerical or supervisory assistance,"

---

40. G.S. 105-296(h).

41. G.S. 132-1.10. Records containing Social Security numbers and other personal identifying information are still public records subject to disclosure. If such records are requested, the government *must* disclose the records after redacting the confidential information.

42. G.S. 132-6.2(b).

then the responding government may charge a "special service charge" to produce the requested documents.[43] This special service charge may include labor and other overhead.

10. How long must tax records be retained?

That a document is a public record and therefore subject to disclosure under public records law does not mean that the tax office must keep the record forever. The question of retention is separate from the question of disclosure.

Minimum standards for records retention are set by the Division of Archives and History in the North Carolina Department of Cultural Resources (DCR) in its *Records Retention and Disposition Schedules* for county and municipal governments.[44] The sections that concern tax administration identify well over 100 different types of tax records and their retention requirements. For example, attachment and garnishment records must be retained for three years after final settlement, while tax revaluation records must be maintained for the lesser of either ten years or two revaluation cycles. Records with only short-term reference value, such as appointment reminders and drafts of letters, can be destroyed after their reference value ends.

Destruction of public records in violation of the DCR retention schedules is a criminal act.[45] Before destroying any public record in reliance on these schedules, tax officials should confirm that their governing board has approved this act by formally adopting the DCR retention schedules. The DCR retention schedules create *minimum* standards, meaning that local governments are free to adopt retention periods longer than, but not shorter than, those issued by the DCR.

---

43. *Id.*
44. Available at www.records.ncdcr.gov/local/default.htm.
45. G.S. 121-5(b) and G.S. 132-3.

11. What is the settlement, and when is one required?

The annual settlement is the tax collector's final accounting to the governing board for work over the past tax year. It is both a financial report detailing all of the funds received by the tax collector and a summary of the collection practices and remedies employed by the tax collector. In some respects, the annual end-of-fiscal-year settlement is simply a more formal and final version of the collection reports that the tax collector is required to provide the governing board each month.[46]

The annual settlement consists of several reports that must be made after the close of the fiscal year on June 30 but before being charged with taxes for the new fiscal year.[47] These reports are

1. a list of delinquent property taxes from the most recent fiscal year owed by taxpayers who own real property in the jurisdiction,[48]

2. a list of delinquent property taxes from the most recent fiscal year owed by taxpayers who do not own real property in the jurisdiction,[49]

3. a financial report for the most recent fiscal year's taxes that balances all of the amounts charged to the tax collector for collection, including taxes, discoveries, penalties, fees and interest, against (i) the amounts actually collected, (ii) taxes that are a lien on real

---

46. The tax collector's duties include submitting to the governing board at each of its regular meetings "a report of the amount [he or she] has collected on each year's taxes with which [he or she] is charged, the amount remaining uncollected, and the steps [he or she] is taking to encourage or enforce payment of uncollected taxes." G.S. 105-350(7).

47. G.S. 105-373(a). The order of collection and the new fiscal year's tax receipts must be charged to the tax collector by September 1. G.S. 105-152(a). If the new fiscal year's tax receipts are charged to the tax collector before the prior year's settlement occurs, the governing board risks personal financial and criminal liability. G.S. 105-352(d).

48. G.S. 105-373(a)(1)(a). The same list must be provided to the governing board in February and then advertised. G.S. 105-369(a). For a detailed discussion of the advertising requirement, see Chapter 9.

49. G.S. 105-373(a)(1)(b). In connection with this list, the tax collector must state under oath that he or she has made "diligent efforts" to collect these taxes from the taxpayers' personal property, including efforts to make collection outside of the taxing unit pursuant to G.S. 105-364. This list may be advertised, but the cost of that advertisement cannot be passed along to the delinquent taxpayers as can the cost of advertising the list of delinquent taxes that are a lien upon real property.

property, (iii) taxes that were discounted, (iv) taxes that were released or placed on the insolvents list by the governing board (see Question 13 below for more on the insolvents list), and (v) taxes that are on appeal to the Property Tax Commission.[50]

Uncollected taxes from the most recent fiscal year can either be "recharged" to the tax collector or charged to another person for collection.[51] Most jurisdictions make the tax collector responsible for the collection of these "old" delinquent taxes, but some appoint a deputy tax collector solely for this purpose. Whoever is so charged must provide an end-of-year accounting for these taxes at the close of the next fiscal year and every year after that unless and until the governing board relieves him or her from the collection obligation through the insolvents process described below.[52]

In addition to the annual end-of-fiscal-year settlements, "transitional" settlements are required (i) when a tax collector's term ends in the middle of the fiscal year and the tax collector will not be reappointed[53] and (ii) when a vacancy occurs in the middle of a tax collector's term due to resignation or removal.[54] These transitional settlements are important for both the departing and incoming tax collectors. Departing tax collectors wish to demonstrate that they left their offices on sound financial footing. Incoming tax collectors want any previously existing financial problems documented so that they are not held responsible for misconduct that did not occur on their watch. Importantly, the fact that the governing board approves a settlement does not absolve the departing tax collector from liability for irregularities existing at the time of settlement but discovered at a later date.[55] In other words, a tax collector cannot escape responsibility for misconduct simply by hiding irregularities from the governing board at settlement time.

---

50. G.S. 105-373(a)(3). Tax collectors "may not seek collection of taxes or enforcement of a tax lien" relating to taxes that are under appeal to the Property Tax Commission. G.S. 105-378(d).

51. G.S. 105-373(a)(4). If another person is given the responsibility for collecting past years' delinquent taxes, he or she must "give bond satisfactory to the governing body" just as does the tax collector.

52. G.S. 105-373(b).

53. G.S. 105-373(c).

54. G.S. 105-373(d).

55. G.S. 105-373(e).

12. When and how is the tax collection percentage calculated?

The Machinery Act does not require the tax collector to calculate a collection percentage. That said, every jurisdiction that levies property taxes calculates and relies on this statistic for two important purposes. First, local government governing boards and managers use the statistic to evaluate the tax collector's performance. Second, the Local Government Budget and Fiscal Control Act[56] requires that the collection percentage be used as a benchmark when budgeting for the next fiscal year. When calculating its budget for next year, a local government cannot assume it will collect a higher percentage of its tax levy than it did this year.[57]

Collection percentages are calculated multiple times throughout the tax year. Tax collectors maintain running year-to-date collection percentages for the current fiscal year's taxes to use in their monthly reports to their governing boards.[58] Budget officials will need the current fiscal year's collection percentage in April or May to estimate property tax collections for the next fiscal year. And the tax collector will want to provide the board with a final collection percentage for the just-ended fiscal year when the collector creates the annual settlement reports in July or August.[59]

The Tax Collection Percentage for Budget Purposes

Of the various collection percentage calculations, the one used for budget purposes is the most perplexing because of its timing. The relevant statute reads, "The estimated percentage of collection of property taxes shall not be greater than the percentage of the levy actually realized in cash as of June 30 during the preceding year."[60] The intent of this provision was to prevent budget officials from overestimating tax collections when they balance the

---

56. G.S. Chapter 159, Article 3.

57. G.S. 159-13(b)(6) ("The estimated percentage of collection of property taxes [for the budgeted year] shall not be greater than the percentage of the levy actually realized in cash as of June 30 during the preceding fiscal year.").

58. G.S. 105-350(7) requires monthly reports of the amount collected on each year's taxes, the remaining uncollected, and the steps being taken to "encourage or enforce payment of uncollected taxes." While a collection percentage is not explicitly made part of this report, it is almost always included.

59. Although G.S. 105-373, the settlement statute, does not explicitly require the tax collector to produce a collection percentage, nearly all tax collectors do so in order to best inform their boards about the tax office's performance throughout the year.

60. G.S. 159-13(6).

budget for the next fiscal year. In other words, when a local government prepares its budget for the next fiscal year it cannot assume that it will collect a higher percentage of its tax levy than it did in the current fiscal year.[61]

The timing concern arises of course because budgets are normally prepared before the new fiscal year begins.[62] Budget officials will seek a collection percentage from the tax collector before the current fiscal year ends, usually in April or May. How can the tax collector provide a collection percentage for a fiscal year that is yet to end?

Some local governments avoid the timing problem by using the collection percentage from the last complete fiscal year rather than the current, ongoing fiscal year when making a budget for the coming fiscal year. For example, in April of 2012 a county might use the collection percentage from the completed 2010–2011 fiscal year when preparing its 2012–2013 budget. However, this approach misinterprets the phrase "the preceding fiscal year" as used in G.S. 159-13(6). The phrase is used from the perspective of the fiscal year *for which* the budget is created, not the fiscal year *in which* the budget is created. In the above example, the county should use an estimated collection percentage for the 2011–2012 fiscal year when creating the 2012–2013 budget. Using the collection percentage from the 2010–2011 fiscal year for the 2012–2013 budget would violate the statutory mandate and inappropriately base the coming year's budget on statistics and economic conditions that would be more than a year out of date by the time the budget takes effect.

The best approach is to use an estimated collection percentage for the current unfinished fiscal year that is based on the current year-to-date collection percentage plus an adjustment for estimated collections through June 30. This adjustment could be based on actual collections for the same time period in the previous year or on the average amount of collections in the same time period for the past several fiscal years. Regardless of the method chosen, the tax collector must provide to the budget officials a tax collection percentage that reflects twelve months of collections, not just a collection percentage that reflects a partial fiscal year.

For example, assume that on May 1, 2011, the budget officer asks the tax collector for the tax collection percentage to be used in the budget for the

---

61. See David M. Lawrence, *Local Government Finance in North Carolina*, 2d ed. (Chapel Hill: UNC School of Government, 1990), 140.

62. G.S. 159-11(b) requires that the budget for the coming fiscal year be submitted to the governing board by June 1.

2011–2012 fiscal year. The tax collector should provide the budget officer with an estimated collection percentage for the entire 2010–2011 fiscal year, despite the fact that two months remain. This estimate should include actual collections from July 1, 2010, through May 1, 2011, plus the collections that are expected to be received from May 2, 2011, through June 30, 2011.

The Tax Collection Percentage Calculation

In theory, the collection percentage calculation is simple. The numerator is the total amount of taxes collected as of the close of business on June 30 for the just-ended fiscal year's taxes. The denominator is the total amount of taxes levied during the just-ended fiscal year. Divide the numerator by the denominator and you have the collection percentage for the just-ended fiscal year.

In practice, the calculation can become quite complex. A number of the complicating factors are addressed below. But keep in mind that the budgetary purpose of the collection rate is to provide an estimate of how much of next year's principal tax levy will be paid by taxpayers within the next fiscal year. As a result, the general rule to follow when calculating the collection rate is to include only those taxes and payments that are part of the *principal tax levy* for the fiscal year in question.

Appeals to the county board of equalization and review (BOER) and the Property Tax Commission (PTC)

The Machinery Act forbids the use of enforced collection actions for taxes that are under appeal to the BOER and the PTC.[63] For this reason, many collectors exclude taxes under appeal from the total amount of taxes levied for the fiscal year. While logical from the collector's perspective, this approach distorts the calculation for use as a budgeting tool. Excluding these taxes inappropriately inflates the collection percentage for next year's budget because it ignores the fact that some taxes will be appealed and therefore uncollectible every year.

---

63. G.S. 105-378(d). Prior to 2011, this provision applied only to PTC appeals. S.L. 2011-3 extended the ban on enforced collections to include taxes appealed to the BOER.

Bankruptcies

Taxes owed by taxpayers subject to a pending bankruptcy proceeding are exempt from enforced collection actions due to the automatic stay imposed in all bankruptcy cases.[64] Accordingly, some tax collectors exclude bankruptcies from their collection percentage calculation for the same reason they exclude property tax appeals. But just like PTC appeals, bankruptcies should be included in the collection rate percentage because excluding them would inappropriately assume that the local government will not experience any uncollectible bankruptcy filings next year.

Interest

Because interest is not part of the principal tax levy, it should not be included in the collection rate percentage calculation. The denominator should not include any accrued interest nor should the numerator include any interest payments.

Fees and Costs

Advertising fees, service fees, and foreclosure costs should be excluded from the collection rate calculation for the same reason interest should be excluded. None of these additional charges are part of the principal tax levy, and therefore they should not affect the collection rate for budgetary purposes.

Releases

Because releases reduce the principal tax levy, any taxes that were released by either the board of equalization and review or by the local government's governing board should be removed from the total tax levy (the denominator) used for the collection rate calculation.

Registered Motor Vehicle Taxes

Under the system in place as of this writing, there is a lag between the application for/renewal of a registration, the notification of that registration by the Division of the Motor Vehicles to the county assessor, and the actual billing of taxes on the motor vehicle being registered. To reflect this lag, the Local Government Budget and Fiscal Control Act mandates that for

---

64. For more details on property taxes and bankruptcy, see Chapter 16.

budgetary purposes the collection rate calculation should include in the tax levy (the denominator) only those motor vehicle taxes that were levied by March 31.[65] But the statute does not define exactly which RMV taxes meet this deadline. The Machinery Act states that a tax on a registered motor vehicle is generally part of the tax levy for the fiscal year in which the tax becomes due.[66] Taxes on most registered motor vehicles become due the first of the fourth month after a registration is applied for or renewed.[67] Taken collectively, it appears that the statutes require a collector to include in the tax levy for purposes of calculating the collection rate all taxes on registered motor vehicles that became due between July 1 and March 31. This approach would capture all new registrations and renewals from the previous March through November. However, the total amount of tax collections (the numerator in the collection rate calculation) should include all payments received as of June 30 for the nine-month motor vehicle levy. Essentially, the Local Government Budget and Fiscal Control Act allows collectors twelve months to collect nine months of motor vehicle taxes for purposes of calculating a collection rate.

Regardless, many if not most collectors across the state use twelve months of RMV levies when calculating the collection percentage. Obviously, if they are making the calculation in April or May they will be estimating RMV levies for the remainder of the fiscal year. Although this approach does not follow the specific procedure proscribed in the Local Government Budget and Fiscal Control Act, it is acceptable because it will produce a *lower* collection percentage for budgeting purposes than will the statutory procedure described by the act. A local government may not rely on a collection percentage *higher* than the one calculated using statutory procedure, but it can rely on a lower percentage. Doing so will necessitate a higher tax rate than would otherwise be needed to produce the same budgeted revenue goal, however. For that reason, elected officials generally prefer using as high a collection rate as legally permitted for budgeting purposes. Collectors concerned about that issue should consider adopting the statutory approach

---

65. G.S. 159-13(b)(6).

66. G.S. 105-330.5(d). If the tax notice is prepared after the due date, then the tax is considered part of the levy for the fiscal year in which the tax notice is prepared.

67. G.S. 105-330.4(a). The four-month rule applies to taxes on vehicles under the staggered registration system. Taxes on vehicles registered under the annual or calendar year system become due on May 1.

and using only nine months of RMV levies in their collection percentage calculations.

Discoveries

If they are "made" prior to January 1, discoveries should be included in the denominator of the collection rate calculation because they are part of the principal tax levy for the year that ends the following June 30.[68] The Machinery Act considers a discovery to have been "made" on the date "the abstract is made or corrected."[69] When this provision was first drafted, tax abstracts were maintained in paper form. Counties have long since turned to electronic tax records, of course, meaning that now a discovery should be considered made on the date the tax office changes the taxpayer's electronic record to reflect the newly discovered property and its value.[70] Although a subsequent taxpayer appeal may change the value of the discovery, it will not change the date on which the discovery is deemed "made" or the tax year in which the discovery will be included.

Payments on all discoveries made prior to January 1 should be included in the numerator for the collection percentage calculation. Discoveries made on January 1 or later (and the related payments) become part of the next year's tax levy and therefore should not be included in the collection rate calculation for the just-ended fiscal year.

Discovery (Late Listing) Penalties

For a variety of reasons, these penalties should not be included in the collection rate calculation. Just like interest, fees, and costs, discovery penalties are not part of the principal tax levy, and the collection rate calculation focuses only on the principal tax levy. Further, the North Carolina Constitution requires that all penalties must be provided to the county schools and not deposited into the taxing unit's general fund.[71] The taxing unit should not

---

68. G.S. 105-312(i).

69. G.S. 105-312(d).

70. The discovery bill should be created at the same time the electronic abstract is made or changed. This bill might not be collectible for an extended period if the taxpayer appeals the discovery, but nevertheless the tax obligation exists and should be delivered to the collector for collection to begin when all appeals end.

71. See N.C. CONST. art. IX, § 7, and Shea Riggsbee Denning, "Public School Funding in the Summer of 2005: *North Carolina School Boards Association v. Moore,*" *Local*

include in its budget calculations billings or collections that do not benefit its bottom line. Finally, discovery penalties are one-time charges often waived by the governing board.[72] Including such billings in the collection percentage would inappropriately skew the budget process.

Discounts

Because discounts are reductions to the principal tax levy, they should be subtracted from the total tax levy (the denominator) in the collection percentage calculation.

Insolvents

As discussed in the next section, the insolvents list will include all taxes that are not liens on real property and unlikely to be collected. But these taxes must remain as part of the denominator for the collection percentage calculation because they remain a part of the principal tax levy for the current year.

Although interest, fees, costs, and discovery penalties should be removed from the numerator and denominator for the collection rate calculation, those figures should be communicated to budget officials so that they can anticipate these revenues when budgeting for next year. Similarly, discounts are removed from the collection rate calculation but should be communicated to budget officials so that they can account for equivalent reductions in the tax levy next year.

Sample Tax Collection Calculation

Assume that it is May 15, 2011, and Carolina County's budget officer has requested the current year's tax collection rate for use in the budget process. The relevant statistics are below. Note there are no insolvents for the current tax year because that determination is made by the board at settlement. "RMV" stands for "registered motor vehicles." All discovery charges, penalties, and payments relate to discoveries made between July 1, 2010, and December 31, 2010.

Government Law Bulletin No. 108 (Nov. 2005), available at www.sog.unc.edu/pubs/electronicversions/pdfs/lglb108.pdf.

72. The governing board has complete discretion to waive some or all of a discovery bill, including penalties, so long as it does so before the taxpayer pays the discovery bill. G.S. 105-312(k).

2010–2011 Principal Tax Levy (real and personal, non-RMV)	$10,000,000
July 1–March 31 Principal Tax Levy (RMV)	$1,000,000
Discounts	$50,000
Releases	$30,000
Pending PTC Appeals	$40,000
Bankruptcies	$50,000
Total Collected on 2010–2011 Principal Taxes through 5/15	
(real and personal, non-RMV)	$9,800,000
(RMV)	$800,000
Estimated Payments on *all* 2010–2011 Principal Property Taxes from 5/15 to 6/30	$50,000
Interest Paid	$75,000
Interest Accrued but Unpaid	$50,000
Discoveries	$200,000
Discovery Payments	$180,000
Discovery Penalties	$25,000
Discovery Penalties Paid	$20,000
Fees and Costs Assessed	$10,000
Fees and Costs Paid	$7,000

First, calculate the total principal tax levy for 2010–2011 by adding the non-RMV tax levy, the RMV tax levy, and discoveries. Ignore interest, discovery penalties, fees, and costs because none of those items is part of the principal tax levy for budget purposes. Note that the RMV levy includes only those taxes that became due by March 31.

2010–2011 Principal Tax Levy (real and personal, non-RMV)		$10,000,000
July 1–March 31 Principal Tax Levy (RMV)	+	$1,000,000
Discoveries	+	$200,000
Total		$11,200,000

Because discounts and releases reduce the principal amount of taxes levied this year, subtract these items from this number. Ignore pending PTC appeals and bankruptcies because even though those taxes are not collectible at this time, they are still part of the principal tax levy.

		$11,200,000
Discounts Taken	−	$50,000
Releases	−	$30,000
Total Tax Levy for 2010–2011		**$11,120,000**

Next, calculate the total collections for 2010–2011 taxes by adding the actual year-to-date payments for principal taxes on non-RMV property, payments of taxes on RMVs, and payments on discoveries. Then add the estimated collections on *all* 2010–2011 principal property taxes for the remaining weeks in the current fiscal year. Ignore all payments and estimated payments for interest, discovery penalties, fees, and costs because those payments are not for principal taxes.

Total Collected on 2010–2011 Principal Taxes thru 5/15		
(real and personal, non-RMV)		$9,800,000
(RMV)	+	$800,000
Discovery Payments	+	$180,000
Estimated Payments on *all* 2010–2011 Principal Property Taxes from 5/15 to 6/30	+	$50,000
Total Collections for 2010–2011 Taxes		**$10,830,000**

Finally, divide the total collections for 2010–2011 taxes by the total tax levy for 2010–2011.

Total Collections for 2010–2011 Taxes	$10,830,000
	÷
Total Tax Levy for 2010–2011	$11,120,000
2010–2011 Tax Collection Percentage	**97.39%**

The Tax Collection Percentage for Settlement Purposes

Although not required, tax collection percentages are routinely calculated by tax collectors as part of the settlement process. The settlement collection percentage calculation should be the same as described above with one exception: there will be no need to estimate tax collections for May and June because the calculation will take place in July or August after the fiscal year has ended.

All payments for principal taxes and discoveries from the just-ended fiscal year that were received between July 1 and June 30 should be included. The best approach is to include only payments that are actually received in the tax office or in an off-site lockbox or other designated payment site by midnight on June 30. Some jurisdictions follow the "postmark rule" and include all payments that are postmarked by June 30 regardless of when they actually arrive in the tax office. While this approach is of course appropriate when calculating interest and discounts,[73] this author believes that the tax collection percentage calculation should be based on actual receipts and not postmark dates.

If the board designates certain taxpayers as insolvent for the current tax year, the taxes owed by those taxpayers must remain in the total tax levy (the denominator for the collection percentage calculation). See the next section for more details on the insolvency process.

Many tax collectors present multiple tax collection percentages to the board at settlement, an approach that is entirely appropriate. For example, a tax collector may present the basic tax collection percentage as described above but also calculate a collection percentage that takes into account those taxes that are not collectible because they are under appeal to the Property Tax Commission or are owed by taxpayers involved in pending bankruptcy proceedings. If that were done for the Carolina County example above, the tax collection rate would rise from 97.39 percent to 98.19 percent because the total tax levy (the denominator) would be reduced by the $40,000 taxes under appeal to the PTC and by the $50,000 owed by taxpayers in bankruptcy proceedings.

Tax collectors often wish to present collection percentages that include all items with which they have charged for collection. Such a calculation would include including interest, discovery penalties, fees, and costs. Tax collectors

---

73. G.S. 105-360(d).

also routinely present separate collection percentages for non-RMV taxes and RMV taxes because RMV collections usually lag well behind non-RMV collections. Also common are collection percentages for prior years' taxes: one for the most recent prior fiscal year and one for all remaining prior years' taxes up to a maximum of ten total years worth of taxes including the fiscal year that just ended. For example, in the Carolina County situation above the collector might provide one or more collection percentages for 2010–2011 taxes, a collection percentage for 2009–2010 taxes, and a cumulative collection percentage for taxes levied from 2001 through 2008.

13. What is the "insolvents list"?

Adding a taxpayer to the insolvents list is the first step for the tax collector to be relieved of responsibility from collecting a tax, a process commonly called writing off a tax. Essentially, the insolvents list is a mechanism for the governing board to conclude that the tax collector has exhausted all available options for collecting a tax.

After the tax collector provides as part of the annual settlement a list of taxpayers owing delinquent taxes that are not a lien on real property, the governing board may add any or all of those taxpayers to the insolvents list. This is usually done at the request of the tax collector after he or she has provided the required sworn statement that every remedy permitted under law has been employed in unsuccessful efforts to collect the delinquent taxes.

If the board agrees with the tax collector that the taxes cannot be collected, it can approve the request to add the taxes to the insolvent list. Doing so permits the tax collector to list these taxes as a credit in the annual settlement against the taxes with which he or she has been charged for collection. However, if the board disagrees with the tax collector and believes that further collection efforts are appropriate for some or all of these taxes, then the tax collector (and/or the entity that provided the tax collector's bond) can be held liable for the uncollected taxes. Either way, the tax should count against the tax collector's collection percentage, a calculation that is not required by the Machinery Act but has become a standard component of tax collectors' year-end reporting.

After a tax has been on the insolvents list for five years, the governing board is permitted (but not required) to relieve the tax collector of responsibility for collecting the tax. This decision does not release the *taxpayer* from responsibility for the tax: the taxpayer still owes the tax and still has a duty to pay the tax, and the tax collector must still accept payment of the tax if offered.[74] However, the tax collector responsible for the taxes need no longer include them on subsequent annual settlements. Perhaps more importantly, the tax will no longer affect that tax collector's collection percentage for prior tax years.

Because motor vehicle taxes do not create liens on real property and are generally more difficult to collect, the Machinery Act provides an expedited write-off process for these taxes. The governing board may relieve the tax collector of responsibility for the collection of motor vehicle taxes that are one or more years past due "when it appears to the board that the taxes are uncollectible."[75] Motor vehicle taxes that are written off under this provision can be removed from the tax collector's annual settlement and not counted against the applicable collection percentage.

14. Are tax collectors automatically relieved of the obligation to collect taxes that are more than ten years old?

No. The Machinery Act bars the use of enforced collection remedies for taxes that are more than ten years past due.[76] But that statute of limitations affects only the use of attachment and garnishment, levy and sale, and foreclosure. It does not automatically relieve the tax collector of the obligation to collect taxes that are more than ten years past due. The only formal method for relieving a tax collector of the collection responsibility is through the insolvents process described above.

That said, the practice in many if not most jurisdictions is for the taxing unit to write off taxes that are more than ten years old and relieve the collector from the responsibility for collecting these taxes. This is usually accomplished by "re-charging" the tax collector with only the ten most recent years of taxes each year when new property taxes are levied. Technically, this does not relieve the tax collector of responsibility for taxes more than ten years

---

74. A taxpayer can be released from the obligation to pay a particular tax only under G.S. 105-381, when the tax in question was imposed due to clerical error or was illegal. For more details on this topic, see Chapter 12.

75. G.S. 105-373(h).

76. G.S. 105-378(a).

old because the original charge of those taxes remains valid without the need for a "re-charge" of those same taxes each year.

15. What is the revenue-neutral tax rate (RNTR), and when must it be calculated?

The RNTR is a figure intended to provide taxpayers with a basis for comparing a local government's property tax rates before and after a countywide reappraisal of real property.[77] Although the calculation of the RNTR is normally the responsibility of a local government's finance or budget staff, it is helpful for tax officials to have a basic understanding of the process.[78]

The RNTR must be calculated and published whenever a reappraisal of the local government's real property occurs.[79] It represents the rate that would generate the same amount of revenue from the new postreappraisal tax base as would have been generated by the current year's tax rate had the reappraisal not occurred. In normal economic times, a local government's tax base will increase as the result of a real property reappraisal. If so, then the RNTR will be less than the tax rate for the current tax year because the same amount of revenue can be generated with a lower tax rate if the tax base grows.

In 2011, several counties conducting reappraisals experienced the extremely rare phenomenon of a shrinking tax base due to the recession. For example, Carteret County, which had last reappraised its real property near the height of the market in 2007, saw its total tax decrease by roughly

---

77. G.S. 159-11(e).

78. For a detailed analysis of the RNTR calculation process, see Christopher B. McLaughlin and William C. Rivenbark, "Statement of Revenue-Neutral Tax Rate: Questions and Answers," *Local Finance Bulletin* No. 39 (Aug. 2009), available at www.sogpubs.unc.edu/electronicversions/pdfs/lfb39.pdf.

79. Real property tax value reappraisals must occur at least every eight years. G.S. 105-286. Most counties reappraise their real property on four- or eight-year cycles. See N.C. Department of Revenue, Property Tax Division, *Sales Assessment Ratio Studies as of January 1, 2010*, available at www.dornc.com/publications/sales_assessment/2010_sales_assess_ratio.pdf (last visited May 13, 2011). If a municipality lies in more than one county, it must calculate and publish a RNTR whenever any of those counties reappraises its real property.

22 percent after its 2011 reappraisal.[80] According to experienced tax officials, only once before—Dare County in the early 1990s—had even one North Carolina county seen its tax base shrink after reappraisal. When it does, of course, that means that the RNTR will be *higher* than the current tax rate because the county would need to raise its tax rate to maintain the same revenue levels.

The RNTR must be calculated and published when a reappraisal occurs, but the local government need not adopt that rate as its tax rate for the new fiscal year. If the local governing board adopts a postappraisal tax rate that is higher than the RNTR, that means it has raised taxes on its taxpayers even if the new tax rate is lower than the current year's tax rate.

Often local governing boards choose to adopt the RNTR, which can lead taxpayers to erroneously conclude that their tax bills will not change for the new fiscal year. While adoption of the RNTR should ensure that local government's tax revenues remain constant in the aggregate, it does not guarantee that each individual tax bill will not remain constant for the new fiscal year. Taxpayers who live in areas that appreciated more than the average property in the jurisdiction usually will see increased tax bills, while taxpayers whose neighborhoods appreciated less than the average property usually will see decreases. Tax collectors whose jurisdictions adopt the RNTR should be prepared for taxpayer questions and complaints about this issue.

---

80. Conversation with Carteret County tax administrator, May 17, 2011. Henderson and Lincoln counties also experienced substantial decreases in their tax bases following their 2011 reappraisals.

Chapter 2

The Property Tax Collection Calendar

This chapter lists the key dates for the collection of property taxes on real property and personal property other than registered motor vehicles. The term "current fiscal year" refers to the fiscal year that opened on July 1 of the previous calendar year. The term "new fiscal year" refers to the fiscal year that begins on July 1 of the calendar year. For example, if the calendar were applied to 2012, the "current fiscal year" would be the 2011–2012 fiscal year that began on July 1, 2011. The "new fiscal year" would be the 2012–2013 fiscal year that begins on July 1, 2012.

If a deadline for action by taxpayers falls on a weekend or holiday, that deadline is extended to the next business day.[1] For example, if January 5 falls on a Saturday, then the last day for a taxpayer to pay taxes from the current fiscal year "at par" (in other words, without interest) would be extended to Monday, January 7. Interest would accrue on Tuesday, January 8.

Not every date relevant to property tax administration is included below. For example, on the first day of every month, an additional .75 percent interest accrues on delinquent taxes.[2] Readers seeking a more comprehensive calendar should consult the version issued by the School of Government around January 1 each year.[3]

Finally, please also remember the "postmark rule": payments sent by mail are considered received by the tax office as of the date of the United States Postal Service postmark stamped on the envelope.[4] If the postmark on a tax

---

1. G.S. 105-395.1.

2. G.S. 105-360(a)(2).

3. See, for example, Christopher B. McLaughlin, "2011 Property Tax Calendar," *Property Tax Bulletin* No. 159 (Dec. 2010), available at www.sog.unc.edu/pubs/electronicversions/pdfs/ptb159.pdf.

4. G.S. 105-360(d).

payment is before the date on which another month (or the first month) of interest accrues, then interest should not accrue on the taxes satisfied by that payment regardless of when the payment is actually received by the tax office.

January

1	Value, ownership, taxable status, and situs of real and personal property determined for the new fiscal year.[5]
	Liens for taxes from the new fiscal year attach to all real property in the taxing unit. These liens include taxes on the real property itself plus taxes on all personal property owned by the same taxpayer in the taxing unit.[6]
5	Last day to pay taxes from the current fiscal year without interest (in other words, "at par.")[7]
6	2 percent interest accrues on unpaid real and personal property taxes from the current fiscal year.[8]
	Unpaid taxes on real and personal property from the current fiscal year become delinquent and enforced collections remedies (foreclosure, attachment, levy) may begin.[9]
31	Last day of listing period for the new fiscal year. Unless this date is extended by the governing board, taxpayers must list all taxable personal property and improvements to real property by this date.[10]
	Last day for taxpayers to submit timely applications for exemptions and exclusions other than the three residential property tax relief exclusions (elderly and disabled, circuit breaker, and disabled veterans) for the new fiscal year. This application deadline is extended automatically if the listing period is extended.[11] Upon a showing of "good cause" by a taxpayer, a late application may be approved by the governing board.[12]

---

5. G.S. 105-285.
6. G.S. 105-355(a).
7. G.S. 105-360(a).
8. *Id.*
9. G.S. 105-365.1(a).
10. G.S. 105-307(a).
11. G.S. 105-282.1(a).
12. G.S. 105-282.1(a1).

February

1st Monday County tax collector must report to the county commissioners all delinquent taxes from the current fiscal year that are liens on real property.[13]

2nd Monday Municipal tax collector must report to the governing board all delinquent taxes from the current fiscal year that are liens on real property.[14]

March

1 Tax collector must advertise delinquent taxes from the current fiscal year that are liens on real property between March 1 and June 30.[15]

2 Last date to which the listing period may be extended in a nonreappraisal year.[16]

April

1 Last date to which the listing period may be extended in a reappraisal year.[17]

1st Monday Earliest date for first meeting of board of equalization and review to hear valuation, ownership, taxable status, and situs appeals for the new fiscal year. Assessor must publish three notices of this meeting at least ten days prior.[18]

May

1 Deadline for local governing board to adopt resolution approving discounts for early payment of property taxes (i.e., before September 1). Resolution must specify the amounts of the discounts and the periods of time for which they are applicable. Discount schedule must be approved by the N.C. Department of Revenue and remains in effect for all future tax years unless and until it is repealed by the local governing board.[19]

1st Monday Latest date for first meeting of board of equalization and review to hear valuation, ownership, taxable status, and

---

13. G.S. 105-369(a).

14. *Id.*

15. G.S. 105-369(c).

16. G.S. 105-307(b)(1).

17. G.S. 105-307(b)(2).

18. G.S. 105-322(e).

19. G.S. 105-360(c).

situs appeals for the new fiscal year. Assessor must publish three notices of this meeting at least ten days prior.[20]

June

1 — Budget officer must file with the governing board the proposed budget including the property tax rate for the new fiscal year by today.[21] Until that occurs, tax collector is not required to accept prepayments of taxes from the new fiscal year.[22]

Last day to submit timely applications for the three residential property tax relief exclusions (elderly and disabled, circuit breaker, and disabled veterans) for the new fiscal year.[23] Upon a showing of "good cause" by a taxpayer, a late application may be approved by the governing board.[24]

30 — Current fiscal year ends.[25]

July

1 — New fiscal year begins.[26]

Governing board should adopt final budget and property tax rate for new fiscal year by today.[27]

Last day for county board of equalization and review to adjourn in a nonreappraisal year. Taxpayers must submit appeals of current year's tax assessments before the board adjourns.[28]

After July 1 and before being charged with taxes for new fiscal year, the tax collector must make a sworn report to the governing board showing a list of unpaid taxes on real and personal property for the prior fiscal year. The tax collector must also make settlement for the taxes from the prior fiscal year before being charged with taxes for the new fiscal year.[29]

---

20. *Id.*
21. G.S. 159-11(b).
22. G.S. 105-359(b).
23. G.S. 105-277.1(c).
24. G.S. 105-282.1(a1).
25. G.S. 159-8(b).
26. *Id.*
27. G.S. 159-139(a).
28. G.S. 105-322(e) (adjournment date) and (g)(2)(a) (appeal deadline).
29. G.S. 105-373(a).

August

31   Last day to pay property taxes from the new fiscal year with a discount adopted by the governing board under G.S. 105-360(c).

September

1   Property taxes from the new fiscal year become due.[30]

Last day to initiate enforced collection remedies (foreclosure, attachment, levy) for taxes that were originally due on this date ten years prior.[31]

On or before today, tax receipts for the new fiscal year shall be delivered to tax collector. Before tax receipts are delivered, collector shall have delivered duplicate receipts for prepaid taxes to finance officer, provided a collector's bond for the new fiscal year approved by governing body, and made annual settlement for taxes from the prior fiscal year.[32]

December

1   Last day for county board of equalization and review to adjourn in a reappraisal year. Taxpayers must submit appeals of current year's tax assessments before the board adjourns.[33]

31   Last day for taxpayers to submit late applications for exemptions or exclusions for the new fiscal year.[34] Upon a showing of "good cause" by a taxpayer, a late application may be approved by the governing board.[35]

---

30. G.S. 105-360(a).

31. G.S. 105-378(a). For example, September 1, 2010, was the last day on which enforced collection remedies could begin for taxes from the 2000–2001 fiscal year that were originally due on September 1, 2000.

32. G.S. 105-352.

33. G.S. 105-322(e) (adjournment date) and (g)(2)(a) (appeal deadline).

34. G.S. 105-282.1(a1).

35. *Id.*

Payment of Property Taxes

Chapter 3

Payment of Property Taxes

This chapter discusses the law governing the payment of property taxes, including electronic payments, discounts, interest, and certificates of taxes owed.

1. What is the deadline for mailing property tax bills?

Surprisingly, the Machinery Act does not require that any type of property tax bill be prepared or distributed to taxpayers. For obvious reasons every taxing unit chooses to send bills to its taxpayers, usually in August after the governing board sets its budget and tax rate. But the failure to mail a bill does not affect the underlying tax obligation.

The Machinery Act charges all persons who own real or personal property "with notice that such property is or should be listed for taxation . . . . This notice is conclusively presumed, whether or not such persons have actual notice."[1] In other words, the fact that a property owner never receives a tax bill does not relieve that property owner from responsibility for taxes on his or her property.[2]

This chapter updates information published as *Property Tax Bulletin* No. 156 (Sept. 2010).

1. G.S. 105-348.

2. Further, G.S. 105-394 excuses mistakes made by the tax office in the listing, billing, or collection process. For more details about that provision, see Chapter 11.

2. How must property taxes be paid?

The Machinery Act requires property taxes to be paid in "existing national currency," meaning cash. Taxpayers cannot pay their taxes with deeds to real property, notes, payments in kind (i.e., bartering), or through the forgiveness of an obligation owed to the taxpayer by the taxing unit.[3] That said, numerous exceptions exist to this rule.

All local governments are permitted to accept checks and electronic payments, as described in Question 3.[4] In lieu of payments, all local governments are also permitted to forgive an obligation arising from "a lease or another contract" between the taxpayer and the taxing unit entered into before the start of the fiscal year for which the taxes were levied.[5] A few local governments are authorized by local bills or their charters to accept deeds to real property as payment of property taxes and special assessments. These include the city and county of Durham and the cities of Salisbury, Wilmington, and Winston-Salem.[6]

3. What are the rules for accepting checks and electronic payments?

To make payment of tax bills as easy as possible, all local governments now accept checks. A growing number accept credit card payments and electronic fund transfers directly from taxpayers' bank accounts. Tax offices can charge taxpayers a fee for the use of these electronic payment options.[7]

---

3. G.S. 105-357(a).

4. G.S. 105-357(b).

5. G.S. 105-357(a). This offset authority was added to the Machinery Act by S.L. 2005-134.

6. 1959 N.C. Sess. Laws ch. 720 (Winston-Salem); 1973 N.C. Sess. Laws ch. 429 (city of Durham); 1985 N.C. Sess. Laws ch. 910 (Farmville, Wilmington, Salisbury, Durham County). See also 1987 N.C. Sess. Laws ch. 740 (Elkin town charter); 1987 N.C. Sess. Laws ch. 262 (Ahoskie town charter); 1989 N.C. Sess. Laws ch. 957 (Reidsville city charter).

7. This includes convenience fees for payment by credit card, which for many years were prohibited by the contractual agreement between the card issuers and governments accepting these payments. In the mid-1990s, credit card issuers began to permit government clients to charge convenience fees for internet transactions. In the past few years, the issuers also began to permit convenience fees for face-to-face transactions, with some restrictions. VISA, for instance, limits government convenience fees

Most tax collectors immediately issue an official tax payment receipt without waiting for the check or electronic payment to clear. They do so at their own risk. If the check or credit card payment is later denied, the tax lien for the taxes included on that receipt may be unenforceable against lienholders or buyers who relied in good faith on that incorrect receipt.[8] With this in mind, the tax collector should act quickly after learning that a check or electronic payment has been denied. To eliminate any future good faith reliance on the incorrect tax receipt, the tax collector should immediately issue a corrected receipt to the original taxpayer and to any subsequent buyers or lienholders of the property.

A denied electronic payment triggers a penalty of 10 percent of the payment, with a minimum penalty of $25 and a maximum of $1,000.[9] The penalty is added to the principal amount of taxes owed and accrues interest if it remains unpaid after the delinquency date. The penalties apply to payments "returned or not completed because of insufficient funds or nonexistence of an account of the drawer."[10] Likely the General Assembly also intended for the penalty to apply when the taxpayer stops payment on a check or electronic payment, because the impact on the tax collector is identical.

This penalty does not apply to a dishonored check or electronic funds transfer if the taxpayer had sufficient funds in another bank account. The statute does not describe how the taxpayer would prove that funds were available elsewhere, but presumably he or she would have to provide a bank statement or similar financial record. This exception applies only to the dishonored payment penalty, not to interest charges that may accrue due to the delayed payment. If the taxes owed are delinquent, interest would continue to accrue until final payment is received.

Unlike other fees and costs added to property taxes, the tax collector may reduce or waive entirely the penalty for dishonored checks and electronic

---

for face-to-face transactions to $3.95. For a more detailed discussion of this issue, see Kara Millonzi's October 19, 2009, post on *Coates' Canons*, the School of Government's Local Government Law blog, http://sogweb.sog.unc.edu/blogs/localgovt/?p=1051.

8. G.S. 105-357(b)(1).

9. G.S. 105-357(b)(2). This penalty is exclusive, meaning that the $25 bad-check penalty imposed under a provision in North Carolina's version of the Uniform Commercial Code, G.S. 25-3-506, does not apply to checks offered in payment of property taxes.

10. G.S. 105-357(b)(2).

payments "upon making a record of the reasons therefore."[11] In other words, tax collectors can forgive the penalty for any reason they desire. To avoid allegations of favoritism, the tax collector should make the waiver process as objective as possible by working with the governing board to develop a list of situations, if any, that would justify a waiver of the penalty.

4. What is a "lockbox" agreement?

The term "lockbox" generally refers not to an actual locked box, but to a contractual agreement with a local bank to accept and process tax payments on behalf of the tax collector. These agreements are explicitly authorized by the Machinery Act.[12] Payments received by the lockbox are considered received by the tax collector for purposes of calculating discounts and interest. Banks serving as lockboxes should make it a practice to keep a copy of the envelopes in which payments are received so they can apply the postmark rule for calculating interest. See Questions 9, 10, and 11 for more details on interest calculations.

Some jurisdictions maintain an actual locked box outside their offices or elsewhere in the jurisdiction in which taxpayers may drop tax payments. These drop boxes should provide clear notice to taxpayers when payments deposited there will be processed by the tax office. See Question 11 for more on this issue.

5. Must the tax collector remedy small underpayments or overpayments?

Yes, unless the governing board passes a resolution permitting the tax collector (1) to treat small underpayments as full payments and (2) not to refund small overpayments unless the taxpayer requests a refund by the end of the fiscal year.[13] The overpayment provision applies only to mailed or elec-

---

11. G.S. 105-358(a). This statute describes the penalty that may be waived or reduced as that "imposed on giving a worthless check," but this waiver authority likely extends to penalties applied to dishonored electronic payments as well.

12. G.S. 105-357(b).

13. G.S. 105-357(c).

tronic payments; in-person overpayments should be corrected at the time of payment.

The statute defines *small* as $1 or less. If the underpayment is more than $1, the tax collector must pursue collection of the entire outstanding amount. If the overpayment is more than $1, the tax collector must refund the entire overpayment.

The governing board must adopt the necessary resolution by June 15 for it to be effective for the fiscal year that opens July 1. Once adopted, the resolution applies to all tax payments, even those for prior years' taxes, and is effective until repealed. Tax collectors subject to such resolutions should keep records of the overpayments and underpayments and account for them in the annual settlement.

6. Must the tax collector pursue collection of minimal tax bills?

Yes, unless the governing board directs its tax officials not to collect minimal taxes, defined as bills for which the combined taxes and fees of the taxing unit and all other taxing units for which it collects total $5 or less.[14] As with the underpayment/overpayment resolution, the minimal tax resolution must be adopted by June 15 to be effective for the fiscal year that opens July 1. Once adopted, the resolution is effective until repealed.

The minimal tax threshold applies only to the original principal amount of taxes, not to subsequent interest, fees, or costs. For example, assume a taxpayer's original tax bill was $100. The taxpayer mails a $100 payment on January 10, at which time the account has accrued $2 in interest. The outstanding $2 in interest must be collected by the tax collector even if a minimal tax resolution is in effect, because the principal taxes originally owed were well over the minimal tax threshold of $5. And the $2 underpayment is too large to be forgiven through the process described in Question 5.

---

14. G.S. 105-321(f). The governing board may choose a lower threshold and is in fact expected to set the threshold at "the estimated cost to the taxing unit of billing the taxpayer for the amounts due on a tax receipt or notice." But in practice most taxing units set their minimal tax threshold at $5, the maximum permitted by the statute.

7. When do discounts apply, and how are they calculated?

A discount is a reduction in a tax obligation in return for payment prior to September 1, the due date for taxes on real and personal property other than registered motor vehicles.[15] Unlike interest charges discussed in Question 9, discounts are optional, not mandatory. Each taxing unit may make its own decision regarding the availability and the amount of discounts.

If a local government wishes to offer discounts, it must accomplish three tasks.[16] First, it must adopt by May 1 an ordinance or resolution specifying the discount amounts and when they apply. Second, it must submit the discount ordinance or resolution to the Department of Revenue for approval.[17] Third, it must publish the discount schedule in a newspaper with "general circulation" in the unit.[18] Once a discount schedule is adopted, it remains in effect for all future tax years unless it is subsequently repealed and must be applied to all payments made during the discount period even if the taxpayer does not request the discount.

The Machinery Act requires that discounts end on September 1 but is silent as to their size or start dates. Most local governments that offer discounts set the rate at 1 or 2 percent and offer them only in July or August or both. If the ordinance or resolution does not indicate when discounts first become available—perhaps the ordinance reads, "A discount of 1% shall apply to all payments made prior to September 1"—then presumably the discount must begin whenever the tax office begins accepting prepayments, as discussed in Question 8.

Discounts are simple to administer when they apply to full payments made after the tax receipts. For example, assume the governing board adopts a 2 percent discount for payments made in August. If Tom Taxpayer wants to pay his $100 tax obligation on August 15, he will receive a discount of $2 and be required to pay only $98 to satisfy his tax obligation in full.

---

15. G.S. 105-360(c).

16. G.S. 105-360(c)(1)–(3).

17. G.S. 105-360(c) states that the department may reject the discount schedule if "the discounts or the periods of time for which discounts are allowed are excessive or unreasonable." Presumably the department must review a subsequent increase in a previously approved discount schedule but not a subsequent decrease, because if the department has already determined that a discount at a certain level is not excessive then a discount at a lower level would also be acceptable.

18. For a discussion of the "general circulation" requirement, see Chapter 9.

Discounts are more complicated when partial payments are involved. Assume the same facts as above but that Tom mails a payment of $50 on August 15. Instead of a $50 balance on his original tax obligation of $100, the balance should be reduced to $49 to account for the 2 percent discount on his $50 payment. If Tom pays the balance prior to September 1, he would be entitled to a discount on that payment as well and could satisfy the full tax obligation with a payment of $48. (The first payment of $50 plus the second payment of $48 would equal $98, the amount owed after applying the 2 percent discount to the original $100 tax obligation.) If Tom pays the balance on or after September 1, he would not receive the discount on the second payment and would owe $49.

8. What are prepayments?

Prepayments are payments of taxes made before the tax receipts have been delivered by the governing board to the tax collector for collection.[19] Essentially, prepayments are tax payments made before the final tax rate has been set and before tax bills have been calculated.

Prepayments need not be accepted until the budget officer files the annual budget estimate with the governing board and the board's clerk, which should occur by June 1.[20] At this point, the tax collector will be able to estimate taxpayers' obligations with reasonable accuracy based on the tax rate proposed in the budget estimate.

Prepayments end once the new tax receipts can be calculated, a process that cannot begin until the governing board adopts a tax rate for the new fiscal year. The adoption of a tax rate is subject to several different deadlines. The Local Government Budget and Fiscal Control Act requires that the tax rate be included in the annual budget ordinance, which must be adopted by July 1, the start of the fiscal year.[21] The Machinery Act provides that a property tax must be levied by adoption of a tax rate by August 1[22] and that the tax receipts must be delivered to the tax collector for collection

---

19. G.S. 105-359(a).

20. G.S. 105-359(b) (acceptance of prepayments); G.S. 159-11(b) (filing of annual budget estimate).

21. G.S. 159-13(a).

22. G.S. 105-347.

by September 1 each year.[23] That said, there are no statutory penalties for missing these deadlines, and local governments that cannot resolve budget disputes routinely operate under interim budgets without adopting a new tax rate well past these dates.[24] As a result, the prepayment period sometimes stretches into the new fiscal year.

Prepayments are by definition estimates, meaning that the taxpayer's final tax obligation might differ from the prepayment amount. For that reason, a receipt for a prepayment should state that it represents an estimate of the tax obligation and that the lien on real property for the taxes owed will not be released until the final tax obligation is completely satisfied.[25]

When the final tax obligation is determined, excess prepayments must be refunded to the taxpayer without interest. If taxes remain outstanding, the balance due should reflect the discount or interest applicable at the time the balance is paid.

The following examples illustrate how these rules work in practice. Assume Tina Taxpayer wishes to prepay her 2011 Carolina County property taxes in June 2011. Carolina County offers a 2 percent discount for all tax payments made prior to September 1. Because the county commissioners have not yet adopted a final budget and tax rate, the tax collector estimates Tina's 2011 taxes to be $1,000. Tina pays $980, which represents the estimated tax less the 2 percent discount. In late July, after the final budget and tax rate is adopted, the tax collector determines that Tina's actual 2011 taxes are $950. The tax collector must refund $49, which is the difference between the amount Tina paid ($980) and her actual tax obligation less the 2 percent discount ($950 × 0.98, or $931). Tina is entitled to the discount on her actual taxes because she prepaid the estimated taxes during the discount period.

What happens when the final tax bill is more than the estimated tax prepayment? Consider the above example again, but assume instead that Tina's actual 2011 property taxes turn out to be $1,100. Tina owes $100 in additional taxes, because she paid estimated taxes of only $1,000. (In fact, she paid only $980 due to the discount, but that payment satisfied $1,000 of

---

23. G.S. 105-321(c).

24. G.S. 159-16 authorizes the use of an interim budget so that the local government can continue to pay ordinary expenses prior to the adoption of the final budget ordinance.

25. G.S. 105-359(d).

the tax bill.) If she does not pay the $100 balance by January 5, 2010, it will incur interest, as discussed in Question 9.

9. When does interest accrue, and how is it calculated?

For taxes on real property and personal property other than registered motor vehicles, interest begins on January 6 of the fiscal year for which the taxes are levied.[26] For example, 2010 property taxes begin accruing interest on January 6, 2011. January 5 is the last day for taxpayers to pay the current fiscal year's tax "at par," meaning without interest, unless January 5 falls on a weekend or holiday. In that situation, the last day to pay taxes at par will be the next business day.[27] For example, if January 5 falls on a Saturday, the last day to pay the current fiscal year's property taxes at par is Monday, January 7, and interest begins on Tuesday, January 8.

The Machinery Act sets the interest rate at 2 percent for the first month and 0.75 percent for each additional month.[28] Interest is not prorated within a month; that is, the full month's interest charge accrues on the first day of that month. For example, if Terry Taxpayer pays her 2010 taxes on February 1, 2011, she will be charged 2.75 percent interest: 2 percent for January and 0.75 percent for February.

The weekend and holiday rule applies to the accrual of additional months of interest the same as it applies to the initial interest accrual on January 6. If the last day of the month falls on a weekend or holiday, then the taxpayer has until the next business day to pay outstanding taxes without accruing an additional month's interest. For example, if January 31 were to fall on a Saturday, then taxpayers would have until Monday, February 2, to pay delinquent taxes without accruing interest for the month of February.

Because the Machinery Act defines *taxes* as "the principal amount of any property tax or dog license tax and costs, penalties, interest," interest applies to not only the principal taxes owed but also to all costs and penalties relating to those taxes. Penalties such as those for late listing under the discovery

---

26. G.S. 105-360(a).
27. G.S. 105-395.1.
28. G.S. 105-360(a)(1), (2).

provisions[29] and for bad checks under the electronic payment provisions[30] should be added to the principal taxes owed when calculating interest. The same applies to costs such as those for advertising tax liens[31] and for providing notice of attachments and garnishments.[32] However, interest is not compounded, meaning it does not accrue on previous interest charges.

Partial tax payments must first be applied to penalties, costs, and interest, and then to the principal amount of taxes.[33] Assume Tracy Taxpayer owes $1,000 in taxes, which become delinquent on January 6. Tracy sends the tax office a payment of $1,000 on January 15. As of that date, Tracy owed $1,020, the principal amount of taxes plus 2 percent interest for January. The tax collector must apply the $1,000 payment first to the $20 interest charge and then to the principal taxes, leaving $20 in taxes outstanding. If Tracy calls the tax office on May 1 to learn how much is owed, the answer would be $20.60: $20 in principal taxes and $0.60 in interest. The interest would total 3 percent: 0.75 percent for February, March, April, and May.

10. What is the postmark exception for interest and discounts?

Normally, payments must be actually received by the tax office to qualify for a discount or stop the accrual of interest. However, payments made by mail are considered received by the tax office on the postmark date for purposes of calculating discounts and interest.[34] If the payment has no postmark or the postmark does not contain a date, then the payment is considered received when it actually arrives in the tax office.

For example, assume Tony Taxpayer mails his 2010 property tax payment on January 1, 2011. The payment arrives in the county tax office on January 10, with a January 3 postmark. Tony's payment is considered received as of January 3. Interest would not accrue on Tony's account, assuming his payment satisfied the tax obligation in full.

---

29. G.S. 105-312(h).

30. See Question 3.

31. G.S. 105-369(d).

32. G.S. 105-368(g). Currently, the fee is $30 per service, meaning most garnishments and attachments require $60 in fees: $30 for service on the taxpayer and $30 for service on the garnishee (i.e, the bank or employer).

33. G.S. 105-358(b).

34. G.S. 105-360(d).

Taxpayers sometimes seek aid from the postmark exception when problems arise with the use of third-party bill-paying services such as those offered through most major banks' websites. Reliance on this provision is misplaced. Consider a tax payment received on January 8 from a bank on behalf of a taxpayer. Unless that payment has a postmark of January 5 or earlier, interest must accrue on the account even if the taxpayer provides proof that the bank deducted the tax payment from the taxpayer's account on January 5 or earlier. The fact that the bank delayed mailing of the payment does not justify a waiver of the interest charge under the postmark exception. The same would be true if the tax payment was deducted from the taxpayer's account on January 4 but sent to the tax office by the bank electronically on January 6 or later. The taxpayer, not the tax office, bears the risk of using a third-party bill payer.

11. When should interest accrue for payments received in lockboxes or drop boxes?

Lockboxes, the common name for arrangements under which local banks accept tax payments, should be viewed as the equivalent of the tax office for purposes of interest accrual. If a payment is received by the lockbox prior to January 6, no interest should accrue. The same is true for discount calculations. If a payment is received by the lockbox prior to September 1, that payment should receive the benefit of whatever discount the taxing unit may offer.

The postmark rule also applies to lockboxes to the same extent it applies to tax offices: if a payment sent to the lockbox carries a postmark from January 5 or earlier, that tax account should not accrue interest regardless of when it actually arrives at the lockbox. This fact makes it imperative that the bank serving as the lockbox save copies of the envelopes in which it receives tax payments for at least for two to three weeks following January 6.

In contrast, a drop box—literally a locked box outside the tax office or at a separate location—is not necessarily the equivalent of the tax office. Tax offices are free to post disclaimers on or near drop boxes indicating that payments deposited in those boxes will not be processed until the following business day. The postmark rule need not apply to payments deposited in a drop box that clearly indicates when payments deposited in the drop box will be processed by the tax office.

12. When is a local government required to pay interest on overpayments?

In general, local governments are not required to pay interest on refunds of property taxes made pursuant to G.S. 105-381.[35] However, interest must be added to overpayments that result from decisions by the county board of equalization and review or the state Property Tax Commission that lower tax assessments. The issue is made more complex by the fact that interest on such overpayments varies depending on the body that renders the decision to lower a tax assessment.

Overpayments resulting from decisions by the county board of equalization and review accrue interest according to the same rates charged to taxpayers who fail to pay their taxes by January 6: 2 percent for the first month and .75 percent for each subsequent month.[36] Overpayments resulting from decisions by the state Property Tax Commission accrue interest at the same rate set by the North Carolina Department of Revenue (DOR) for late state income tax refunds.[37] In both situations, interest begins to accrue from the later of the date the tax was paid or the date the tax would have been delinquent, usually January 6 of the fiscal year in which the tax was levied. Interest continues to accrue until five days after the refund check is mailed.

For example, assume Wanda Wolfpack files a timely appeal of the 2012 assessment of her home in Carolina County. As is permitted, while the appeal is pending the county sends Wanda a tax bill based on the original assessment. Wanda pays this $2,000 tax bill in September 2012. If the Carolina County Board of Equalization and Review rules for Wanda in December 2012 and cuts her assessment in half, Wanda will be entitled to a $1,000 refund, but no interest will be due if the county pays this refund prior to January 6, 2013.

Assume instead that Wanda loses at the county board of equalization and review but prevails before the state Property Tax Commission in July 2013. The county will be required to pay interest on Wanda's overpayment at the rate set by the DOR, from January 6, 2013, through five days after the refund check is mailed.

---

35. See Chapter 12 for more details on refunds and releases.

36. G.S. 105-360(d), added to the Machinery Act by S.L. 2011-3.

37. G.S. 105-290(b)(4). That rate is set every six months as required by G.S. 105-241.21. As of June 2011, the rate was 5 percent per year and had been at that rate since 2008.

13. What are the special rules for accruing interest against taxpayers who are serving in the military?

In general, active duty military servicemembers are subject to the same interest provisions as are other taxpayers. However, special rules exist for a servicemember deployed in support of U.S. military operations in Afghanistan or Iraq: taxes owed by such a taxpayer do not become delinquent and therefore do not accrue interest until ninety days after the taxpayer's deployment ends.[38] Note that the servicemember need not be deployed in Afghanistan or Iraq; the location of deployment is irrelevant so long as the servicemember is deployed somewhere other than his or her home base in support of operations in one of those two countries. As discussed in Chapter 6, federal law greatly limits enforced collection options against active duty military servicemembers after this ninety-day waiting period ends.

14. What are the special rules for charging interest on property taxes owed by public service companies?

Public service companies such as airlines, railroad companies, and electric and gas companies are subject to unique listing and appraisal procedures found in Sections 105-333 through 105-344 of the North Carolina General Statutes. Essentially, public service company property is listed and appraised by the N.C. Department of Revenue and then allocated to the counties.[39] Counties and municipalities may then levy taxes on this property as they do all other property in their jurisdictions.

If a public service company "fails or refuses to pay" local property taxes, the taxing unit may bring a civil action against the company in state court after giving the company written notice via certified or registered mail at least fifteen days prior.[40] If the taxing unit prevails, the judgment must include attorneys' fees, a penalty of 50 percent of the taxes owed, and interest

---

38. See S.L. 2003-300 and S.L. 2001-508.

39. For a detailed discussion of this process, see Shea Riggsbee Denning, *A Guide to the Listing, Assessment, and Taxation of Property in North Carolina* (Chapel Hill, N.C.: UNC School of Government, 2009), 100–105. (This publication is available for purchase at http://shopping.netsuite.com/s.nl/c.433425/it.A/id.1907/.f.)

40. G.S. 105-344.

on the taxes and penalty at an annual rate of 9 percent from the date the tax was due, which normally would be September 1.

This statute leaves several questions unanswered. When can the taxing unit initiate a collection action? Presumably not until after the taxes become delinquent on January 6, but the statute is silent on this issue. Can the taxing unit use traditional Machinery Act remedies of attachment and garnishment and foreclosure instead of pursuing a civil action? Probably not. The statute does not explicitly make a civil action the exclusive remedy, but the specific collection remedy for public service companies likely trumps the Machinery Act's general collection remedies. Can the regular Machinery Act interest apply to taxes owed by public service companies? Again, probably not. As with the civil action requirement, the specific interest rules for public service companies likely trump the Machinery Act's general interest provisions.

15. Can taxpayers rely on statements by the tax office to avoid a tax obligation?

Generally not. Most statements by the tax collector regarding the amount of taxes owed on a particular property do not bind the taxing unit or affect its ability to collect those taxes, even if the tax collector's statement is inaccurate. Oral statements can never be the basis for avoiding enforcement of a tax lien.[41] In two instances written statements by the tax office can affect the enforceability of a tax lien.

The first instance involves a receipt issued for a tax payment made by a check or electronic payment that is later dishonored, discussed in Question 3. The second instance involves a written certification of the taxes owed made by the tax office under G.S. 105-361. Errors in this certificate can extinguish a tax lien and create liability for the tax collector.[42]

The Machinery Act grants the right to request a binding certificate of taxes only to individuals or entities who

- own the property,
- occupy the property,

---

41. G.S. 105-361(d).
42. G.S. 105-361(b).

- have a lien on the property,
- have a legal interest or estate in the property,
- are under contract to purchase or lease the property or to provide a loan secured by the property, or
- serve as an authorized agent or attorney for one of the above parties.[43]

When one of these parties requests a statement of taxes owed, the tax office must provide a binding certificate.[44] The statute does not specify the form of this certificate other than requiring that it be in writing. That said, tax offices should develop a form specifically for this purpose and keep copies of all such forms issued. An excellent example of this type of form is included as Appendix 3A. Note that the form includes regular real property taxes as well as deferred taxes, taxes on personal property owned by the same taxpayer in the jurisdiction, and special assessments.

If a party subsequently relies on the certificate, the tax lien for any taxes or special assessments omitted from that certificate is extinguished. The tax obligation remains, but the lien on the real property no longer exists, meaning foreclosure is no longer an option to collect the omitted taxes.

The statute defines reliance to mean one of three actions:

- paying the taxes and assessments listed on the certificate,
- purchasing or leasing the real property,
- lending money secured by a lien on the real property.

For example, assume that Parcel A is owned by Able, who requests a certificate of taxes owed in July 2010. The tax office provides the certificate but fails to include taxes for the 2010 fiscal year.[45] If Able pays the taxes included

---

43. G.S. 105-361(1)(a)–(f). Any party may obtain information regarding the amount of property taxes outstanding on a particular parcel under public records law. But only these six types of entities may rely on that information to avoid enforcement of a tax lien.

44. G.S. 105-361(c) establishes a penalty of $50 for failure to provide the required certificate. But the penalty can be recovered only through a civil action filed by the party requesting the certificate and thus is unlikely ever to apply.

45. G.S. 105-361 makes clear that taxes for the current fiscal year must be included on the certificate. If a certificate is requested before the current year's taxes are finalized, the certificate should include an estimated amount for the current year's taxes along with a notation that the amount has been estimated and is subject to later adjustment.

on the certificate, then the lien for 2010 taxes is no longer enforceable against Parcel A because Able relied on the certificate by paying the taxes listed on that document. The tax collector will still be able to pursue collection of the 2010 taxes on Parcel A using attachment and garnishment or levy and sale against the *personal* property of whoever owns Parcel A on January 6, 2011 (the delinquency date), and all subsequent owners.[46] But the tax collector may not foreclose on Parcel A to collect the 2010 taxes.

16. Can taxpayers rely on information posted on the tax office website to avoid a tax obligation?

Only if the governing board passes a resolution allowing taxpayers to rely on information on the tax office website as it if were a written certification.[47] But even then the tax office may post disclaimers on the website limiting the accuracy of the information. For example, the website may state that the information contained therein only reflects transactions up to a certain date. In that case, taxes added to the property in question after the effective date listed on the website would still be a lien on that property even though they were not reflected on the website.

17. Can the register of deeds refuse to register a deed if property taxes are owed on the property being transferred?

Yes, in most counties. As of the 2011 legislative session, seventy-three counties are authorized to prohibit the register of deeds from accepting a deed transferring real property until the tax collector first certifies that there are no property tax liens on the property that is the subject of the deed.[48] This

---

46. The responsible taxpayer for taxes on real property is the owner of record as of the date of delinquency and all subsequent owners. G.S. 105-365.1(b)(1).

47. G.S. 105-361(e).

48. G.S. 161-31(b). These seventy-three counties are Alamance, Alexander, Anson, Beaufort, Bertie, Brunswick, Buncombe, Burke, Cabarrus, Camden, Carteret, Caswell, Catawba, Cherokee, Chowan, Clay, Cleveland, Currituck, Dare, Davidson, Davie, Duplin, Durham, Edgecombe, Forsyth, Gaston, Gates, Graham, Granville, Greene, Halifax, Harnett, Haywood, Henderson, Hertford, Hyde, Iredell, Jackson, Johnston, Jones, Lee, Lenoir, Lincoln, Macon, Madison, Martin, McDowell, Montgomery, Nash, Northampton, Onslow, Pasquotank, Pender, Perquimans, Person, Pitt, Polk, Robeson,

certification must cover all property taxes the tax collector is responsible for collecting, which could include county taxes, municipal taxes, special service district taxes, rural fire district taxes, and supplemental school board taxes. If the county tax collector is not responsible for collecting taxes levied by a municipality, then delinquent taxes owed to that municipality cannot be the basis for the refusal to certify a deed.[49] The statute makes no reference to liens for special assessments, meaning that outstanding special assessments are not sufficient justification for a tax collector to refuse to certify a deed for registration.

This requirement may be avoided if the closing attorney certifies that he or she will pay the outstanding taxes at closing. Unfortunately, the statute does not mention how the outstanding taxes can be recovered if the closing attorney fails to make good on that promise. The county would retain Machinery Act remedies against the property and its owners, of course. But can any remedies be used against the offending attorney? Without specific authorization in the Machinery Act, it seems unlikely that the tax collector would be permitted to target the attorney's money or property to satisfy the outstanding taxes. The funds the attorney handles at closing are appropriate for attachment because they are funds due to the delinquent taxpayer and not the attorney. If a particular attorney routinely breaks the promise to pay outstanding taxes, the best approach would be to hand that attorney a notice of attachment for the closing funds the next time that attorney submits a deed for registration.

If the tax collector mistakenly certifies a deed for registration, would that error be binding on the county and extinguish the lien for the omitted taxes? Likely not, because nothing in the deed certification statute indicates that the process affects the existence or enforceability of liens on the property. This provision is intended to limit the authority of the register of deeds, not the tax collector. If a buyer seeks assurance that the property is free from all tax liens, he or she must proceed under the Machinery Act's certification process as described in Question 15.

Rockingham, Rowan, Rutherford, Stanly, Surry, Swain, Transylvania, Tyrrell, Vance, Warren, Washington, Wayne, Wilson, Yadkin, and Yancey.

49. The only exception to this rule is Duplin County. Local bill S.L. 2010-24 authorized Duplin County to adopt a resolution that prohibits the recording of a deed unless the tax collector certifies that all taxes, both county and municipal, have been paid, even if the county does not collect taxes for a particular municipality.

18. Can a local government refuse to issue a building permit if property taxes are owed on the property that is the subject of the permit?

No, unless the local government is one of the twenty that has received such authority under a local bill. As of the 2010 legislative session, only Alexander, Alleghany, Anson, Bertie, Catawba, Chowan, Currituck, Davie, Gates, Greene, Lenoir, Lincoln, Iredell, Stokes, Surry, Tyrrell, Wayne, and Yadkin counties and the towns of Columbia and Edenton had been granted the authority to withhold building permits (or any other type of permit) due to outstanding property taxes.[50]

Currituck County is the only local government authorized to withhold the issuance of a special use permit or conditional use permit under its zoning regulations if the applicant owes delinquent property taxes.[51]

---

50. G.S. 153A-357(c), as modified by S.L. 2005-433 (Greene, Iredell, Lenoir, Wayne, and Yadkin counties), S.L. 2006-150 (Davie and Lincoln counties), S.L. 2007-58 (Gates County), S.L. 2009-117 (Alexander, Alleghany, Anson, Bertie, Catawba, Chowan, Stokes, Surry, and Tyrrell counties), and S.L. 2010-30 (Currituck County); G.S. 160A-417, as modified by S.L. 2009-68 (towns of Columbia and Edenton).

51. G.S. 153A-340(c2), added to the statutes by S.L. 2010-30 and applicable to Currituck County only.

Appendix 3A

GASTON COUNTY

OFFICE OF THE TAX COLLECTOR

STATEMENT OF TAXES DUE

GC STD -1

2010 02 25

Per NCGS 105-361, on the request of any of the persons prescribed in Section(1), below, and upon the condition prescribed by Section (2), below, the tax collector shall furnish a written certificate stating the amount of any taxes and special assessments for the current year and for prior years in his hands for collection (together with any penalties, interest, and costs accrued thereon) including the amount due under G.S. 105-277.4(c) if the property should lose its eligibility for the benefit of classification under G.S. 105-277.2 et seq. that are a lien on a parcel of real property in the taxing unit.

Section 1

I ___________________________, hereby affirm that I am qualified to request a Statement of Taxes Due for the property identified in Section (2) as one of the persons identified below:

Any of the following persons shall be entitled to request the certificate:

☐ An owner of the real property;

☐ An occupant of the real property;

☐ A person having a lien on the real property;

☐ A person having a legal interest or estate in the real property;

☐ A person or firm having a contract to purchase or lease the property or a person or firm having contracted to make a loan secured by the property;

☐ The authorized agent or attorney of Name ________________ Phone ____________ of any person described above.

Signature ________________________________ Phone ________________ Date ____________

Section 2

Duty of Person Making Request. – With respect to taxes, the tax collector shall not be required to furnish a certificate unless the person making the request specifies in whose name the real property was listed for taxation on January 1 for each year for which the information is sought. With respect to assessments, the tax collector shall not be required to furnish a certificate unless the person making the request furnishes such identification of the real estate (Parcel ID) as may be reasonably required by the tax collector.

Current Property Information:

Parcel ID __________ Legal Reference: Deed Book / Page ______ / ______ Tax District: ________________

Tax Year	Listing Owner (as of Jan 1 for each year)	Parcel ID	Tax Deferral *	Special Assessments	Real Estate Amt	Bus/Individual Personal Amt	Deferred Amt
1. 2009			☐ ——	☐	$______	$______	$______
2. 2008			☐ ——	☐	$______	$______	$______
3. 2007			☐ ——	☐	$______	$______	$______
4. 2006			☐ ——	☐	$______	$______	$______
5. 2005			☐ ——	☐	$______	$______	$______
6. 2004			☐ ——	☐	$______	$______	$______
7. 2003			☐ ——	☐	$______	$______	$______
8. 2002			☐ ——	☐	$______	$______	$______
9. 2001			☐ ——	☐	$______	$______	$______
10. 2000			☐ ——	☐	$______	$______	$______
				TOTAL	$______	$______	$______

I CERTIFY THAT THE AMOUNT OF TAXES (TOGETHER WITH ANY PENALTIES, INTEREST AND COST ACCURED THEREON) THAT HAVE BEEN

MADE A LEIN ON THE REAL PROPERTY IDENTIFIED ABOVE IS $ ________________ THROUGH AND INCLUDING THE MONTH OF

____________ YEAR ______ . THIS DOES NOT INCLUDE TAXES FOR THE TAX YEAR ________.

Date of Statement: ________________________

____
Tax Collector

____
Prepared By:

* Tax Deferrals include: Historic District (HD); Circuit Breaker (CB); Builder's Inventory (BI); Present Use Value (PUV); Working Waterfront (WW); Wildlife Conservation (WC); Historic Property (HP); Non-profit low-moderate income housing site (NHS)

Chapter 4

Deferred Property Taxes

Deferred Property Taxes

Beginning with the creation of the present-use value classification in the early 1970s, the North Carolina General Assembly has relied increasingly upon deferred property tax programs when seeking to provide tax relief for the state's property owners. As of this publication, there exist eight different deferred property tax programs affecting such diverse property as working water-fronts, wildlife conservation land, and new homes yet to be sold by their builders. Although these programs differ greatly in eligibility requirements and operation, in 2008 the General Assembly codified uniform collection procedures for all deferred taxes. This chapter explains these procedures and answers some frequently asked questions about deferred taxes.

1. What are deferred taxes?

Deferred taxes are taxes that, because of an exclusion, are not due and payable in the year in which they are levied but may become due and payable when the underlying property is no longer eligible for the applicable exclusion. As of the end of the 2009 legislative session, the following eight North Carolina General Statutes address property tax exclusions that could give rise to deferred taxes:

1. G.S. 105-275(29a), a historic district property held as a future site of a historic structure,
2. G.S. 105-277.1B, the property tax homestead circuit breaker,

---

This chapter updates information published as *Property Tax Bulletin* No. 149 (Aug. 2009).

3. G.S. 105-277.1D, home builders' inventory (for tax years 2010 through 2012),
4. G.S. 105-277.4(c), present-use value property,
5. G.S. 105-277.14, working waterfront property,
6. G.S. 105-277.15, wildlife conservation land (beginning in the 2010 tax year),
7. G.S. 105-278(b), historic property, and
8. G.S. 105-278.6(e), nonprofit property held as a future site of low- or moderate-income housing.

Determining eligibility for these exclusions is the responsibility of the assessor, not the tax collector, and is beyond the scope of this chapter. For detailed discussion concerning many of these exclusions, see Shea Riggsbee Denning, *A Guide to the Listing, Assessment, and Taxation of Property in North Carolina* (Chapel Hill, NC: UNC School of Government, 2009).

2. How are deferred taxes collected?

While details vary from exclusion to exclusion, in 2008 the General Assembly codified a number of uniform collection procedures for all eight deferred tax programs.

One statute, G.S. 105-277.1F, includes several uniform deferred tax rules for due dates, interest, and liens. First, deferred taxes become due and payable on the day the property loses eligibility for the relevant exclusion as a result of a disqualifying event. Each exclusion defines "disqualifying event" differently, but for the most part the term references a change in ownership or use of the underlying property. (See Question 3 for more details on disqualifying events.) Second, interest accrues on all deferred taxes as if they had been due and payable in year of levy. For example, 2009 taxes deferred under the circuit breaker exclusion will accrue interest on January 6, 2010—the date of delinquency for all 2009 taxes—regardless of when these deferred taxes become due and payable.[1] Third, the tax for the fiscal

---

1. One of several unique aspects of the circuit breaker is that interest can accrue indefinitely on deferred taxes because a "gap" in eligibility may arise without a disqualifying event. A participating taxpayer may lose circuit breaker eligibility due to an increase in income or a failure to submit the annual application, but because no disqualifying event occurs, the deferred taxes do not become due and payable. This gap could continue for years, meaning that the interest owed when a disqualifying

year that begins in the calendar year of the disqualifying event is calculated as if the property were never eligible for the exclusion that year. For example, if a disqualifying event occurs at any point in 2010, no taxes would be deferred for 2010 and the full tax bill would be due and payable as usual. The 2010 taxes would be due on September 1 and delinquent on January 6, 2011. Fourth, and finally, deferred taxes remain a lien on the underlying property until they are either satisfied through payment or excused by operation of the applicable exclusion.

Another statute adopted in 2008, G.S. 105-365.1, creates uniform rules for the use of enforced collection remedies for all taxes, including deferred taxes. With one exception, deferred taxes become delinquent and subject to enforced collection remedies immediately upon the occurrence of a disqualifying event.[2] That said, most tax collectors would likely first send a bill for the deferred taxes to the responsible party before proceeding with a levy, attachment, or foreclosure.

Consider the application of these uniform rules to the following scenario. A taxpayer begins participating in the present-use value program for agricultural property in 2009 and sells the property to a developer—a disqualifying event—in March 2015. The present-use value exclusion provides that the three most recent years of deferred taxes are due and payable upon the occurrence of a disqualifying event. The deferred taxes plus interest from 2012, 2013, and 2014 would become due and payable and would constitute a lien on the property until satisfied. Interest would have begun to accrue in January 2013 for the 2012 deferred taxes, in January 2014 for the 2013 deferred taxes, and in January 2015 for the 2014 deferred taxes. Enforced collection actions could begin immediately for both the principal taxes and interest. Taxes for 2015 would be calculated with no deferral, due on September 1, 2015, and delinquent in January 2016.

---

event occurs could be substantially larger than the principal taxes. For a detailed discussion regarding eligibility gaps and other unique aspects of the circuit breaker, see Christopher B. McLaughlin, "The Homestead Circuit Breaker: Implications for Local Tax Offices," *Property Tax Bulletin* No. 145 (Oct. 2008), available at www.sog.unc.edu/pubs/electronicversions/pdfs/ptb145.pdf.

2. G.S. 105-365.1(a). The lone exception exists under the circuit breaker when the disqualifying event is the death of the owner. In such a situation, the deferred taxes do not become delinquent until the first day of the ninth month after the date of death. Presumably this delay exists so that the estate can be resolved before enforced collection remedies may begin.

Table 4.1. Deferred Taxes Due and Collectible as of March 2015

Year	Principal Deferred Taxes	Interest	Total Due and Payable as of March 2015
2015	$0 (2015 taxes will be calculated without the deferral)	$0 (taxes not delinquent until) January 2016	$ 0
2014	$10,000	$350 (2% for Jan. 2015, .75% per month for next 2 months)	$10,350
2013	$10,000	$1,250 (2% for Jan. 2014, .75% per month for next 14 months)	$11,250
2012	$10,000	$2,150 (2% for Jan. 2013, .75% per month for next 26 months)	$12,150
Total	$30,000	$3,750	$33,750

Assuming that $10,000 in taxes was deferred each year, Table 4.1 summarizes the taxes that would be collectible as of the disqualifying event in March 2015.

The deferred taxes from 2009, 2010, and 2011 would never become due and payable and would no longer be a lien on the property. This is true of all deferred taxes beyond those that are made due and payable by a disqualifying event. (See Table 4.2, below, for a summary of which deferred taxes become due and payable under each exclusion.) Although these "uncollectible" deferred taxes essentially disappear, this has no impact on a tax collector's annual settlement. The tax collector is never charged with their collection and, therefore, never needs to include these taxes in the settlement calculations.[3]

That said, there are still several reasons for a tax collector to maintain accurate records of all deferred taxes: to facilitate their eventual collection, to keep the board informed about the existence and magnitude of these taxes, and to provide taxpayers notice of these outstanding amounts. At

---

3. A tax collector need only include in the settlement "the total amount of taxes in his hand for collection" for the current and previous tax years. G.S. 105-373(a)(3) and (b). Deferred taxes that never become due and payable are never placed in the tax collector's hands for collection.

present, the circuit breaker is the only deferred tax program that requires the tax collector to provide annual notice of the amount of deferred taxes that are a lien on the property.[4]

3. What is a disqualifying event?

The definition of the term "disqualifying event" depends on the exclusion involved, as does the number of years of deferred taxes that become due and payable upon such an event. Table 4.2, below, provides a brief summary for each of the eight deferred tax exclusions, but tax collectors are strongly advised to refer to the most recent versions of the relevant statutes before initiating collection actions.

4. Who is responsible for deferred taxes that become due and payable?

The general rule regarding responsible taxpayers for real property taxes applies to deferred real property taxes: the taxpayers who may be targeted with enforced collection remedies are the owner of record as of the date of delinquency and all subsequent owners of record.[5]

While seemingly straightforward, this rule can create confusion when the disqualifying event is a transfer of ownership. Consider a residence that has benefited from the circuit breaker for several years while owned by

---

4. G.S. 105-277.1B(h) ("On or before September 1 of each year, the collector shall notify each residence owner to whom a tax deferral has previously been granted of the accumulated sum of deferred taxes and interest."). The statute provides no guidance as to the form of notice, however, meaning tax collectors are free to determine the most efficient and effective method of conveying this information to taxpayers. The deferred taxes and interest could be included on the tax bill or on a separate notice, and the amounts could be broken out by year or could simply be reported as a lump sum.

5. G.S. 105-365.1(b)(1). This is true for all deferred taxes that relate to real property. However, under the circuit breaker program, it is possible for personal property taxes to be deferred when an eligible taxpayer owns and resides in a manufactured home that sits on land owned by another taxpayer. In such a situation, G.S. 105-365.1(b)(2) applies, and the responsible taxpayer is the listing owner in the year the deferred taxes become due. Subsequent owners of the manufactured home could not be subject to enforced collection remedies for the delinquent deferred taxes.

Table 4.2. Property Tax Deferred Tax Exclusions

Exclusion	Disqualifying Event	Number of Years of Deferred Taxes Due and Payable Upon Disqualifying Event
Historic District Property (future site of historic structure) G.S. 105-275(29a)	Historic structure is not moved to the property within five years from the first day of the fiscal year the property was classified under this exclusion.	All, up to the maximum of five
Circuit Breaker G.S. 105-277.1B	(i) Owner dies, (ii) property is transferred, or (iii) property is no longer used as a permanent residence.[a]	Three
Residential Home Builders Inventory G.S. 105-277.1D	(i) Builder transfers the residence; (ii) residence is occupied by the builder or by someone other than the builder with the builder's consent; (iii) five years passed from the time the improved property was first subject to being listed for taxation by the builder; or, (iv) three years passed from the time the improved property was first classified under this exclusion.	All, up to the maximum of three
Present-Use Value Property (agricultural, horticultural, and forestland property) G.S. 105-277.4	Property fails to meet any condition or requirement for the exclusion.[b]	Three
Working Waterfront Property G.S. 105-277.14	Property fails to meet any condition or requirement for the exclusion.	Three
Wildlife Conservation Land G.S. 105-277.15	Property fails to meet any condition or requirement for the exclusion.	Three
Historic Property G.S. 105-278(b)	Change in an ordinance designating a historic property or a change in the property, other than by fire or other natural disaster, that causes the property's historical significance to be lost or substantially impaired.	Three
Future Site of Low- or Moderate-Income Housing G.S. 105-278.6(e)	Nonprofit organization fails to construct low- or moderate-income housing on the site within ten years from the first day of the fiscal year the property was first classified under this exclusion.	All, up to the maximum of ten

[a] Under the circuit breaker, a transfer does not cause a disqualifying event if (1) the property is transferred to a co-owner of the residence or, as part of a divorce proceeding or upon the owner's death, to the previous owner's spouse, and (2) the new owner continues to use the property as his or her permanent residence. G.S. 105-277.1B(i).

[b] Under the present-use value program, no deferred taxes are due and the liens for all deferred taxes are extinguished if the land loses its eligibility due to one of these three events: (i) the land is enrolled in a federal conservation reserve program, (ii) the land is donated to certain land conservation nonprofit organizations, or (iii) the land is donated to a federal, state, or local government entity. G.S. 105-277.4(d).

Taxpayer A. Taxpayer A sells the residence to Taxpayer B, who is neither the spouse of nor the co-owner with Taxpayer A. This transfer would constitute a disqualifying event and cause the three most recent years of deferred taxes to become immediately due, payable, and delinquent. Who is responsible for these deferred taxes, Taxpayer A or Taxpayer B?

The general rule states that the owner as of the date of delinquency is the responsible taxpayer, along with all subsequent owners. In this situation, there are two possible owners of record as of the date of delinquency, which is the day the transfer was recorded and record ownership changed. At the beginning of that day, Taxpayer A was the record owner. At the end of that day, Taxpayer B was the record owner. If Taxpayer A is viewed as the record owner on the date of delinquency for enforced collection purposes, then both Taxpayer A and Taxpayer B—because of the rule concerning subsequent ownership—are responsible for the deferred taxes. But if Taxpayer B is viewed as the owner as of the date of delinquency, then Taxpayer A is not responsible.

Neither the Machinery Act nor North Carolina case law specifically answers this question. To maximize collection options, most tax collectors would conclude that both Taxpayer A and Taxpayer B are responsible. Unless and until a North Carolina court interprets G.S. 105-365.1 differently, this approach is clearly reasonable.

Regardless of how this question is resolved, tax collectors retain a lien on the underlying real property for the deferred taxes. As is true for all real property tax liens, this lien will survive subsequent transfers and may be foreclosed upon without first resorting to remedies against the owner's personal property.

5. What is the statute of limitations for the enforced collection of deferred taxes?

The Machinery Act requires that enforced collections begin within ten years of the original due of the tax being collected.[6] Deferred taxes become due on the date of the disqualifying event.[7] As a result, tax collectors have ten years from the date of the disqualifying event to collect deferred taxes.

---

6. G.S. 105-378(a).
7. G.S. 105-277.1F(b).

For example, assume that Parcel A enters the circuit breaker program beginning with the 2010 tax year. If a disqualifying event occurs on May 1, 2014, then the deferred taxes for 2011, 2012, and 2013 immediately become due and payable on that date. Enforced collections for those deferred taxes must begin by May 1, 2024. However, taxes on Parcel A for the 2014–2015 tax year would be calculated without the circuit breaker deferral, meaning they would due on September 1, 2014, and subject to enforced collection actions until September 1, 2024.

Chapter 5

The Property Tax Lien

Chapter 5

The Property Tax Lien

1. What is a property tax lien?

A property tax lien is the tool a tax collector uses to collect a tax obligation from a taxpayer's property. In technical terms, a lien is "the right to have a demand satisfied out of the property of another."[1] A property tax lien allows the tax collector to satisfy unpaid taxes by selling the taxpayer's real property (through foreclosure) or tangible personal property (through levy and sale) or by collecting intangible property due to the taxpayer (through the attachment of bank accounts, wages, and rents).

2. When does a tax lien attach to property?

A property tax lien is not enforceable against a particular piece of property until it *attaches* to that property. Note that a tax lien attaches to *property*, not to a taxpayer. Once a tax lien attaches to a specific property, it generally remains attached to that property until the taxes that gave rise to the lien are satisfied, regardless of who owns the property at that time. See Question 8 for a detailed discussion of how tax liens are discharged or extinguished.

A property tax lien on *real* property attaches on January 1 of the year the tax is levied.[2] For example, the 2009 property tax liens on real property

---

This chapter updates information published as *Property Tax Bulletin* No. 150 (Oct. 2009).

1. Thigpen v. Leigh, 93 N.C. 47 (1885).

2. G.S. 105-355(a). This is also true for property annexed by a city or town. Annexations cause the municipal tax lien on the annexed property to relate back to January 1 preceding the fiscal year in which the annexation occurred. G.S. 160A-58.10(b). For example, if Blue Devil City annexes property in Carolina County on March 1, 2010,

arose on January 1, 2009, even though those property taxes are levied for the fiscal year that runs from July 1, 2009 to June 30, 2010. This occurs automatically and no further action by a local government is required to make the lien enforceable. However, a property tax lien on *personal* property attaches only if and when the tax collector levies upon or attaches that property for delinquent taxes.

Consider the situation of Tina Taxpayer. She resides in the fictional Carolina County and lists for taxation in that county real property (Parcel A) and personal property (a boat). The lien for 2009 Carolina County property taxes attaches to Parcel A on January 1, 2009. Although the property taxes on Tina's boat also arise on January 1, 2009, there is no tax lien on that boat unless and until the Carolina County tax collector levies upon and seizes it for delinquent property taxes.

3. What taxes are included in the property tax lien?

This depends on the type of property being attached.

Tax Liens on Real Property

A tax lien on real property and related improvements[3] includes taxes payable in the fiscal year of levy as well as deferred taxes that are not yet due and payable under such programs as the homestead circuit breaker and the present-use value program.[4] This lien also includes property taxes on all *personal* property owned by the same taxpayer in the taxing unit, excluding registered motor vehicles.[5]

Consider again Tina Taxpayer, who lists in Carolina County a parcel of real property (Parcel A), a boat, and a registered motor vehicle. The tax lien

---

the lien on the annexed territory for 2009 taxes (which cover the period July 1, 2009, to June 30, 2010) relates back to January 1, 2009. The 2009 municipal taxes will be prorated for the annexed properties. The 2010 municipal taxes will be levied in full with the lien attaching as of January 1, 2010.

3. Taxes on improvements to and separate rights in real property are a lien on the real property regardless of whether those improvements and separate rights are owned and listed by another party. G.S. 105-355(a)(2).

4. See G.S. 105-277.1B(h) (circuit breaker) and G.S. 105-277.4(c) (present-use value). For a detailed discussion of the collection of deferred taxes, see Chapter 4.

5. G.S. 105-330.4(c) provides that taxes on registered motor vehicles do not become a lien on real property owned by the same taxpayer.

on Parcel A will include the taxes on the real property itself and taxes on the boat but not taxes on the vehicle.

What if Tina listed in Carolina County two parcels of real property (parcels A and B) as well as her boat and vehicle? Because taxes on personal property create a lien on all real property owned by the same taxpayer in the same taxing jurisdiction, the property taxes on Tina's boat would be a lien on *both* parcels of real property listed by Tina. The boat taxes may be collected only once, of course, but the tax collector would have the option of enforcing the lien on either parcel of real property.

However, taxes on Parcel A will not create a lien on Parcel B, or vice-versa. Taxes on one parcel of real property do not become a lien on other parcels of real property owned by the same taxpayer in the same jurisdiction. If Tina pays the 2009 taxes on Parcel A and her boat, the entire tax lien on Parcel A is extinguished. If the taxes on Parcel B become delinquent, the tax collector may foreclose on Parcel B but has no lien and therefore no remedy against Parcel A to collect taxes on Parcel B.

When determining which taxes should be included in the real property tax lien, tax collectors must be careful to distinguish between separate taxpayers. Confusion often arises when spousal, corporate, and partnership taxpayers are involved. Property owned jointly by husband and wife is listed separately from property owned individually by either the husband or the wife.[6] Taxes on personal property owned individually by either a husband or a wife do not become a lien on real property listed by the husband and the wife as tenants by the entirety. Similarly, taxes on personal property listed by a corporation or partnership do not become a lien on real property listed by a shareholder of the corporation or partner in the partnership—even if the corporation or partnership is owned and controlled exclusively by that one shareholder or partner.

A local government's tax lien on real property also may include other debts owed by the taxpayer that for collection purposes are granted a status similar to that of property taxes. These debts may include special assessments,[7] solid waste fees,[8] and costs incurred by the local government

---

6. G.S. 105-302(c) (rules for listing real property) and G.S. 105-306(c) (rules for listing personal property).

7. G.S. 153A-200(c) (counties) and G.S. 160A-233(c) (cities).

8. G.S. 153A-293 (counties) and G.S. 160A-314.1 (cities).

to eliminate public nuisances[9] or violations of minimum housing standards[10] on the taxpayer's property. Different attachment rules apply to these liens, which are discussed in more detail in Question 7.

Tax Liens on Personal Property

A tax lien on personal property may include any and all property taxes owed by the owner of the property as well as other debts with similar collection status such as special assessments.

Return to the example of Tina Taxpayer, who lists in Carolina County two parcels of real property, a boat, and a registered motor vehicle for 2009 property taxes. There are no property tax liens on either the boat or the vehicle unless and until the Carolina County tax collector levies upon and seizes them under G.S. 105-312 to satisfy delinquent taxes. If the 2009 property taxes on Tina's boat become delinquent and the tax collector were to levy upon and seize Tina's vehicle to satisfy those taxes, the tax collector would have a lien on the vehicle as of the date of seizure. The tax collector would have no lien upon Tina's boat even though the boat was the property that generated the unpaid taxes.

4. What happens to the tax lien if the property changes hands?

Transfers of ownership do not extinguish tax liens. With few exceptions, once a lien attaches to property it remains attached to that property until either the underlying taxes are paid or the tax collector sells or forecloses upon the property. See Question 8 for a complete list of situations in which the tax lien is discharged or extinguished.

Because personal property must be either physically secured or seized by the tax collector for a tax lien to attach, it is rare for the ownership of the property to change after the lien attaches. If personal property were transferred after being levied upon by the tax collector, the tax lien would remain attached to the property in the hands of the new owner.

However, real property often changes hands when it is already subject to a lien, because the tax lien on real property arises as a matter of law on January 1 of each year. If the lien is not satisfied at transfer, it remains attached to

---

9. G.S. 153A-140 (counties) and G.S. 160A-193 (cities).
10. G.S. 160A-443(6) (covers both counties and cities).

that property in the hands of the new owner. The transfer of real property cannot extinguish an existing tax lien. But there is one circumstance in which a transfer can *create* a tax lien. This occurs when real property that is completely or partially exempt from property tax as of January 1 is transferred prior to July 1 (the start of the tax year) to an owner who does not qualify for an exemption. In such a situation, the property is taxable in the hands of the new owner for the entire year and the resulting tax lien relates back to January 1.[11]

The reverse is not true. Property that is taxable as of January 1 remains taxable for the entire tax year even if it is sold to an exempt owner before the tax year begins. The tax lien is not extinguished simply because the new owner is exempt from property taxes. The tax lien remains enforceable against that new owner unless that new owner is a government or related agency. In such a case, the tax lien is not enforceable against the governmental owner but remains attached to the property and enforceable against subsequent nongovernmental owners.[12] Although a tax collector may not enforce a tax lien against a governmental owner, under G.S. 105-385(c) governments and related agencies are obligated to satisfy all outstanding tax liens whenever they purchase real property. This obligation is triggered only by a purchase, not by a gift or by a transfer by will, and can be enforced through a civil lawsuit against the governmental owner.[13]

A few examples might help illustrate these principles. Assume that as of January 1, 2009, Parcel A is owned by the Very Expensive School for Rich Kids, an educational organization exempt from property taxes. If the Very Expensive School sells Parcel A to Tina Taxpayer prior to July 1, 2009, the property is taxable for the entire 2009 tax year and the tax lien attaches and relates back to January 1, 2009. If the sale to Tina occurs on or after July 1, 2009, Parcel A is exempt from property taxes for the entire 2009 tax year.

---

11. G.S. 105-285(d).

12. *See* Vaughn v. Bd. of Comm'rs of Forsyth County, 118 N.C. 636 (1896) (government property exempt from seizure and sale by creditors).

13. Nor does G.S. 105-385(c) apply when the federal government seizes property in a forfeiture action. Thankfully for local governments, federal marshals have a policy of paying all outstanding local taxes on property seized in forfeiture actions. *See Letter* from Walter B. Edmisten, United States Marshal, Western District of North Carolina, to Mecklenburg County Tax Assessor, January 8, 1999. (Copy available in author's files.)

Continuing with the same example, assume Tina Taxpayer lists Parcel A for taxation in Carolina County for 2010 but then sells Parcel A to the Slightly Less Expensive School for Upper-Middle-Class Kids, another educational organization exempt from property taxes, in March 2010. The property would remain taxable for the 2010 tax year and the lien for 2010 property taxes would remain attached to Parcel A and enforceable against the Slightly Less Expensive School if the 2010 taxes are not paid by their delinquency date of January 6, 2011.

If Tina instead sells Parcel A to the North Carolina Department of Revenue (DOR) in March 2010, the property still remains taxable for the 2010 tax year and the tax lien remains attached. Under G.S. 105-385(c), the DOR is obligated to satisfy the 2010 tax lien at closing. If the DOR fails to satisfy this obligation, the tax collector's only remedy against the DOR would be a civil lawsuit. The tax lien could not be enforced against the DOR, although it would remain attached to the property if the taxes remain unpaid and enforceable against subsequest nongovernmental owners.

5. What if the property loses value or is destroyed after the tax lien attaches?

The taxable value of all property, both real and personal, is determined as of January 1 of each year.[14] Changes in value after that date have no effect on the tax obligation relating to that property even if the entire property is destroyed before the tax year begins. Because the underlying tax obligation is not affected by a subsequent change in value of the property, the related tax lien is also unaffected and remains enforceable even if the property subject to the lien is completely destroyed.

Here are two examples demonstrating these rules. First, assume that Carolina County assigns Parcel A a 2010 tax value of $200,000, representing $50,000 for the land and $150,000 for a house on that land. If the house is completely destroyed by fire on March 1, 2010, the listing taxpayer remains responsible for the tax owed on the entire $200,000. Carolina County retains a lien on the real property for the entire tax bill.

Second, consider a boat listed for taxes in Carolina County that sinks to the bottom of the ocean twenty miles off the coast of North Carolina on

---

14. G.S. 105-285(b) and G.S. 105-285(d).

March 1, 2010. Despite the fact that the boat is unrecoverable, the listing taxpayer remains obligated for the 2010 taxes. The tax collector had no lien on the boat, because the boat had not been levied upon—and could not have been levied upon because the 2010 taxes were not yet delinquent. But if the taxpayer also listed real property in Carolina County, the tax collector would still have a lien on that real property for the taxes on the boat. And if those taxes become delinquent, the tax collector could foreclose on the real property or seize or attach the taxpayer's personal property to satisfy the taxes on the boat, despite the fact it now rests on the bottom of the Atlantic Ocean.

Similar questions arise when a parcel of real property is subdivided after the tax lien attaches. Which tax liens should attach to the subdivided parcels? Under the definition of "responsible taxpayer" in G.S. 105-273-(17), the owner of one subdivided parcel could be held responsible for the entire tax lien on the undivided parcel. However, in practice, most tax offices would seek to enforce only a portion of the entire lien on the undivided parcel, based on the relative tax values of the subdivided parcels.

6. How do discoveries affect tax liens on real property?

Discoveries occur when the assessor learns of property that was not listed for taxation.[15] Discovery bills are considered part of the tax levy for the fiscal year that opens in the calendar year the discovery is made.[16] Therefore the discovery of personal property creates a lien on the real property owned by the same taxpayer in the same jurisdiction as of January 1 of that year.[17]

For example, assume Suzie Seahawk owns Parcel A and a boat in Carolina County. The assessor discovers in 2011 that Suzie failed to list the boat for 2008 taxes. The discovery bill for the 2008 taxes and penalties will be part of the 2011–2012 tax levy and will be delinquent on January 6, 2012, the same date on which "regular" 2011–2012 taxes will become delinquent. The lien for the 2008 taxes and penalties on the boat will be a lien on Parcel A relating back to January 1, 2011.

---

15. G.S. 105-312. For more details on discoveries, see Chapter 11.

16. G.S. 105-312(i).

17. G.S. 105-355(a).

What happens if the owner of the discovered property transfers real property between the date on which the discovered personal property should have been listed and the date of the discovery? For example, consider again the facts of the Suzie Seahawk hypothetical above. Assume that Suzie sold Parcel A to Billy BlueDevil in 2010. When the assessor discovers the boat in 2011, Suzie no longer owns Parcel A, meaning the discovery taxes and penalty cannot become a lien on Parcel A. If Suzie owns other real property in Carolina County, the discovery bill will become a lien on that other real property. If not, the discovery bill will not be secured by a lien on any real property, despite the fact that the 2008 taxes on the boat would have been secured by a lien on Parcel A had Suzie satisfied her listing obligations back in 2008. Billy will not be responsible for discovered taxes on the boat.

The result is different when the discovery involves improvements to real property rather than personal property. Assume that instead of a boat, the assessor discovers in 2011 a garage on Parcel A that has not been listed for taxation since it was built in 2007. Suzie owned Parcel A until 2010, when she sold it to Billy. In this situation, the discovery bills for 2008, 2009, and 2010 should be issued in the name of Suzie because she was the record owner of Parcel A and the discovered improvement during those years. The 2011 discovery bill will be issued in the name of Billy, the current record owner of the property. But *all* of the discovery taxes and penalties will be a lien on Parcel A as of January 1, 2011, because the discovered improvement existed on Parcel A as of that date. As a result, Billy will ultimately be responsible for the entire amount if Suzie does not pay the discovery bills issued in her name. Most assessors would send Billy copies of all of the discovery bills, even those that are billed to Suzie, so that he has notice of his possible liability. Billy is sure to be furious that he may have liability for Suzie's failure to list the garage, but his recourse is against Suzie, not the tax office.

7. Are tax liens paid before other liens on the same property?

Often but not always.

Property can be subject to multiple liens at the same time. These competing liens can arise from a number of different sources:

- deeds of trust on real property such as mortgage loans,
- security interests in personal property such as motor vehicle loans,

- judgment liens arising from private lawsuits against the taxpayer,
- state tax liens,
- federal tax liens,
- other local government tax liens for property taxes or special assessments.

When multiple liens exist, the order of payment is determined by the *priority* of the liens. Liens with higher priority—"senior" liens—are paid before liens with lower priority—"junior" liens.[18] Typically, the Machinery Act makes property tax liens senior to other liens. But this is not always the case. Sometimes priority will be determined by the dates the competing liens *attached* to the property, a situation described as "first in time, first in right." In general, the earlier a lien attaches, the more senior it is.

When a lien holder enforces a lien, that lien and all junior liens are extinguished regardless of whether the property produces enough cash to satisfy those liens.[19] Senior liens are not extinguished and remain attached to the property after the sale unless they are paid in full with sale proceeds.

The following three tables summarize the priority rules that govern liens for taxes and other obligations that are treated like property taxes for collection purposes, such as special assessments and public nuisance abatement costs.

Table 5.1 covers liens on real property. To use this table, first find the type of lien held by the tax collector in the left-hand column. Then read across that row to determine the priority of that lien relative to other types of liens that might also be attached to the same property. Note that this table distinguishes between property tax liens representing taxes on the real property itself and property tax liens representing taxes on other personal property.

---

18. 51 Am. Jur. 2d *Liens* § 70 (2000).

19. For real property, see Dixieland Realty Co. v. Wysor, 272 N.C. 172, 158 S.E.2d 7 (1967) (foreclosure of senior mortgage extinguishes junior mortgages and liens), and G.S. 1-339.68 (real property sold at execution subject only to senior liens). For personal property, see 51 Am. Jur. 2d *Secured Transactions* § 643 (2003) (sale of collateral by secured creditor discharges the security interest on which the sale is made and all junior liens but does not affect senior liens), 51 Am. Jur. 2d *Liens* § 62 (2000) (sale of property by the creditor holding lien on that property extinguishes that lien), and G.S. 25-9-622 (acceptance of collateral in full or partial satisfaction of the secured obligations extinguishes all junior liens on the collateral.)

Table 5.1. Real Property: Priority of Local Government Liens

Type of Lien	Other Local Real Property Taxes	Other Local Personal Property Taxes	Other Local Special Assessments	State Taxes[a]	Federal Taxes[b]	Private
Real property taxes (G.S. 105-356(a))	Equal dignity	Equal dignity	Senior	First in time, first in right	Senior	Senior
Personal property taxes (G.S. 105-356(a)) Solid waste fees (G.S. 153A-293 or G.S. 160A-314.1) Nuisance abatement (G.S. 153A-140 or G.S. 160A-193)	Equal dignity	Equal dignity	Senior	First in time, first in right	First in time, first in right	Senior
Special assessments (G.S. 153A-200(c) or G.S. 160A-233(c))	Junior	Junior	Equal dignity	Junior	Junior	Senior
Minimum housing standards repair/ demolition[c] (G.S. 160A-443(6)(a))	Junior	Junior	Equal dignity	Junior	Junior	Senior

Note: Find the lien in the left-hand column and read across to determine its relative priority.

[a] Carteret County v. Long, 349 N.C. 285, 507 S.E. 2d 39 (1998), and G.S. 105-241(d).

[b] 26 U.S.C. § 6323.

[c] This category refers only to liens on the specific real property that required repair or demolition. Under G.S. 160A-443(6)(b), a local government that incurs repair or demolition costs to enforce minimum housing standards is also granted liens on certain other real property owned by the same owner. However, these additional liens are not granted any preferential priority. They are junior to liens for local taxes and special assessments and first in time, first in right as to all other liens.

These liens have different priorities relative to federal tax liens (discussed more below).

"Equal dignity" means that the two liens have the same priority, are paid at the same time upon foreclosure sale, and share proportionately in the proceeds if the sale does not produce enough cash to satisfy both liens entirely. All property tax liens have the same priority and are of equal dignity with all other property tax liens and liens for solid waste fees and nuisance abatement costs, which are granted the same collection status as property taxes.

For example, assume that Carolina County and Blue Devil City both have property tax liens on Parcel A—$600 for the county and $400 for the city. These two liens are of equal dignity and have the same priority regardless of when they arose. The county's lien could be from 2009, and the city's lien could be from 2001, or vice-versa; the two liens would have still have the same priority. If the property is eventually foreclosed upon either by the city or by the county (or by both) for nonpayment of taxes, the two tax liens would be paid at the same time from the sale proceeds.[20] If the foreclosure sale produced $100 after costs and fees, the city and county will share these proceeds in proportion to their liens — $60 for the county and $40 for the city.

"Senior" means that the lien in the left-hand column has priority over the other lien on the property. A property tax lien on real property always has priority over a special assessment lien and private lien such as a deed of trust (mortgage) even if one of these liens has attached to the real property before the property tax lien. For example, assume that in 2006, Blue Devil City levies a special assessment on Parcel A. If Carolina County forecloses on Parcel A for delinquent 2008 taxes, the county's property tax lien has priority over the city's special assessment lien despite the fact that the tax lien arose two years after the special assessment lien.

"Junior" means that the lien in the left-hand column has a lower priority than the other lien on the property. A special assessment lien always has a priority lower than that of local, state, and federal tax liens, regardless of which lien attached first.

"First in time, first in right" means that the first of the two liens to attach and become "perfected" — in other words, enforceable against other liens — has priority. For example, a local government property tax lien is first in

---

20. Although the details of the foreclosure process exceed the scope of this chapter, note that this statement is true only if both the city and the county participate in the foreclosure action. G.S. 105-374 and G.S. 105-375.

Table 5.2. Real Property: Attachment/Perfection Dates for Liens

Type of Lien	Date of Attachment/Perfection
Real property tax lien (G.S. 105-356(a))	January 1 of the year in which the taxes or fees are levied
Personal property tax lien (G.S. 105-356(a)) Solid waste fee lien (G.S. 153A-293 or G.S. 160A-314.1)	(tax liens become "choate" on the date the local government adopts its budget ordinance, for purposes of determining priority of personal property taxes liens relative to federal tax liens)
Special assessment lien (G.S. 153A-200(c) or G.S. 160A-233(c))	Date on which the governing board confirms the assessment roll
Nuisance abatement lien (G.S. 153A-140 or G.S. 160A-193) Minimum housing standards repair/ demolition lien (G.S. 160A-443(6)(a) and (b))	Date on which costs are incurred
State tax lien (G.S. 105-241(d)) Federal tax lien (26 U.S.C. § 6323(f) and G.S. 44-68.12)	Date on which lien is recorded in the clerk of superior court

time, first in right compared with a lien for unpaid state income or sales taxes.[21] If Carolina County forecloses on Parcel A for delinquent 2008 property taxes, the county's property tax lien would be senior to state tax liens that attached to Parcel A after January 1, 2008—the date on which the 2008 property tax lien attached to real property—and junior to state tax liens that attached before that date.

To determine which lien first attached and became perfected, use Table 5.2.

Two unique aspects of federal and state tax liens bear discussion. First, unlike local property tax liens, state and federal tax liens must be recorded in the appropriate superior court in order to be enforceable against other liens.[22] Second, when determining the priority of local tax liens as compared to a federal tax lien on real property, the local tax collector must distinguish between the lien for taxes on the real property itself and the lien for taxes

---

21. Carteret County v. Long, 349 N.C. 285, 507 S.E.2d 39 (1998).
22. G.S. 105-241 and 26 U.S.C. § 6323(f)(1).

on personal property owned by the same taxpayer. The lien for taxes on the real property always has priority over a federal tax lien, regardless of which lien attached first.[23] However, the lien for taxes on personal property is first in time, first in right relative to a federal tax lien, based on a comparison of the date the federal tax lien was recorded in the appropriate superior court and the date the local tax lien became "choate"—when it became specific as to the property and the amount of taxes secured.[24] Local property taxes become specific when the local budget ordinance is adopted and the tax rate finalized, which is required to occur before July 1.[25]

For example, assume that the federal government records a tax lien against Parcel A in Carolina County Superior Court on February 1, 2009. Carolina County holds a 2009 property tax lien against Parcel A, consisting of $600 in taxes on Parcel A and $100 in taxes on a boat owned by the same taxpayer. The federal lien would be junior to the $600 county lien for taxes on Parcel A but would be senior to the $100 county lien for taxes on the boat, which were not choate on February 1, 2009, because the county had yet to adopt its tax rate.

Table 5.3 addresses the priority of tax liens on personal property. As with Table 5.1, find the type of lien held by the tax collector in the left-hand column. Then read across that row to determine the priority of that lien relative to other types of liens that might also be attached to the same property. The terms "equal dignity," "first in time, first in right," "senior," and "junior" have the same meanings as in Table 5.1.

Note that Table 5.3 distinguishes between a lien for taxes on the property that is the subject of the lien (in row 1) and a lien for taxes on other real or personal property (in row 2). The former is always senior to both state tax liens and private liens (such as those held by finance lenders). The latter is first in time, first in right to both state tax and private liens based on when it attaches.

Use Table 5.4 to determine the date of attachment for a lien on personal property that is first in time, first in right as to other liens.

Unlike a property tax lien on real property, a property tax lien on personal property does not attach automatically on January 1. Local property

---

23. 26 U.S.C. § 6323(b)(6) and G.S. 105-346(a)(1).

24. United States by and through Internal Revenue Service v. McDermott, 507 U.S. 447, 449 (1993).

25. G.S. 159-13(a).

Table 5.3. Personal Property: Priority of Local Government Liens

Type of Lien	Other Local Real Property Taxes	Other Local Personal Property Taxes	Other Local Special Assessments	State Taxes	Federal Taxes	Private
Personal property taxes on the property subject to lien (G.S. 105-356(b))	First in time, first in right	First in time, first in right	Senior	Senior	First in time, first in right	Senior
Personal property taxes on other property (G.S. 105-356(b)) Real property taxes (G.S. 105-356(b)) Solid waste fees (G.S. 153A-293 or G.S. 160A-314.1) Nuisance abatement (G.S. 153A-140 or G.S. 160A-193)	First in time, first in right	First in time, first in right	Senior	First in time, first in right	First in time, first in right	First in time, first in right
Special assessments (G.S. 153A-200(c) or G.S. 160A-233(c))						
Minimum housing standards repair/ demolition (G.S. 160A-443(6)(a))	Junior	Junior	First in time, first in right	First in time, first in right	First in time, first in right	First in time, first in right

Note: Find the lien in the left-hand column and read across to determine its relative priority.

tax liens—and other liens collectible as property taxes—attach to personal property only when a tax collector levies upon the property (for tangible personal property like boats, motor vehicles, and equipment) or provides notice of attachment and garnishment (for intangible property like bank accounts and wages). The same is true of state tax liens. A federal tax lien

Table 5.4. Personal Property: Attachment/Perfection Dates for Liens

Type of Lien	Date of Attachment/Perfection
Real property tax lien (G.S. 105-356(a))	Date on which *tangible* personal property is levied upon or
Personal property tax lien (G.S. 105-356(a))	Date on which *intangible* personal property is attached/garnished
Solid waste fee lien (G.S. 153A-293 or G.S. 160A-314.1)	
Special assessment lien (G.S. 153A-200(c) or G.S. 160A-233(c))	
Nuisance abatement lien (G.S. 153A-140 or G.S. 160A-193)	
Minimum housing standards repair/ demolition lien (G.S. 160A-443(6)(a))	
State tax lien (G.S. 105-241(d))	
Federal tax lien (26 U.S.C. § 6323(f) and G.S. 44-68.12)	Date on which lien is recorded in the clerk of superior court

is perfected and enforceable against other lien holders when the federal government records its lien in the appropriate superior court.

An example might help illustrate the rules listed in Tables 5.3 and 5.4. Assume that in 2010 the DOR levies upon the boat owned by Tina Taxpayer in Carolina County for unpaid 2007 state income taxes. While this boat is in the hands of the county sheriff awaiting sale, Carolina County levies upon the boat for delinquent 2009 property taxes owed by Tina. The county's lien represents taxes on Tina's real property as well as property taxes on the boat itself. When Tina purchased the boat in 2005, she financed it with a loan from Big Bank. The bank recorded a security interest in the boat to secure the loan. What are the relative priorities of these liens?

Applying the rules listed in Tables 5.3 and 5.4, the county tax lien representing taxes on the boat itself has the highest priority, despite the fact that the county's liens were the last to attach. The county tax lien representing taxes on Tina's real property is first in time, first in right to both the state tax lien and Big Bank's lien. Both the state tax lien and Big Bank's lien have priority over the county tax lien for real property taxes because they attached before the county's tax lien. Between the state tax lien and Big Bank's lien, the first to attach has priority, meaning that Big Bank's lien is senior.[26] Simply put, the relative priority of these four liens is:

1. Carolina County's lien for property taxes on the boat,
2. Big Bank's security interest,
3. DOR's lien for unpaid income taxes,
4. Carolina County's lien for real property taxes.

8. When is a tax lien discharged, extinguished, or made unenforceable?

This can occur in a number of situations, the most obvious of which is the payment of the taxes that gave rise to the lien. Below is a list of events that can cause a tax lien to "unattach" from property or become unenforceable. Numbers 1, 2, 3, and 4 discharge or extinguish the lien entirely; when one of these events occurs, the lien no longer exists. Numbers 5, 6, and 7 render the tax lien unenforceable against some or all parties with a legal interest; the lien still exists, but it has limited or no utility for a tax collector.

1. Payment of the taxes, interest, and costs that gave rise to the lien.[27]
2. Release by the governing board of the taxes, interest, and costs under G.S. 105-381.
3. Sale through foreclosure or levy and execution by the taxing unit or by a senior lien holder.[28]
4. By order of a federal bankruptcy court judge.[29]

---

26. G.S. 105-241(d).

27. G.S. 105-362(a) (real property liens); G.S. 105-366; and G.S. 1-339.57 (personal property). Note that under 105-363, a co-owner of real property may release his or her share of the property from the tax lien by paying the appropriate percentage of the total taxes, interests, and costs that are a lien on the property.

28. *Supra*, n. 19.

29. A bankruptcy court judge can order that property subject to a local tax lien be sold "free and clear" of all liens, with the lien to attach to the proceeds. However, there is no guarantee that there will be proceeds to which a lien can attach, because often a creditor may be permitted to purchase the property by "bidding" and releasing its

5. Reliance on a certificate of taxes owed and issued by the tax collector under G.S. 105-361 or a tax receipt for payment by check or electronic means under G.S. 105-357(b)(1) (unenforceable against the party that relies on the documents and against all subsequent innocent purchasers).
6. Transfer of the property to a government or related agency (unenforceable against the government or related agency).
7. Application of the Machinery Act's statute of limitations, G.S. 105-378(a), which bars enforced collection actions more than ten years after the original due date of the underlying taxes (unenforceable against all parties).

Number 1 deserves special mention when it involves satisfaction of a tax lien on real property that includes both real and personal property taxes. Under G.S. 105-362(a), a taxpayer who wishes to discharge the tax lien on his or her real property must pay not only the taxes on that real property but also pay all personal property taxes that are included in that lien. However, if a prospective buyer or person with a legal interest in that same real property wishes to discharge the tax lien, that person must pay only the taxes on the real property plus a proportionate part of the personal property taxes included in that lien.

Here's how it works. Assume Tina Taxpayer lists for 2009 taxes in Carolina County two parcels of real property (Parcel A and Parcel B) as well as a boat. Parcel A and Parcel B each have tax values of $100,000. If Tina wishes to discharge the 2009 tax lien on Parcel A, she must pay the 2009 taxes on Parcel A plus *all* of the taxes owed on the boat. Now assume that Wanda Wolfpack is under contract to purchase Parcel A. If she wishes to discharge the lien on Parcel A, Wanda must pay the taxes on Parcel A plus a *proportionate part* of the taxes on the boat. This proportion is calculated by dividing the assessed value of the real property in question by the assessed value of all real property listed in the county by the same taxpayer. In this situation, Parcel A represents 50 percent of the assessed value of all real property listed in Carolina County by Tina Taxpayer ($100,000/$200,000). Wanda, therefore, must pay 50 percent of the taxes on Tina's boat, in addition to the taxes on Parcel A, to discharge the tax lien on Parcel A.

---

claims against the debtor. 11 U.S.C. 363(f) and (k). For a detailed discussion of how a bankruptcy filing affects the tax collection process, see Chapter 16.

9. Can a private party enforce a tax lien?

Yes, in limited circumstances.

Contrary to a persistent myth, a person cannot gain rights to real property simply by paying the taxes owed on that real property. That said, special rules apply to co-owners, lien holders, and other parties who *already* have a legal interest in a particular piece of real property. Under G.S. 105-363 and G.S. 105-386, if an interested party pays the outstanding taxes on the real property, that party "steps into the shoes" of the taxing authority and is entitled to enforce the tax lien through judicial proceedings. That party cannot, however, use Machinery Act remedies, such as attachment or garnishment, to enforce the lien.

For example, assume that Terry Tarheel holds a properly recorded mortgage lien on Parcel A, which is owned by Debbie Duke. If Terry pays the outstanding taxes on Parcel A, she will immediately possess an additional lien on Parcel A in the amount of taxes paid. However, if the taxes are paid by Debbie's brother or any other party who has no legal interest in the property, that person will not automatically gain a lien on Parcel A.

Chapter 6

Attachment and Garnishment

Attaching bank accounts and garnishing wages are increasingly popular enforcement remedies for tax collectors, with good reason. Under the Machinery Act the attachment and garnishment process is extremely efficient. It permits the tax collector to seize bank accounts, wages, rents, real estate closing settlements, sale proceeds, or any other funds payable to the taxpayer simply by providing notice to the taxpayer and the party holding those funds. If that party does not pay the seized funds to the tax collector, it becomes responsible for the outstanding taxes.

The attachment and garnishment process is far from a silver bullet, of course. It requires information about where the taxpayer banks, works, or conducts business, information that the taxpayer generally does not want to volunteer. It requires the cooperation of banks and employers, which are usually more worried about their customers and employees than they are about unpaid property taxes. And, unlike most sales at foreclosure or levy, it leaves the property that generated the delinquent taxes in the hands of the offending taxpayer, perhaps increasing the likelihood that tax collectors will have to use enforced collection remedies in multiple tax years.

This chapter focuses on the law governing the attachment and garnishment process. For details about the mechanics of the process, see the comprehensive North Carolina Tax Collectors Association's *Collections Procedure Manual* available on the NCTCA website at www.nctca.org.

This chapter updates information published as *Property Tax Bulletin* No. 152 (Feb. 2010).

1. When may a tax collector use attachment and garnishment?

Attachment and garnishment may be used whenever the tax collector is authorized to pursue enforced collection remedies against personal property under G.S. 105-366.[1] This remedy may be employed to collect property taxes on any type of property, be it real or personal, or a registered motor vehicle. No additional order from the governing board or a court is required, because the order of collection made by the board when it delivered the tax receipts to the collector serves as the equivalent of a judgment and execution against taxpayers' property.[2]

The general rule is that tax collectors may not employ enforced collection remedies until unpaid property taxes become delinquent. Most property taxes become delinquent on the date interest begins to accrue.[3] Deferred taxes become delinquent on the date a disqualifying event occurs.[4]

Enforced Collection before Delinquency

Tax collectors need not always wait until the date of delinquency to begin enforced collection efforts against personal property, however. G.S. 105-366 permits a tax collector to take action before the date of delinquency when the taxpayer

1. is about to remove the property from the taxing unit,
2. is about to transfer the property to another taxpayer,
3. is in imminent danger of becoming insolvent,
4. goes out of business, or

---

1. Although in other contexts the terms "attachment" and "garnishment" have distinct meanings, the Machinery Act uses them interchangeably. This chapter does likewise.

2. G.S. § 105-321(b).

3. G.S. 105-365.1(a)(1). Property taxes on property other than registered motor vehicles accrue interest beginning on January 6 following the year in which the taxes were levied. G.S. 105-360(a). Property taxes on motor vehicles accrue interest on the first day of the first month following the date the taxes were due, unless the tax bill is prepared after the due date, in which case the taxes accrue interest on the first day of the second month after the bill is prepared. G.S. 105-330.4(b).

4. G.S. 105-365.1(a)(2). For taxes deferred under the circuit breaker program, G.S. 105-277.1B, the date of delinquency is nine months after the date of the disqualifying event if that event is the death of the owner. G.S. 105-365.1(a)(3). For a more detailed discussion about the circuit breaker program and the seven other deferred tax programs, see Chapter 4.

5. transfers the major part of its inventory, supplies, or fixtures to another taxpayer other than in the ordinary course of business.

G.S. 105-366(c) requires that the tax collector have "reasonable grounds for believing" that the taxpayer is about to take the actions described in numbers 1, 2, and 3. Although North Carolina courts have yet to interpret the exact meaning of this "reasonable belief" requirement, it is safe to assume that it would require something more than an unconfirmed rumor or gossip.

Numbers 4 and 5 are commonly referred to as the "going out of business" provisions. G.S. 105-366(d) authorizes not only "early" enforced collection actions in these instances but also collection actions targeting the new owner of the property, if the tax collector begins the action within six months of the sale or transfer of the property. For more details on this "going out of business" exception, see Question 4, below.

Order of Remedies

Often a tax collector has potential collection remedies against real property, through foreclosure, and against personal property, through attachment and garnishment or levy and sale. If so, the tax collector normally has the discretion to choose which remedy to use first. The Machinery Act describes only two scenarios in which a tax collector must first target personal property:

1. when the governing body orders a tax collector to do so and
2. when the taxpayer or a lienholder requests that the tax collector do so and provides a written statement "describing the personal property to be proceeded against and giving its location."[5]

Tax collectors who proceed first against real property must remember that the Machinery Act bars all collection remedies against personal property once a foreclosure complaint is filed.[6] After starting a foreclosure action,

---

5. G.S. 105-366(a)(1) and (2). It is unclear exactly what remedy a taxpayer would have against a tax collector who violated these mandates. Subsection (a) states, "No foreclosure of a tax lien on real property may be attacked as invalid on the ground that payment of the tax should have been procured from personal property." If a taxpayer cannot object to a foreclosure action because the tax collector should have proceeded first against the taxpayer's personal property, these mandates seem to lack teeth.

6. G.S. 105-366(b).

the tax collector may not pursue any other collection remedies other than those available under the Set-Off Debt Collection Act.[7]

Appeals

Local governments may not use *any* enforced collection remedies if an appeal of the assessment that generated the delinquent taxes is pending before the county board of equalization and review, the state Property Tax Commission, or the courts.[8] Interest continues to accrue on the account while the appeal is pending.[9] Once the taxpayer's appeal is resolved, the local government may immediately begin enforced collection actions for any remaining delinquent taxes.

2. What kinds of intangible property may be attached or garnished?

The Machinery Act places no limitation on kinds of intangible property that may be subject to attachment and garnishment. Wages, other compensation, rents, bank deposits, and "any other intangible personal property" may be targeted by the tax collector to satisfy delinquent taxes.[10] Bank account and weekly or monthly wages are of course the most common and reliable sources of funds, but tax collectors should consider all possible debts that might be owed to the delinquent taxpayer. If the taxpayer owns rental property, the tenants may be served notices of attachment and be required to pay their monthly rents to the tax collector instead of their landlord.[11] If

---

7. G.S. Chapter 105A. This act provides local governments the ability to attach and garnish a taxpayer's state income tax refund or lottery winnings. It specifically makes these remedies "in addition to and not in substitution for" any other collection remedies available to the local government. G.S. 105A-3(a). See Chapter 8 for more details.

8. G.S. 105-378(d). S.L. 2011-3 extended this provision to cover taxes appealed to the county board of equalization and review.

9. See Chapter 3 for more details on interest.

10. G.S. 105-368(a).

11. Not surprisingly, tenants are usually less than thrilled to receive a notice of attachment for fear that the landlord will respond punitively if they satisfy the attachment obligation. Although no state law expressly protects tenants in this situation, at least two could offer some relief. G.S. 75-51, which makes it an unfair trade practice to attempt to collect a debt by means of any "unfair threat or coercion," could apply to a landlord who threatened to evict a tenant who complied with a legal attachment. A tenant's compliance with an order of attachment could also trigger protection under

the taxpayer is closing on the sale of real estate, the closing attorney can be served with a notice of attachment and be required to first satisfy outstanding taxes before delivering the proceeds of the sale to the seller. If another city or county department owes the delinquent taxpayer funds due to a contractual obligation or an overpayment, that department may be served with a notice of attachment and be required to direct those funds to the tax collector instead.

The remedy is not entirely without limits, however. State and federal laws exempt a variety of payments and benefits from attachment by creditors. Funds that are off-limits to tax collectors include:

1. Social Security benefits;[12]
2. federal railroad retirement benefits, federal railroad unemployment and sickness benefits, civil service retirement system benefits, and federal employee retirement system benefits;[13] federal military veterans' benefits;[14]
3. North Carolina state and county public assistance payments, including those for Work First, foster care, adoption assistance, food and nutrition services, and Medicaid;[15]
4. North Carolina unemployment benefits;[16]
5. North Carolina teacher and state employee retirement benefits;[17]
6. North Carolina workers' compensation;[18] North Carolina local government retiree benefits;[19] and
7. retirement savings plans covered by the federal Employee Retirement Income Security Act, which includes most pension, profit sharing, and 401(k) savings plans.[20]

---

the retaliatory eviction provisions, G.S. 42-37.1, which offers tenants defenses to a summary eviction proceeding.

12. 42 U.S.C. § 407.

13. 42 U.S.C. § 1383(d)(1), 45 U.S.C. § 231m(a), 45 U.S.C. § 352(e), 5 U.S.C. § 8346(a), and 5 U.S.C.§ 8470.

14. 38 U.S.C. § 5301.

15. G.S. 108A-36. Medicaid payments to providers and recipients are also exempted from attachment by 42 C.F.R. § 447.10.

16. G.S. 96-17(c).

17. G.S. 135-9.

18. G.S. 97-21.

19. G.S. 128-31.

20. 29 U.S.C. § 1056(d)(1); 26 U.S.C. § 401(a)(13)(A).

All seven of these categories of benefits are exempt from attachment prior to payment. That is, a tax collector may not send a notice of attachment to the agency or institution responsible for paying these benefits and ask that future benefits be paid first to the tax collector.

However, the first five categories—Social Security benefits, federal retiree benefits, veterans' benefits, state and county public assistance payments, and unemployment benefits—are exempt also from attachment *post payment.* As a result, these benefit payments can be exempt from attachment even after they are received by a taxpayer and deposited into a bank account.

If a bank account contains only exempt benefit payments, that account should be exempt from attachment for delinquent taxes. But what if a bank account contains exempt benefits as well as other, nonexempt funds? For the most part, no clear guidance exists on this issue. The North Carolina unemployment benefits antiassignment clause explicitly states that the protection from attachment terminates when the benefits are mingled with other funds.[21] This means that if a taxpayer deposits any funds from a nonexempt source into a bank account that also contains unemployment benefits, the entire bank account would be subject to attachment. But the antiassignment clauses for such federal benefits as Social Security and for North Carolina public assistance are less explicit. For years, tax collectors, banks, and taxpayers haggled over exactly what portion, if any, of a commingled bank account could be attached for delinquent taxes.

In 2011 the federal government issued regulations that attempted to clarify the attachment and garnishment process for exempt federal benefits, such as Social Security.[22] Under the new regulations, the burden of determining whether the attached account contains exempt federal benefits falls on the bank rather than on the taxpayer or the taxing unit. The applicability of this new process to tax garnishments remains in question, however, because the regulations cover only court-ordered garnishments and those issued by child support enforcement agencies.[23] As this chapter

---

21. G.S. 96-17(c).

22. 76 Fed. Reg. 9939 (Feb. 23, 2011). The interim final rule became effective May 1, 2011.

23. The regulations define "garnishment order" as "a writ, order, notice, summons, judgment, or similar written instruction *issued by a court* or a State child support enforcement agency, including a lien arising by operation of law for overdue child support, to effect a garnishment against a debtor." *Id.* (emphasis added).

describes, in North Carolina bank accounts can be garnished without the need for a court order.

Before the regulations took effect, most observers assumed they would apply to property tax garnishments because the orders of collection issued by governing boards to local tax collectors are the equivalent of court orders.[24] But after receiving many inquires on the issue, the United States Treasury Department advised that the absence of an actual court order means that the new regulations will *not* apply to local tax garnishments.[25]

Nevertheless, local tax collectors need to understand the new attachment procedure created by the regulations for three reasons. First, some banks still may choose to apply the new procedure to all garnishments.[26] Second, the new regulations were not yet final as of mid-2011. They were released as "interim final rules" subject to further changes after a public comment period. Depending on the comments received, the regulations could be extended to cover tax garnishments. Third, even if the new regulations are never applied to local tax garnishments North Carolina tax collectors could eliminate much of the confusion around this issue by consistently applying the regulations' procedure when attaching bank accounts that contain exempt federal benefits or state and county public assistance payments.[27]

---

24. G.S. 105-321(b) states that orders to collect have "the full force and effect of a judgment and execution against the taxpayers' real and personal property."

25. Conversation with Natalie H. Diana, senior counsel, Office of Chief Counsel, U.S. Treasury, Financial Management Service (May 2, 2011).

26. That may be good news for tax collectors because it relieves them of the obligation to determine the existence and exempt status of federal benefits. But it may be a risky approach for a bank. The Machinery Act makes the bank, as garnishee, liable for any funds removed from the garnished account after receiving notice of the tax garnishment. The new federal regulations trump that state law by requiring banks to wait to freeze the account until after conducting the two-month lookback described above. Banks are absolved of liability if the account holder withdraws money from the account between the notice date and the date of the lookback review. However, banks are protected by the federal regulations only for garnishments explicitly covered by those regulations. If a bank were to apply the lookback procedure to a state tax garnishment that is not covered by the new regulations, the bank could be held liable under the Machinery Act for any funds withdrawn after the bank received the garnishment notice but before it completed the lookback review.

27. The lookback review should *not* be applied to state unemployment benefits that were deposited into accounts that contain other funds, because state law explicitly makes those benefits subject to attachment when they have been mingled with other funds. G.S. 96-17(c).

The new regulations require banks to conduct an account review within two days of receiving a notice of attachment to determine if any exempt federal benefits have been deposited into the attached account during a two-month "lookback period."[28] If so, then the bank must protect from attachment and allow the taxpayer access to the lesser of (i) the amount of exempt federal benefits deposited into the account during the lookback period and (ii) the balance of the account as of the date of the account review. Any funds in excess of this protected amount must be frozen from taxpayer access immediately and distributed to the garnishor (i.e., the taxing unit) in a timely fashion. Note that the lookback procedure applies whenever the bank account contains exempt benefits and not only when exempt benefits are mingled with other funds.

Here is how this procedure should work in practice. Assume that Big Bank receives a notice of attachment on Big Bank on May 1, 2012, for Billy BlueDevil's savings account. Within two business days, Big Bank must conduct an account review for the previous two months. Assuming Big Bank conducts the review on May 2, the lookback period would begin on May 1 and extend back to March 1.

If no exempt federal benefits were deposited in Billy's account at Big Bank during the lookback period, then Big Bank must proceed as usual with the attachment by freezing the entire account and forwarding the attached funds to the creditor that initiated the attachment.

Assume instead that Big Bank learns that $4,000 of Social Security benefits had been deposited into Billy's account during the lookback period, $2,000 per month in March and April, and that there was $5,000 in the account on the date of the review. Big Bank would then be obligated to protect from attachment and continue to make available to Billy $4,000. The remaining $1,000 would be subject to attachment, meaning Big Bank immediately must block Billy's access to $1,000 of the account and then remit that amount to the creditor that initiated the attachment.

---

28. To accomplish this task, banks will rely heavily on identifiers placed on electronic deposits and fund transfers by the Automated Clearinghouse (ACH), the electronic network for banking in the United States. The lookback period runs from the day before the account review is conducted to the corresponding date two months earlier. For example, if the account review were conducted on November 16, the lookback period would run from November 15 to September 15.

What if Big Bank learns that $4,000 of Social Security benefits had been deposited into Billy's account during the lookback period but only $3,000 was in Billy's account on the date of the account review? In that case the entire account would be protected from attachment and remain available to Billy, and there would be no unprotected funds available for attachment.

HUD Rent Payments

Although federal and state *benefit* payments are often exempt from prepayment attachment, the same is not true of federal and state *rent* payments. For example, the federal Department of Housing and Urban Development operates a Section 8 housing program that subsidizes landlords who make housing available to certain low-income individuals. If a Section 8 landlord owes delinquent property taxes, the Section 8 rent payments from the federal government to the landlord should be subject to attachment. Similarly, rent paid by the county and/or the federal government to a private landlord to lease a building for use by the county's Women, Infants, and Children (WIC) program also should be subject to attachment for delinquent taxes owed by the landlord.

3. Whose intangible personal property may be subject to attachment and garnishment?

The answer depends on the type of tax being collected.

For property taxes on real property, the responsible taxpayers are the owner of record on the date of delinquency and all subsequent owners.[29] A responsible taxpayer is defined as the person or entity whose property may be targeted for collection efforts. For real property taxes that were not deferred, this means that the tax collector may attach wages or bank accounts of the owner as of January 6 in the fiscal year for which the taxes were levied and of all subsequent owners. For real property taxes that were originally deferred, the responsible taxpayers are the owner of the real property on the date the disqualifying event occurs and all subsequent owners.

---

29. G.S. 105-365.1(b)(1). This is true for taxes arising in 2006 and subsequent years. For taxes from 2005 and earlier, the responsible taxpayer for real property taxes is the owner of record as of the listing date—the same rule that currently applies to personal property taxes.

For property taxes on personal property other than registered motor vehicles, the responsible taxpayer is the owner of record as of the listing date, January 1 prior to the beginning of the fiscal year for which the taxes were levied.[30] Subsequent owners are not responsible for taxes on personal property, unless the "going out of business" provisions in G.S. 105-366(d) apply. (More on this issue below in Question 4.)

For property taxes on registered motor vehicles, the responsible taxpayer is the owner of record as of the date on which the current vehicle registration is renewed or the date on which a new registration is applied for.[31]

Here is how these rules work in practice. Assume Tina Taxpayer lists real property (Parcel A), a boat, and a registered automobile for 2009 taxation in Carolina County. Tina fails to pay any of her 2009 property taxes. In February 2010 Tina sells Parcel A, the boat, and the automobile to Cindy Citizen. If the Carolina County tax collector wishes to use the attachment and garnishment process to collect these outstanding taxes, whose intangible personal property may be targeted, Tina's or Cindy's?

For the taxes on Parcel A, the record owner as of January 6, 2010, and all subsequent owners are the responsible taxpayers. This means both Tina and Cindy may be subject to attachment and garnishment for the taxes on Parcel A. For the taxes on the boat, only the listing taxpayer is responsible.[32] This means only Tina may be subject to attachment and garnishment for the taxes on the boat. For the taxes on the registered automobile, only the owner as of the date the registration was renewed is the responsible taxpayer. Assuming Tina renewed the registration in 2009, only Tina's intangible personal property may be subject to attachment and garnishment for taxes on the automobile.

---

30. G.S. 105-365.1(b)(2).

31. G.S. 105-365.1(b)(3).

32. Note that because Tina listed both the boat and Parcel A in Carolina County, the taxes on the boat create a lien on Parcel A. G.S. 105-355(a). Although Cindy's personal property may not be subject to enforced collection remedies to satisfy the taxes on the boat, the tax collector could enforce the county's lien on Parcel A through a foreclosure action to satisfy the taxes on the boat. For a more detailed discussion of tax liens on real property, see Chapter 5.

Owner of Record

Before deciding which taxpayer to target with enforced collection remedies, G.S. 105-365.1 requires a tax collector to determine the "owner of record" as of either the listing date (for personal property), the delinquency date (for real property), or the date on which a motor vehicle registration was renewed or applied for. The Machinery Act does not define the term "owner of record," nor have the courts. How, then, is a tax collector expected to make this determination? Thankfully, record ownership of most taxable property can be determined by documents such as titles, deeds, and court orders.

For personal property that is subject to title documents, such as motor vehicles, airplanes, and boats, the owner of record should be the party whose name is on the title document as of the relevant date. Title documents do not exist for many types of taxable personal property, however. For example, when one landscaper sells used lawnmowers to another landscaper, no title documents change hands. If there is a contract or sales receipt involved, that document could serve as proof of record ownership. But when no such documents exist, ownership as of a particular date may more difficult to prove. Possession is generally considered the "strongest evidence of ownership,"[33] but what if both landscapers claim *not* to have had possession of the property as of the listing date? The best solution would seem to be for the assessor to keep the property listed in the name of the original owner until that owner provides proof that ownership has been transferred to another party.[34]

For real property, the owner of record is the party identified in a document recorded either in the county register of deeds office or in Superior Court. Normally, ownership of real property is transferred by deed. A valid deed transfers title from the grantor to the grantee regardless of when or if it is recorded.[35] However, that transfer is not effective against lienholders, such as the county tax office, until that transfer is recorded with the register

---

33. Boyce v. Williams, 84 N.C. 275 (1881).

34. For example, see G.S. 105-312(f), which creates a presumption that property discovered in the hands of a taxpayer should be listed in that taxpayer's name for the preceding five years unless that taxpayer can demonstrate that another taxpayer owned the property and therefore had the duty to list it for taxation in any of those years.

35. Patterson v. Bryant, 216 N.C. 550, 5 S.E.2d 849 (1939).

of deeds.[36] Similarly, a consent agreement between divorcing spouses that calls for the transfer of real property to one of the soon-to-be ex-spouses must be incorporated into a divorce judgment and recorded with the register of deeds to change the owner of record.[37]

When the owner of real property dies, tax officials should not change the owner of record until the clerk of superior court records either a certificate of probate (if the owner died with a will)[38] or a final accounting by the personal representative for the estate (if the owner died intestate without a will).[39] Under intestacy law title passes to the heirs effective as of the date of death, even if the heirs are not identified until much later.[40] For example, if an owner dies on December 15, 2009, but the heirs are not determined until February 1, 2010, the heirs are the owner of record as of the listing date (January 1) for 2010 taxes and the delinquency date for 2009 taxes (January 6), even though they were not identified until a month later.[41]

---

36. G.S. 47-18(a).

37. G.S. 1-228. Even then, the divorce judgment needs to include or incorporate an adequate description of the real property and indicate that the transfer is effective as of the date of the judgment for that transfer to be effective against third parties. *See* Martin v. Roberts, 177 N.C. App. 415, 628 S.E.2d 812 (2006) (consent order in divorce proceeding did not transfer title to real property because it lacked a legal description of the property and it contemplated a future conveyance, not a completed conveyance). For example, a judgment of divorce containing the following provisions would be sufficient to transfer ownership without the recording of a deed: "The Wife hereby conveys and releases unto the Husband all of her right, title and interest in said real property. The legal descriptions contained in the deed wherein the parties took title to the property are incorporated herein by this reference. This is a completed conveyance and does not remain executory; however, to further evidence this transaction the Wife shall execute and deliver to Husband a quitclaim deed for the property." Compare that language to the following provision, which likely would not be sufficient to transfer ownership: "It is agreed that Wife convey to Husband all right, title and interest she may have in and to said lot or parcel of real estate. The parties agree to execute for one another such documents of title or other documents as may be necessary to accomplish the purposes of this agreement."

38. G.S. 31-39.

39. G.S. 28A-21-2; 28A-23-1.

40. G.S. 28A-15-2.

41. Note that upon the death of the owner, real property may be listed in the names of "the heirs" (for an owner that died without a will) or "the devisees" (for an owner who died with a will) until probate proceedings begin. Once such proceedings begin and the court names an executor or administrator, the property may be listed in the

Married Taxpayers

Tax collectors must take care to target the property of the responsible taxpayer and not property that is owned by related taxpayers. This is especially true for married taxpayers. Real property owned by a husband and wife as tenants by the entirety is considered to be owned by the marital unit, not by the husband and wife individually.[42] This means that there may be three different taxpayers involved with a married couple: the husband for property he owns individually, the wife for property she owns individually, and the marital unit for real property they own as tenants by the entirety and for personal property they own jointly.[43]

Property owned by a husband or wife individually is not subject to enforced collection actions for unpaid taxes on real property owned jointly by the husband and wife. If a husband and wife own a tract of land as tenants by the entirety, the tax collector may not garnish the husband's wages or the wife's wages to satisfy the taxes on the land. Although many tax collectors may follow a different practice, technically wages belong to the individual spouse and not to the spouses jointly and therefore are not property owned by the responsible taxpayer. However, if those individual wages are deposited into a joint bank account, then that joint account could be attached by the tax collector to satisfy the taxes on the land because the bank account is property of both spouses. A joint bank account also may be attached for the tax obligation of an *individual* spouse, because each spouse has the right to withdraw all of the funds in a joint account.

Corporations

A corporation is a separate legal entity from its shareholders, officers, and incorporators.[44] This means that property owned by a corporation is not subject to enforced collection actions for taxes owed by a shareholder, even

---

name of the executor or administrator in his or her fiduciary capacity until the court confirms the heirs or devisees with title to the real property. G.S. 105-302(c)(6).

42. Davis v. Bass, 188 N.C. 200 (1924).

43. Only real property may be owned as tenants by the entirety. However, *personal* property owned jointly by a husband and wife should also be considered to be owned by the marital unit and not by the husband and wife individually. This follows from the requirement in G.S. 105-306(c)(7) that personal property owned by a husband and wife be listed under both their names as an undivided interest.

44. See G.S. 55-6-22 (shareholders not liable for the acts of the corporation).

if that shareholder owns the entire corporation. The reverse is also true: property owned by a shareholder is not subject to enforced collection actions for taxes owed by a corporation. These principles apply to "traditional" corporations organized under G.S. Chapter 55, to professional corporations organized under G.S. Chapter 55B, and to limited liability companies organized under G.S. Chapter 57C.

How can a tax collector collect a delinquent tax from a corporation that has gone out of business or no longer owns any assets? Unfortunately, the answer is often, "with difficulty, if at all." If the corporation formally dissolves by filing articles of dissolution with the secretary of state, then it is required to provide notice to all creditors.[45] Creditors who do not receive the required notice are authorized to satisfy the obligations owed to them from assets that were distributed at dissolution to the corporation's shareholders.[46] Often no formal dissolution occurs, however: the shareholders simply distribute the corporation's assets and stop doing business under the corporate name. In this situation a tax collector may have no viable collection options other than attempting to convince a court to disregard the corporate form and hold the shareholders liable for the corporation's debts. Known as "piercing the corporate veil," this remedy is rarely granted by the courts. It generally applies only in egregious cases when the controlling shareholder uses the corporation as the shareholder's "instrumentality" to shield activities in violation of public policy or statute.[47] Before attempting to attach a shareholder's intangible property based on this theory, a tax collector would be wise to consult with his or her local government's attorney.

Unlike corporations, sole proprietorships are not separate legal entities from their owners. Taxpayers who run businesses but have not incorporated those businesses are personally liable for taxes on property owned by those businesses.[48]

---

45. G.S. 55-14-06 and G.S. 55-14-07.

46. G.S. 55-14-08 and G.S. 57C-6-09.

47. *See* State v. Ridgeway Brands Mfg., LLC, 362 N.C. 431 (2008) (permitting state to proceed with attempt to pierce the corporate veil based on controlling shareholders' efforts to avoid required payments to state tobacco litigation settlement escrow fund).

48. See G.S. 105-306(6) (property held in connection with a sole proprietorship must be listed in the name of the owner, not in the name of the business).

Partnerships

Partnerships, like corporations, are required to list their property for taxation separately from that of their owners. However, unlike corporate shareholders, partners may be targeted by enforced collections resulting from the partnership's tax obligations. G.S. 105-366(8) permits a tax collector to attach and garnish the intangible personal property of a partner to satisfy the taxes on property owned by the partnership but only after the tax collector has exhausted all remedies against the partnership's property.

4. How do the "going-out-of-business" provisions work?

As mentioned above, G.S. 105-366(d) creates exceptions to the rules about when and against whom enforced collection remedies against personal property may be pursued. These provisions are triggered when a merchant or retailer goes out of business or transfers the "major part of its stock of goods, materials, supplies or fixtures, other than in the course of business." For the purposes of these provisions, "retailer" is broadly defined to include retail sellers of tangible personal property as well as manufacturers and producers of tangible personal property.[49]

Within thirty days of the transfer, the parties must satisfy the taxes on the transferred property that are due or will become due on September 1 of the year of the transfer. If not, then the tax collector is permitted to levy or attach *any* personal property of the taxpayer to whom the property was transferred, so long as the levy or attachment occurs within six months of the transfer. The collector may also attach any property held by the taxpayer that originally owned the equipment.

For example, assume Blue Devil Chickens Inc. sells its poultry processing equipment to Tar Heel Turkeys Inc. on March 1, 2010, when the 2009 taxes on the equipment are delinquent. If the parties do not satisfy *both* the 2009 and 2010 taxes on the transferred equipment by April 1, 2010, then the tax collector is permitted to satisfy those taxes by attaching any personal property held by Blue Devil Chickens. The collector may also attach any personal property held by Tar Heel Turkeys so long as that attachment occurs within six months of the transfer, which in this case would be September 1, 2010.

---

49. G.S. 105-164.3(35).

This is true even though the 2010 taxes normally would not be delinquent until January 6, 2011. If the tax collector fails to act before September 1, 2010, then Tar Heel Turkeys is no longer subject to Machinery Act remedies for the 2009 and 2010 taxes and may be held responsible only through a civil lawsuit.

5. May the tax collector attach or garnish funds in a different county?

Yes. G.S. 105-321(b) makes the governing board's order of collection the equivalent of a court judgment. Court judgments may be executed against property located anywhere in the state.[50] This means attachment can occur anywhere in the state. The tax collector should use the sheriff in the county where the funds reside to serve the notice of attachment rather than relying on certified mail. The process can be even simpler for out-of-county bank branches, if the bank in question also has a branch in the tax collector's county. In that situation the tax collector may serve a notice of attachment on the branch in the tax collector's county to reach any account held at *any* other branch of that bank, be it in another county or even another state.[51]

Although some tax collectors have had success convincing out-of-state employers to honor North Carolina notices of attachment, such employers are under no obligation to do so. The tax collector has no ability to enforce a notice of attachment outside state borders.

6. Are members of the United States military subject to garnishment and attachment?

Not usually. Both state and federal law restrict a tax collector's ability to use enforced collection remedies against military personnel.

Under state law taxes on property owned by military personnel serving in Iraq or Afghanistan do not accrue interest or become delinquent until

---

50. G.S. 1-308.

51. Letter from N.C. Attorney General to Aubrey S. Tomlinson Jr. (Dec. 10, 1987), available at www.ncdoj.com/About-DOJ/Legal-Services/Legal-Opinions.aspx?Page=1.

ninety days after their deployment ends.[52] Tax collectors therefore must wait until 90 days after a servicemember's deployment in Iraq or Afghanistan ends to initiate any enforced collection remedies for taxes that became due during that deployment.

Under the federal Servicemembers' Civil Relief Act (SCRA), tax collectors may not sell the tangible personal property or real property of military personnel to satisfy a tax obligation without a court first determining that the servicemember's military service did not materially affect his or her ability to pay the taxes.[53] Even if a court grants permission to sell the property, the servicemember has the right to redeem the property—in other words, to reverse the sale—up to 180 days after his or her military service ends.

A separate section of the SCRA permits a court to stay or vacate an attachment or garnishment up to ninety days after the servicemember's military service ends.[54] Further, the federal garnishment statute forbids a garnishment of a servicemember's pay unless the garnishment has been "determined by a final judgment of a court of competent jurisdiction."[55] In North Carolina that would generally not happen until after a garnishee has refused to respond to a notice of garnishment and the tax collector initiates a civil lawsuit in state court.

In light of these provisions, tax collectors are wise to refrain from any enforced collection actions against active-duty military personnel until well after their deployment or military service ends. Waiting may increase the risk of the taxpayer removing his or her property from the state, but the local government's interests will not otherwise be harmed. Interest will accrue as usual if the servicemember is not deployed in Iraq or Afghanistan. Equally important, the period during which a taxpayer is a member of the active-duty military does not count against the Machinery Act's ten-year statute of limitation.[56] Even if a taxpayer is in the military for more than ten years, the tax collector will be still be able to rely on enforced collection methods to recover those taxes after the taxpayer's military service ends.

---

52. S.L. 2001-508, S.L. 2003-300.
53. 50 U.S.C. app. § 501.
54. 50 U.S.C. app. § 204.
55. 5 U.S.C. § 5520a(k)(2)(A).
56. 50 U.S.C. app. § 206.

7. How can a tax collector locate the taxpayer's intangible property?

Tax collectors have developed many creative solutions to this problem, including saving copies of checks used to pay taxes, obtaining employers' names from the Employment Security Commission, and searching the N.C. Escheat Fund.[57]

Many tax collectors also use the authority granted by the Machinery Act to require employers to disclose the names and addresses of all employees "who may be liable for taxes."[58] This provision has led to two ongoing disagreements between tax offices and some employers.

The first concerns state employers. They are concerned that providing the addresses of their employees to a tax collector will violate their obligations under the state personnel records provision that makes employee addresses confidential.[59] In 1983 the state attorney general concluded that an exception to these provisions permitted a state agency to share employees' addresses with a local tax collector to assist collection efforts.[60] However, recent conversations with state attorneys indicate that the attorney general's office no longer honors that 1983 opinion and is advising state agencies to not release addresses to local tax collectors. Absent another reversal of course by the attorney general, a local tax collector may need to accept only employees' names from state agencies. The collector can proceed with an attachment if a match results, even though without the address the collector will be less certain that the delinquent taxpayer and the state employee are one and the same.

The second disagreement focuses on whether an employer can require a list of delinquent taxpayers from the tax collector to which the employer can then compare its employee list or whether the employer must simply turn over its complete employee list. The spirit of G.S. 105-368(i) seems to favor the latter, seeing that *all* employees "may be liable for taxes" now or at some point in the future. However, because the provision is not entirely clear on

---

57. Details on these and other productive approaches are described in the *Collections Procedures Manual* at www.nctca.org.

58. G.S. 105-368(i).

59. G.S. 126-22 and 126-23.

60. Opinion of attorney general to Dr. Sarah T. Morrow, secretary of Department of Human Resources, 52 Op. N.C. Att'y Gen. 85 (1983), available at www.ncdoj.com/About-DOJ/Legal-Services/Legal-Opinions.aspx?Page=1.

this issue, tax collectors may wish to cooperate with employers as much as possible to expedite the garnishment process.

8. What notice is required to initiate an attachment or garnishment?

The tax collector must serve notice of an attachment and garnishment on both the taxpayer and the garnishee—that is, the bank, employer, or other party that holds the funds due the taxpayer. The Machinery Act allows notice to be served personally or through one of the methods permitted by Rule 4 of the North Carolina Rules of Civil Procedure.[61] "Personal service" means that the notice is hand-delivered by an employee in the tax collector's office, the sheriff, or a deputy sheriff. The most commonly used method under Rule 4 is service by registered or certified mail, return receipt requested. First-Class Mail is *not* one of the authorized methods of service, nor is e-mail. That said, if a tax office routinely serves a large number of attachment notices on a major bank or employer and that garnishee requests that it be provided notice electronically so that it can more easily and quickly comply with the attachment, it seems reasonable to do so even though it may not satisfy the technical service of process requirements.

Service by publication is permitted under Rule 4 when the tax office does not have valid addresses for the parties, but that is generally only effective for missing taxpayers, not missing garnishees. If the tax office cannot locate the bank or employer that holds the taxpayer's funds, the attachment is unlikely to be successful.

Timing

The Machinery Act is silent as to the appropriate timing of notices with respect to the taxpayer and the garnishee. Experience suggests that it makes most sense to serve a bank before serving the taxpayer, so that the taxpayer does not have the opportunity to withdraw funds from the targeted account before the bank freezes that account. This delay in serving the taxpayer is especially important in light of the federal regulations regarding the

---

61. G.S. 105-368(b); G.S. 1A-1, Rule 4(j). S.L. 2011-145 § 31.26(d) raised this fee from $15 to $30.

attachment of federal benefits, such as Social Security, that were issued in 2011. Under these new procedures (discussed in detail in Question 2 above), a bank must continue to provide customer access to attached accounts until completion of the mandatory account reviews to determine if the accounts contain exempt federal benefits. The account review can occur as late as two business days after the bank receives the notice of attachment, meaning tax-payers will have much more opportunity to withdraw attached funds before banks freeze their access. As discussed above, it is unclear whether these new regulations will apply to local tax garnishments. But in case they do, the best practice will be for the tax collector to wait two business days after giving notice of attachment to the bank before giving notice to the taxpayer. In contrast, it is best to serve an employee before serving the employer, in the (perhaps overly optimistic) hope that the employee will be prompted to pay the tax bill to prevent his or her employer from learning of the employee's tax problems.

Fees

G.S. 105-368(g) requires that the fee for service of the notice of attachment be the same as that charged in civil lawsuits, which is currently $30 per service.[62] The fees are added to the amount of taxes to be recovered by the attachment. Normally, this will be $60: $30 for service on the taxpayer and $30 for service on the garnishee. However, if multiple notices of attach-ment are serviced simultaneously on one garnishee, then only one $30 fee is charged for service on that garnishee. That fee is then allocated equally among the delinquent taxpayers. For example, assume that ABC Corp. employs ten delinquent taxpayers. If the tax collector attaches the wages of all ten of these taxpayers simultaneously, then the total service fee will be $330: $30 for the one service on ABC Corp. plus $300 for the ten services on the individual taxpayers. Each taxpayer will have $33 added to the taxes they owe: $30 for their individual service plus $3 for one-tenth of the fee for the single service on ABC Corp. If the sheriff's office serves the notices, then the fees collected must be paid to the sheriff's office. If the tax office serves the notices, the tax office retains the fees.

---

62. G.S. 7A-311(a)(1). Prior to August 1, 2011, the fee was $15 per service. S.L. 2011-145 (sect. 31.26(d)) raised the fee to $30 per service.

Who Must Be Served

Both the taxpayer and the garnishee must receive notice. If the tax collector is attaching a joint bank account, all account holders should receive notice. Rule 4 of the North Carolina Rules of Civil Procedure provides detailed procedures for service on corporations, partnerships, and associations. Generally, service on those parties should be made to an officer, director, managing agent, general partner, or other individual authorized to accept service. For banks, the usual practice is to serve the branch manager.

G.S. 105-368(h) mandates different procedures for service on state and local employers. For a local government employee, the statute requires service on "the officer charged with making up the payrolls of the political subdivision." For example, to garnish the wages of a county employee, in most cases service should be made on the county finance officer. For a state employee, the statute requires service on "the head or chief fiscal officer of the department, agency, instrumentality or institution by which he is employed." In practice, however, many state agencies will prefer that service be made on the office responsible for payroll. For example, if a School of Government faculty member is responsible for delinquent property taxes (Perish the thought!), technically the statute requires notice be served either on the UNC–Chapel Hill chancellor or the UNC–Chapel Hill vice-chancellor for finance and administration. But collectors at the Orange County tax office who have extensive experience garnishing the wages of UNC employees report that the standard practice is to serve UNC–Chapel Hill Payroll Services with the notice of garnishment. The better the communication between the garnishee and the tax office, the more effective and efficient the garnishment will be.

Federal employees are also subject to garnishment for local taxes, although federal law modifies the standard process and priority.[63] Federal agencies have thirty days, rather than ten days, to respond to a notice of garnishment and must give priority to garnishment orders for child support and alimony, regardless of when the notice was served. See Question 9, below, for more on priority of garnishments.

---

63. 5 U.S.C. § 5520a.

Contents of Notice

The notice must contain as much identifying information about the taxpayer as the tax office possesses, including Social Security number; the amount of taxes, interest, fees, and penalties owed by the taxpayer, broken out by year; the name of the taxing unit(s) that levied the taxes; a description of the property to be attached, such as wages or bank accounts; and a copy of G.S. 105-366 and G.S. 105-368. See Figure 6A for a sample notice of attachment from Orange County.

Increasingly, banks are refusing to process an attachment unless the tax office provides a taxpayer's Social Security number. This demand seems to violate a garnishee's obligations under the Machinery Act. If the tax office possesses the taxpayer's Social Security number, the Machinery Act requires the tax office to provide it to the garnishee. But the Machinery Act does not require the tax office to obtain a Social Security number before proceeding with an attachment. Regardless, in the interest of maintaining a cooperative relationship with its garnishees, a tax office might consider doing what it can to obtain taxpayers' Social Security numbers before sending notices of attachment.

9. What are the obligations of the garnishee?

Immediately upon receiving the notice of attachment, the garnishee is liable to the tax collector for all taxes, interest, fees, and penalties identified in the attachment up to the amount of funds the garnishee owes the taxpayer. Within ten days of the notice, the garnishee must either raise an objection to the attachment or provide the attached funds to the tax collector.[64] If the garnishee raises an objection, the tax collector has ten days to respond. If the tax collector does not agree, then the matter must be tried in superior court in the garnishee's home county with the losing party responsible for the winning party's costs and attorneys fees.[65]

The attachment theoretically freezes all funds owed the taxpayer at the time of notice. If a bank were to allow a taxpayer to withdraw funds from an attached account after the bank receives notice of the attachment, the bank could be held liable for the withdrawn funds.

---

64. G.S. 105-368(c) and (d). Objections must be served in writing upon the tax collector by registered or certified mail.

65. G.S. 105-368(g).

Figure 6A

NOTICE OF ATTACHMENT
AND GARNISHMENT

<u>**SAMPLE**</u>

To: | GARNISHEE |

Street ADD
City, State, ZIP

PLEASE REMIT PAYMENT TO:
ORANGE COUNTY TAX COLLECTOR
P.O. BOX 8181
HILLSBOROUGH, NC 27278

The person owing or having in his possession wages, rents, bank deposits, debts, or other property of the taxpayer sought to be attached (hereinafter called garnishee) and the following taxpayer:

To: | TAXPAYER |

Each of you will take notice that pursuant to Sections 105-366 and 105-368 of the General Statutes of North Carolina authorizing the attachment and garnishment of wages, rents, bank deposits, proceeds of property subject to levy, and other intangible personal property, the property described below for the taxpayer is hereby attached to the extent stated below for taxes levied by the County of Orange and which are unpaid.

Year/Bill Number	Account #	Tract #	Total
Total taxes, plus penalties and interest			$
Cost of serving notice			$30.00
Total due and attached			$

(additional interest will accrue monthly on unpaid balance)

The property sought to be attached is [WAGES or FUNDS ON DEPOSIT] due the taxpayer, or subject to his demand, or to become due him during calendar year _____.

Within ten (10) days after service of this notice, the garnishee is directed to answer the notice by sending to the tax collector of Orange County by registered mail a statement that he has no defense or set-off against the taxpayer, and by remitting the amount demanded; or, if the garnishee does offer a defense or set-off, he shall proceed as provided Section 105-368(d) of the North Carolina General Statutes. If the amount due the taxpayer has not matured at the date of service of this notice, the garnishee's statement shall set forth that fact, and the demand shall be paid to the tax collector upon the maturity. If the property attached is wages or other compensation for personal services, the garnishee shall remit to the tax collector ten percent of such compensation per any period, and he shall continue to remit ten percent of the taxpayer's compensation each pay period until the total amount demanded is satisfied. Pursuant to the requirements of G.S. 105-368(b)(5), G.S. 105-366 and 105-368 are printed on the reverse side.

Date Notice Prepared	Orange County Tax Collector

RETURN
(for use in personal service only)

I certify that this notice was received on the ______ day of, ______, ______, and was served as follows:

1. On _______________________________ (garnishee) by leaving a copy with _______________________________ on the ___ day of ___, ___.

Officer

2. On _______________________________ (taxpayer) by leaving a copy with _______________________________ on the ___ day of ___, ___.

Officer

However, the new federal rules for protecting Social Security and similar benefits discussed in Question 2 above changed the obligations of garnishee banks. As discussed above, it is unclear whether these new regulations will apply to local tax garnishments. But for attachments that do fall under their reach, banks will no longer be permitted to freeze accounts immediately. Instead, the bank will apply a freeze until after it conducts the mandatory account review to determine if any exempt federal benefits have been deposited in the attached accounts during the previous two months. The account review must be conducted within two days of the notice of attachment. During the time between the notice of attachment and the account review, the taxpayer will retain access to the attached accounts and can withdraw money without creating liability for the bank.

If the account review determines that there are unprotected funds in the attached accounts, then the bank must immediately freeze those funds and pay to the tax collector within ten days as much of those funds as are needed to satisfy the tax obligation. If the bank permits the taxpayer to withdraw funds from the attached accounts between the date of the account review and the date on which the bank forwards the funds to the tax collector, the bank will be liable for the withdrawals if the funds remaining in the account are not sufficient to satisfy the taxes.

Many banks charge their customers fees whenever they process a notice of attachment. These fees are a matter of contractual agreement between the bank and its customers and should not affect the taxing unit's collection remedies. Technically the fee should not reduce the amount of funds paid by the bank to the tax collector. But in practice most banks first deduct the fee and then pay the balance of the account up to the amount of taxes owed to the tax collector. This practice is probably not worth fighting in light of the tax collector's desire to work closely with local banks.

For employers the garnishment requires them to provide to the taxpayer 10 percent of the taxpayer's gross wages each pay period. "Gross wages" means wages before taxes, retirement contributions, or other voluntary withholdings such as charitable contributions or parking fees. An employee may be subject to multiple garnishments simultaneously, the priority of which will generally be determined by order of attachment.[66]

---

66. For a detailed discussion of the priority of tax liens on wages and other property, see Chapter 5.

Here is how this works in practice. Assume Tina Taxpayer earns $500 in gross wages per pay period and that Carolina County garnishes Tina's wages for a $1,000 delinquent tax bill. Tina is already subject to a state tax wage garnishment of $50 per pay period. Tina's employer must provide to Carolina County $45 per period until the county tax bill is satisfied. This amount is calculated as follows: $500 in gross wages, less the $50 state tax garnishment that has priority because it attached before the local garnishment, leaving $450 in gross wages subject to garnishment, times ten percent.

Unlike other tax garnishments, child support garnishment orders never reduce the amount of gross wages available for a local tax garnishment. In other words, local tax garnishments always have priority over child support orders, for two reasons. First, unlike a notice of garnishment for property taxes, a child support order is not a judgment lien on the taxpayer's property.[67] Second, even if a child support order were the equivalent of a lien, child support garnishments are limited to "disposable income," which excludes amounts withheld for federal, state, and local taxes.[68]

Employers sometimes claim that all state and local tax garnishments are subject to a cumulative 10 percent cap, an assertion that is not supported by the applicable statutes.[69] *Each* tax garnishment is subject to a separate 10 percent cap. As in the above example, each 10 percent cap is applied to the amount of gross wages available after the senior garnishment has been applied.

Employers have also attempted to avoid property tax garnishments by relying on the federal Consumer Credit Protection Act (CCPA), another losing argument. The CCPA limits wage garnishments to 25 percent of disposable income and forbids garnishments from reducing an employee's weekly disposable wages below an amount equal to the wages for thirty hours of work at the federal minimum hourly wage.[70] However, the CCPA exempts

---

67. G.S. 110-136.

68. G.S. 110-129(6).

69. G.S. 105-242, which creates a 10 percent cap for state tax garnishments, is part of Article 9 of G.S. Chapter 105. The definitional section of Article 9, G.S. 105-228.90, makes clear that Article 9 applies only to subchapters I, V, and VIII of G.S. Chapter 105 as well as certain taxes and requirements found in other chapters. Article 9 does *not* apply to Subchapter II of G.S. Chapter 105, which is the local property tax subchapter. Because local property taxes are not covered by Article 9, the restrictions on garnishment in 105-242 do not apply to garnishments for local property taxes.

70. 15 U.S.C. § 1673.

from its restrictions garnishments for state and federal taxes. Although property taxes in North Carolina are levied and collected by local governments, they are a creature of *state* law and therefore should qualify for the CCPA exemption.

10. For how long is an attachment or garnishment effective?

G.S. 105-368(a) obligates the garnishee to turn over all funds "due the taxpayer or to become due to him within the calendar year." Technically, this means that a notice of garnishment should be effective until the taxes have been satisfied or the calendar year ends, whichever comes first.

Despite this limitation, most employers continue to honor the garnishment obligation until the taxes are satisfied without requiring a new notice at the beginning of a new year. In contrast, banks generally assume that their obligation ends when they turn over the funds in their possession at the time of notice. Tax collectors need to decide how forceful they wish to be with banks who take this approach, recognizing the need for a strong working relationship with institutions that can help greatly with the collection process. Clearly, banks must make available all funds that are in their possession from the time of notice until the expiration of the ten-day waiting period. This includes funds that are in the bank's possession but not yet due to the taxpayer, such as a certificate of deposit that will mature before the close of the year. Beyond that, it may be counterproductive for a tax collector to demand that a bank make available funds the taxpayer deposits into the attached account after the ten-day waiting period expires. It is likely better practice simply to serve the bank with a second notice of attachment if the tax collector believes that the bank has received new funds.

11. What should the tax collector do if the garnishee provides more funds than the law requires or permits?

The tax office should keep the funds, unless the taxpayer or the garnishee raises an objection within the ten-day waiting period. This situation may arise when a bank mistakenly attaches the wrong account or an employer forwards more than 10 percent of the taxpayer's wages. Assuming that the tax office was not the source of the error, the tax office is under no obligation to return the funds. In fact a refund may violate the restrictions on refunds and releases found in G.S. 105-380 and G.S. 105-381. Those provisions permit refunds only for illegal actions or clerical errors by the tax office, not for errors by a taxpayer or garnishee. If a bank attaches the wrong account due to its own error, then the bank must resolve that issue with its customer. If an employer garnishes too large a percentage of the taxpayer's wages, then the employer must resolve that issue with its employee. The tax office should not get involved.

The one exception to this rule might be the case in which the taxpayer claims after the fact that the tax collector attached exempt funds such as Social Security benefits or state public assistance payments. If the taxpayer can prove this claim to the satisfaction of the tax office, the funds probably should be returned on the premise that the attachment was void from the beginning and never could have been legally performed by the garnishee. See Question 2, above, for more details on funds exempt from attachment.

12. What is the statute of limitations for use of the attachment and garnishment remedy?

The ten-year limitation on enforced collections found in G.S. 105-378(a) applies to attachments and garnishments. This statute of limitations provides a taxpayer with a defense to any attachment and garnishment that is attempted more than ten years after the tax for which the levy is conducted came due. Property taxes on real property and personal property other than registered motor vehicles become due on September 1 of the fiscal year for which the taxes are levied.

For example, 2000 property taxes on real property became due on September 1, 2000. Any enforced collection action for 2000 property taxes must have been started by August 31, 2010, else G.S. 105-378(a) would provide the taxpayer with a statute of limitations defense to the action.

This statute of limitation requires only that the collection action begin within ten years, not that it be completed within ten years. Accordingly, the statute of limitations is satisfied if the notice of attachment or garnishment is served within ten years of the due date even if funds continue to be paid to the tax collector after the ten-year period expires. An attachment or garnishment may continue indefinitely so long as it begins before the ten-year period ends.

For example, if a tax collector provides notice of wage garnishment on August 30, 2010, for delinquent real property taxes from the 2000 tax year, the statute of limitations is satisfied. The tax collector may continue to receive funds garnished from the taxpayer's wages in September 2010 and beyond without regard for the ten-year limitation.

Chapter 7

Levy and Sale of Tangible Personal Property

Compared to the attachment and garnishment process, seizing and selling a taxpayer's personal property to satisfy delinquent property taxes can be a complicated endeavor. But when real property is not involved and the tax collector cannot locate a taxpayer's bank account or employer, the levy and sale of personal property may be the best collection option available. Indeed, the mere threat of the seizure of a taxpayer's personal property and the likely disruption of that taxpayer's business or everyday life can sometimes produce prompt payment of outstanding taxes.

This chapter discusses the legal issues involved with the levy and sale of personal property and provides several sample forms for use in the process.

1. When and against whom may the levy and sale remedy be employed?

The same rules that apply to the use of attachment and garnishment also apply to the use of the levy and sale remedy.[1] Note that these remedies are not limited to the collection of property taxes; both attachment and garnishment and levy and sale may be used to collect *any* tax levied by a local government, including occupancy taxes and privilege license taxes.[2] The most important of these rules are found in G.S. 105-365.1, which identifies the taxpayers responsible for various types of property taxes and which outlines

---

This chapter updates information published as *Property Tax Bulletin* No. 155 (Aug. 2010).

1. See Chapter 6 for a detailed discussion of these rules.

2. G.S. 153A-147 (general remedies for county taxes); G.S. 160A-207 (general remedies for municipal taxes). See Chapter 15 for more details on the levy and collection of other local taxes.

when enforced-collection remedies can be used against those responsible taxpayers.

The responsible taxpayer for taxes owed on real property is the owner of record as of the delinquency date, normally January 6 of the fiscal year for which taxes have been levied. Successive owners of real property also are personally responsible for taxes that became delinquent while the property was owned by a previous taxpayer. For taxes owed on personal property other than registered motor vehicles, the only responsible taxpayer is the listing taxpayer, that is, the owner of record as of January 1 preceding the fiscal year for which the taxes were levied. Successive owners of personal property are not personally responsible for taxes on property listed in the name of a previous owner. For taxes owed on registered motor vehicles, the responsible taxpayer is the owner of record on the date the vehicle's registration was applied for or renewed. Successive owners of a registered motor vehicle are not personally responsible for taxes on a vehicle that was registered in the name of a prior owner. Some exceptions to these general rules exist, most notably the "going-out-of-business" provisions in G.S. 105-366(d), which allow tax collectors, in certain situations, to use enforced-collection remedies against purchasers of business personal property.

Tax collectors may target *any* personal property owned by the responsible taxpayer with the levy and sale remedy regardless of the type of property taxes owed. For example, a tax collector may levy upon and sell a taxpayer's automobile for property taxes owed on that automobile or for property taxes owed on real property or other personal property owned by that same taxpayer.[3] The tax collector can also target for levy and sale property that was transferred by the responsible taxpayer to a close relative[4] or property held by the estate of a deceased taxpayer[5] or personal property of a partner for the tax obligations of a partnership.[6] A detailed discussion of all of the provi-

---

3. G.S. 105-366(b)(1). The reverse is not always true. Taxes owed on a registered motor vehicle are not a lien on that taxpayer's real property, meaning that foreclosure of real property is not a remedy for the collection of taxes on registered motor vehicles. G.S. 105-330.4(c).

4. G.S. 105-366(b)(2).

5. G.S. 105-366(b)(4).

6. G.S. 105-366(b)(8). This provision requires that the tax collector first exhaust all collection remedies against partnership property before targeting property owned by an individual partner.

sions concerning responsible taxpayers and enforced collections is presented in Chapter 6.

2. Is a court order needed to use the levy and sale collection remedy?

No. The order of collection that must be given to the tax collector each year by the governing board has "the force and effect of a judgment and execution against the taxpayers' real and personal property."[7] In other words, the order of collection is the equivalent of a court order authorizing the tax collector to seize and sell a taxpayer's tangible personal property to satisfy delinquent tax obligations. To minimize possible taxpayer complaints about the tax collector's authority to use this remedy, tax collectors should insist that the order of collection issued by their governing boards contains the following language recommended in G.S. 105-321(b): "[T]his order shall be a full and sufficient authority to direct, require, and enable you to levy on and sell any real or personal property of such taxpayers."

3. Who is authorized to make the levy?

The tax collector, a "duly appointed" deputy tax collector,[8] a sheriff, or, for municipal taxes, a municipal police officer can make the levy and conduct the sale.[9] In the interest of security of both persons and property, however, it makes good sense to involve a law enforcement officer in the process.

If the tax collector prefers that a law enforcement officer actually make the levy rather than simply be present while the tax collector does so, G.S. Chapter 105 (referred to as the Machinery Act) requires that the local governing body first authorize the tax collector to delegate the levy and sale

---

7. G.S. 105-321(b).

8. G.S. 105-367(b). That a tax office employee carries the title of deputy tax collector is not sufficient to bestow on that employee the authority to conduct a levy and sale. To gain such authority, the employee must be appointed as deputy tax collector by the governing board and must take the oath required of tax collectors. See Chapter 1 for more details on the appointment of tax collectors and deputy tax collectors.

9. *Id.*

Figure 7A. Sample Execution Document for Levy against Personal Property for Taxes

TO: The Sheriff of ___________ County:

Whereas, the taxpayer(s) named below has failed to pay _____________ County certain lawfully due taxes for the year(s) set out below:

____

[*name and address of taxpayer(s)*]

____

[*tax years and amounts owed, including interest and penalties*];

and whereas, under the provisions of G.S. 105-321, the ___________ County Board of Commissioners has issued an order of collection having the force and effect of a judgment against the property of the above named taxpayer(s), said order being the provisions of G.S. 105-367(b), the ___________ County Board of Commissioners has issued an order authorizing the Tax Collector to call upon the Sheriff to levy on and sell personal property subject to levy. You are therefore directed to satisfy said claim for taxes, plus the cost of the levy and sale, out of the proceeds from the sale of personal property of the above named taxpayer.

By: ___________________ , ___________________
County Tax Collector

Date: ___________

duties to a sheriff or police officer.[10] After receiving this authorization, the tax collector must "direct an execution" to the law enforcement officer. The Machinery Act does not describe the form for such an execution, but it should identify the taxpayer and the taxes, interest, penalties, and costs owed; request that the law enforcement officer levy upon and sell the taxpayer's personal property to satisfy the amounts owed; and reference the statutory authority for the levy. If the tax collector knows of the existence and location of specific personal property that should be targeted by the law enforcement officer, it would of course be helpful to include that information on the execution document. Buncombe County uses a form similar to that presented in Figure 7A.

---

10. *Id.*

4. How is a levy made?

Neither the Machinery Act nor the General Statutes' execution sale provisions referenced by the Machinery Act describe exactly how a levy must occur. The only guidance available comes from a few state court opinions involving levies, some of which date to the nineteenth century.

Generally, the official making the levy must actually seize the property and remove it from the taxpayer's possession. Assuming the property can be moved, it is not sufficient to leave the property in the taxpayer's possession and simply post a notice indicating that the property has been levied upon. As the North Carolina Supreme Court observed more than 120 years ago, "A seizure is necessary; and if, from the nature of the property (as is the case with the growing crop, but not of the cotton in the gin and crib), an actual seizure be impossible, some act as nearly equivalent to a seizure as practicable, must be substituted for it."[11] If the property cannot be moved, then the official making the levy should both post notice of the levy and take steps to secure the property so that it is no longer under control of the taxpayer.

For example, if the property being levied is a car, it can be towed to a secure county parking lot. Merely placing a parking boot on the vehicle may not be sufficient and also heightens the risk of damage to the car while immobilized in an unsecured area, damage for which the tax collector could be liable. If the property being levied is an airplane, it could be towed to a secure hanger on the airport grounds. If the property being levied consists of computers and cash registers, they should be physically removed from the taxpayer's business location and placed in a secure storage facility. If the property being levied is heavy factory equipment that cannot be moved without great cost or damage to the property, the factory in which the equipment resides should be secured around the clock by an employee of the tax department or the sheriff's department or a private security firm.

The cost of seizing and securing the property, which could include the cost of hiring a moving or towing company, renting storage space, or hiring a security guard, can be recovered from the sale proceeds.[12] Once the

---

11. Long v. Hall, 97 N.C. 286 (1887). *See also In re* Phipps, 202 N.C. 642 (1932) (no levy accomplished when officer merely gave clerk of court notice of levy but left funds to be levied in possession of clerk of court); Rives v. Porter, 29 N.C. 74 (1846) (levy accomplished when officer placed horses subject to levy in owner's barn but slept on the premises to secure the property).

12. G.S. 105-367(d) and G.S. 1-339.70(a).

property is seized and secured, the tax collector has responsibility for it and can be held liable for damage to the property caused by the tax collector's negligence.[13] Immediately upon seizing and securing the property, the tax collector or sheriff should take photographs of the property and/or make a detailed inventory of it to protect against subsequent accusations of damage or loss by the taxpayer. Prior to seizing the property, the tax collector should confirm that the local government has both a secure storage location and adequate insurance for the property. When cars or mobile homes are seized, the best option may be for the tax collector to ask the towing or moving company to store the seized property.

In North Carolina, an officer may not forcibly enter a residence to levy upon personal property.[14] As a result, tax collectors cannot enter a home to levy upon and seize personal property without permission from the homeowner. This prohibition against forced entry likely extends to a garage that is attached to a residence. But such forcible entries as lock picking or window breaking are permitted against buildings that are not residences, including detached garages and barns.[15]

It is a crime to interfere with a public officer making a levy and to refuse to surrender, to remove, or to hide property that has been levied upon.[16] Although tax collectors are permitted to use reasonable force against a taxpayer in order to complete a levy, the wiser course of action if there is any likelihood of encountering a belligerent taxpayer is to involve a law enforcement officer in the process.[17]

It is possible to levy upon property that has been levied upon already by another taxing authority. In such a situation, the second taxing unit need not seize the property and remove it from the possession of the first. For

---

13. 70 AM. JUR. 2D *Sheriffs, Police, and Constables* § 50 (2005).

14. Red House Furniture Co. v. Smith, 310 N.C. 617 (1984).

15. 30 AM. JUR. 2D *Executions and Enforcements of Judgments* § 199 (2005).

16. G.S. 14-223 (obstructing a public officer); G.S. 14-115 (refusing to surrender property or removing property that has been levied upon).

17. State of North Carolina *ex rel.* Peleg S. Rogers & Co. v. Dilliard, 25 N.C. 102 (1842) (permissible to levy horse even if owner is riding said horse). Local legend has it that a former Mecklenburg County tax administrator once chased a private jet down a runway, jumped into the cockpit of the plane, and declared it levied upon. The pilot/delinquent taxpayer threatened to fly the plane out of state but backed down after the administrator threatened to pursue kidnapping charges against the pilot if he did. Though successful in obtaining payment, this procedure is not recommended.

example, assume that Carolina County levies upon a Toyota Camry owned by Wanda Wolfpack to satisfy her outstanding property taxes. If Wanda also owes property taxes to Blue Devil City, Blue Devil City may also levy upon Wanda's car simply by providing notice of levy to the official conducting the levy and sale for Carolina County. For more details on the priority of successive liens on the same real property—in other words, on who gets paid first—see Questions 11 and 12 below.

5. What notice must be given to the taxpayer when property is levied upon?

Surprisingly, no formal notice is required when property is seized for unpaid taxes. That said, most tax and sheriff departments do provide the owner of the property with some documentation at the time of levy. Such notice could spur the taxpayer to pay the outstanding taxes and thereby eliminate the need for levy and sale as well as remind the taxpayer of the potential penalties for interfering with a levy. If a law enforcement officer makes the levy, the taxpayer could be handed a copy of the execution order directed to that officer by the tax collector. If the tax collector makes the levy, the taxpayer could be given the form presented in Figure 7B, an adaptation of that used by Orange County.

6. How must the sale be advertised?

The sale of property levied upon for unpaid property taxes is governed by the laws concerning sales "under execution"—that is, sales of property to enforce court judgments—found in G.S. Chapter 1, Article 29B. Those provisions require that notice of the sale of personal property be posted for ten days immediately preceding the sale "in the area designated by the clerk of superior court."[18] In other words, the only required notice of sale is one that must be posted in the county courthouse. That notice must include the date, hour, and place of sale; a description of the "nature and quantity"

---

18. G.S. 1-339.53.

Figure 7B. Sample Seizure and Levy Form

STATE OF NORTH CAROLINA
COUNTY OF _____________
     v.

____

Take notice that the undersigned has this day, _____________, 20_____, seized and levied upon the following described property:

____

____

for delinquent property taxes in the amount of $ _______________________________

due by you to _______________ County for the year(s) _____________________

and that the undersigned will proceed to sell said property at public auction for cash and apply the proceeds to the payment of said taxes, in accordance with G.S. 105-367 of North Carolina law.

You are further notified that the above described property has been taken into the possession of the undersigned, and you are hereby notified not to remove said property. Such interference is a crime under Section 14-115 of the North Carolina General Statutes.

To redeem your property, you must be prepared to produce proof of identification and pay all costs, such as towing, storage, advertising, and any other costs incurred to date.

This _______ day of _____________, 20_____

/s/

Tax Collector, ____________________________ County _____________________

of the property to be sold; and a reference to the governing body's order of collection, which serves as the execution authorizing the sale.[19]

The Machinery Act also authorizes the tax collector to "advertise the sale in any reasonable manner and for any reasonable period of time he deems necessary to produce an adequate bid for the property."[20] Because the cost of this additional advertising can be added to the cost of sale and recovered from the sale proceeds, most tax collectors will take additional steps beyond the required notice to attract bidders to the sale.

---

19. G.S. 1-339.51.
20. G.S. 105-367(c).

Neither the Machinery Act nor the execution sale provisions require personal notice of the sale to the taxpayer. But as with notice of the actual levy, providing notice to the taxpayer of the sale may help produce payment of the outstanding taxes and eliminate the need for the sale.

For the same reasons, notice should also be given to all parties that hold a lien on the property to be sold, such as a financing company that has recorded a security interest in an automobile. Security interests are also commonly recorded on business equipment, such as computers and inventory. Because these liens could be extinguished when the property is sold for unpaid taxes, the lienholders should receive notice so that they have an opportunity to protect their interests by paying the outstanding taxes or purchasing the property at the sale. See Questions 11 and 12 for a discussion about competing liens on the same property.

7. Must notice be given to the N.C. Division of Motor Vehicles if the property being sold is a car or a mobile home?

Yes. State law requires that no motor vehicle can be sold by a sheriff or a police officer or by any person under "judicial proceedings" without notice being provided to the Division of Motor Vehicles (DMV) at least twenty days prior to the sale.[21] Although a sale by the tax collector under the Machinery Act might not qualify as a judicial proceeding, the safest course of action is to assume that the notice requirement applies to any automobile to be sold for unpaid taxes. The tax collector or sheriff should complete DMV Form LT-101 and submit it to the DMV along with a copy of the execution or order for collection.[22] This notification requirement also applies to mobile homes that are registered with the DMV. (Form LT-101 is reproduced in Appendix 7A.)

---

21. G.S. 20-114(c).

22. N.C. ADMIN. CODE tit. 19A, ch. 03D, § .0404 (sale of motor vehicle under judicial proceedings).

8. When, where, and how must the sale occur?

If prior to the sale date the taxpayer pays all outstanding taxes, costs, and penalties, including the costs of seizing and securing the property, the tax collector and/or sheriff should cancel the sale and return the personal property to the taxpayer.[23]

If full payment is not made, the sale must then be held as indicated in the notice of sale. Sales of personal property can be held on any day except Sunday, in any place in the county, at any time between 10:00 a.m. and 10:00 p.m. (4:00 p.m. for towns with 5,000 or fewer residents).[24] The personal property must be present at the sale, meaning that in cases of large, immovable property the sale should be held where the property is situated.[25]

If the personal property consists of multiple items, the items may be sold individually, in groups, or as a whole, depending on which procedure will produce the highest price.[26] For example, if the property to be sold consists of six personal computers, the tax collector could sell all six computers as one item, sell two groups of three computers, sell three pairs of computers, or sell each of the six computers individually.

The sale must be made in cash to the highest bidder.[27] Immediately upon payment of the high bid, the property must be delivered to the buyer along with a bill of sale or similar record of the transaction.[28] The buyer will take the property free and clear of all liens unless the sale proceeds are not sufficient to satisfy a lien that was senior to the tax lien for which the property was sold. See Questions 11 and 12 below for a discussion of junior and senior liens.

There is no provision for upset bids on personal property as there is for the sale of real property at a tax foreclosure.[29] Nor must the court confirm the sale to the highest bidder.[30] This means that the taxpayer's right to

---

23. G.S. 1-339.57.

24. G.S. 1-339.43 (day of sale); G.S. 1-339.44(c) (place of sale); G.S. 1-339.60 (time of sale).

25. G.S. 1-339.45.

26. G.S. 105-339.46.

27. G.S. 1-339.47.

28. G.S. 1-339.62.

29. G.S. 1-339.64 (upset bid procedure for sale of real property); G.S. 105-374(o) (upset bid procedure for mortgage-style tax foreclosures).

30. G.S. 105-374(p) (confirmation of mortgage-style tax foreclosure sale of real property).

"redeem" his or her property by paying the outstanding taxes and costs ends once the sale has begun.[31]

Another difference between the sale of real property and the sale of personal property for outstanding taxes is that the levy and sale procedures do not authorize the taxing unit to bid at the sale of personal property. This means that the taxing unit cannot set a minimum bid for the property as it can do at a foreclosure sale of real property by submitting a bid for amount of taxes owed.[32] If the highest bid for personal property is one dollar, then the property must be sold for one dollar regardless of how much is owed in taxes and costs.

9. When may a sale of personal property be postponed?

A sale cannot be postponed simply because the bids offered by potential buyers are lower than the amount the taxing unit wanted. The execution sale provisions permit the postponement of a sale in only five situations:

1. when there are no bidders,
2. when the number of bidders is "substantially decreased by inclement weather or by any casualty,"
3. when it is impractical to hold the sale because there are too many other execution sales scheduled for the same time and place,
4. when the tax collector or sheriff cannot hold the sale due to illness or other good reason, and
5. when other "good cause" exists.[33]

The statute does not define "good cause," but almost certainly it requires something more than a disappointingly low sale price. If a sale is postponed under this provision, the official conducting the sale must publicly announce the postponement and on that same day post a signed notice of

---

31. When real property is sold at a tax foreclosure, the taxpayer can terminate the sale and "redeem" his or her property at any point prior to confirmation of the sale. Confirmation cannot occur until after the upset bid period ends, which means that a taxpayer could redeem real property by paying the taxes and costs up to ten days after the initial sale.

32. G.S. 105-376 (taxing unit as purchaser at foreclosure sale).

33. G.S. 1-339.58(a).

the postponement that includes the reason for the postponement as well as the new date and time for the sale.[34]

10. What if the high bidder does not make good on the bid?

If the high bidder does not immediately pay the bid in cash, the sheriff or the tax collector should immediately attempt to resell the property.[35] If no new bids are received, a new sale can be scheduled and advertised as described above (see Question 6).[36] The original high bidder is liable for the difference between the original bid and the eventual sale price minus the expenses of resale.[37] To enforce this liability, however, a taxing unit would need to bring suit against the original bidder in state court; the unit cannot use Machinery Act remedies to collect the difference between the bids.[38]

11. How should sale proceeds be distributed?

Proceeds from the sale of the levied property should be distributed in the following order:

First, to the sheriff, municipal police officer, and/or the tax collector for advertising and sale fees.[39] The sale fees are set by statute and based on the sale price: 5 percent of the first $500 in sale price and 2.5 percent of the remainder of the sale price plus additional "necessary expenses of the sale," such as advertising.[40] For example, if the sale price is $1,000, the sale fee will be $37.50, $25 for the first $500 and $12.50 for the remaining $500 in sale price.

---

34. G.S. 1-339.58(b) and (c).

35. G.S. 1-339.69(a).

36. *Id.*

37. G.S. 1-339.69(c).

38. The setoff debt collection procedure found in G.S. Chapter 105A would be available, however. This procedure permits a local government to attach a debtor's state income tax refund or lottery winnings to satisfy an obligation.

39. G.S. 106-367(d) and G.S. 1-339.70(a).

40. G.S. 7A-311(a)(3). Although this section specifies the fees for sales made by the sheriff, G.S. 105-367(a) also makes it applicable if the levy sale is conducted by the tax collector instead of the sheriff.

Second, to the sheriff, municipal police officer, and/or the tax collector for the cost of caring for the property from the time of levy to the time of sale.[41]

Third, to creditors holding previously existing liens on the property that are senior to the tax lien for which the property was sold, unless the property was sold "subject to" the senior liens.[42] (See Question 12 for a discussion of competing liens on the same property.)

Fourth, to the taxing unit for the taxes, interest, penalties, and costs for which the property was levied upon and sold. The property will be sold free and clear of this tax lien regardless of whether there are sufficient funds to pay all outstanding amounts.[43]

Fifth, to creditors holding liens on the property that are junior to the tax lien for which the property was sold.[44] The property will be sold free and clear of these junior liens regardless of whether there are sufficient funds to pay all outstanding amounts.[45] (See Question 12 for a discussion of competing liens on the same property.) If there are multiple junior lienholders, the best approach may be to provide the surplus funds to the clerk of superior court and allow that official to determine the appropriate priority (see sixth in the sequence, below).

Sixth, to the taxpayer who previously owned the property or, if there are conflicting claims on the surplus funds, to the clerk of superior court so that the clerk can hold a proceeding to resolve those claims.[46] It is not the tax collector's responsibility to referee conflicting claims to surplus funds.

---

41. G.S. 1-339.70(a).

42. 51 Am. Jur. 2d *Secured Transactions* § 643 (2003).

43. 51 Am. Jur. 2d *Liens* § 62 (2000) (sale of property by the creditor holding lien on that property extinguishes that lien).

44. *Id.* at § 94.

45. 51 Am. Jur. 2d *Secured Transactions* § 643 (2003).

46. G.S. 1-339.70(c) and G.S. 1-339.71.

12. Is the tax lien paid before other liens on the same personal property?

Liens generally are paid in the order in which they arose, a process known as first in time, first in right.[47] However, the Machinery Act gives property tax liens on personal property priority over state tax liens and private liens regardless of when they arose if the tax lien is for taxes owed on the property being sold.[48] Liens for property taxes on property other than the property being sold are prioritized under the first in time, first in right rule: liens that arose before the taxing unit levied upon the property (senior liens) are paid before the tax lien, while liens that arose after the taxing unit levied upon the property (junior liens) are paid after the tax lien.[49]

For example, assume that the Carolina County tax collector levies upon Tom Tarheel's Lexus SUV for $1,500 in property taxes and interest owed on that car for 2008, 2009, and 2010. In 2007 Tom had financed his purchase of the Lexus with Big Bank, which still holds a $15,000 security interest in the car. Because the Carolina County's tax lien represents taxes on the Lexus itself, the tax lien will be senior to Big Bank's lien and be paid first even though Big Bank's lien arose first.

Assume that Tom's Lexus has been involved in a couple of wrecks and that at the tax sale conducted by the sheriff it attracts a high bid of only $10,000. The proceeds must first be used to pay the sale fee of $262.50 to sheriff. The tax collector can then deduct the costs of the levy and sale, which in this case amounted to $737.50 for towing, storage, and advertisement of the sale, leaving $9,000 to be distributed. The tax lien of $1,500 is to be paid next, leaving only $7,500 for Big Bank. Big Bank's lien on the car is extinguished even though the sale proceeds are insufficient to satisfy the entire amount Tom owed Big Bank on the car.

Consider these same facts again but assume that Carolina County's $1,500 tax lien represents taxes owed on Tom's real property, not taxes owed on the Lexus itself.[50] In this situation, Big Bank's lien on

---

47. See 51 AM. JUR. 2D *Liens* § 70 (2000).

48. G.S. 105-356(b)(1). Local tax liens on personal property do not have the same priority over federal tax liens on the same property; both liens are subject to the first in time, first in right rule of priority. 26 U.S.C. § 6323.

49. G.S. 105-356(b)(2).

50. Although taxes owed on a registered motor vehicle do not constitute a lien on real property, taxes owed on real property can justify a lien on that same taxpayer's

the Lexus takes priority over Carolina County's lien because Big Bank's lien attached first. The Lexus would normally be sold subject to Big Bank's lien of $15,000, which would discourage bidding on the car as well as reduce the likelihood of the sale producing enough cash to satisfy the outstanding taxes owed by Tom. Whether or not those taxes are completely satisfied, the Lexus would be sold free and clear of Carolina County's tax lien.

For a detailed discussion of the priority of property tax liens on both personal and real property, see Chapter 5.

13. What is the statute of limitations for use of the levy and sale remedy?

The ten-year limitation on enforced collections found in G.S. 105-378(a) applies to this collection remedy. This provision provides a taxpayer with a defense to any levy that is attempted more than ten years after the tax for which the levy is conducted came due. Property taxes on real property and personal property other than registered motor vehicles become due on September 1 of the fiscal year for which the taxes are levied.

For example, 2000 property taxes on real property became due on September 1, 2000. Any enforced collection action for 2000 property taxes must be started by August 31, 2010, or else G.S. 105-378(a) would provide the taxpayer with a statute of limitations defense to the action.

This statute of limitations, however, requires only that the collection action begin within ten years, not that it be completed within ten years. Accordingly, the statute of limitations is satisfied if the property is levied upon ten years even if the actual sale of the property occurs outside of the ten-year period.

For example, if on August 30, 2010, a tax collector levies upon and seizes a taxpayer's car for delinquent real property taxes from the 2000 tax year and the car is then sold in mid-September 2010, the taxpayer would not have a statue of limitations defense to the collection action. It does not matter

---

registered motor vehicle. See G.S. 105-330.4(c) (taxes on registered motor vehicle do not become lien on real property) and G.S. 105-366(b) (tax collector may levy upon any personal property owned by taxpayer who owes delinquent property taxes).

when the actual sale of the car occurs so long as the levy is made before the ten-year period ends.

14. May the tax collector pursue multiple levies and sales of a taxpayer's personal property to satisfy delinquent taxes?

Yes. A tax collector may employ the levy and sale remedy as many times as necessary to satisfy a particular delinquent tax. If the sale of levied property does not produce enough funds to completely satisfy the delinquent taxes owed by the former owner of the levied property, the tax collector may seize, levy upon, and sell more of that taxpayer's personal property to satisfy those taxes. Similarly, the tax collector may pursue a levy and sale of tangible personal property simultaneous with an attachment and garnishment of the taxpayer's intangible personal property, such as bank accounts and wages. However, a tax collector may not employ the levy and sale remedy (or the attachment and garnishment remedy) after a foreclosure action on the taxpayer's real property has been initiated.[51] Even if that foreclosure sale fails to satisfy the delinquent taxes, the tax collector is prohibited from pursuing subsequent Machinery Act remedies against that taxpayer's personal property. After a foreclosure action is initiated, the only remedy remaining for a tax collector is the set-off debt collection procedure discussed in Chapter 8.

---

51. G.S. 105-366(b).

Appendix 7A. DMV Form LT-101

LT-101   Date: ___________________

NOTICE OF SALE OF A MOTOR VEHICLE - 20 DAY ADVANCE NOTICE TO DIVISION OF MOTOR VEHICLES

A.   **DESCRIPTION OF VEHICLE** (Must be fully completed)

MAKE	YEAR MODEL	BODY STYLE	MOTOR NO. (1953 and older – attach pencil tracing)

SERIAL NO. (All models – attach pencil tracing)

STATE & YEAR IN WHICH VEHICLE LAST REGISTERED	LICENSE PLATE NUMBER

B.   **LOCATION OF VEHICLE – SALE DATE** (Must be fully completed)

PLACE STORED	ADDRESS	SALE DATE
PLACE OF SALE	ADDRESS	SALE HOUR

C.   **Notice of Sale under JUDICIAL PROCEEDINGS**

NAME OF COURT AUTHORIZING SEZURE AND SALE (Attach copy of court order and/or judgment and/or execution)

NAME OF OWNER FROM WHOM THE VEHICLE WAS SEIZED	ADDRESS

D.   **Notice of Sale of ABANDONED VEHICLE Pursuant to GS 160A-303 City Ordinance No.**

PLACE STORED	ADDRESS	SALE DATE
PLACE OF SALE	ADDRESS	SALE HOUR

E.   **Notice of Sale for OTHER REASONS** (Explain fully and cite statutory provision)

F.   **NAME AND ADDRESS OF AGENCY OR DEPARTMENT SELLING VEHICLE**

NAME	STREET ADDRESS OR BOX NUMBER
CITY, STATE, ZIP	SIGNATURE AND OFFICIAL POSITION

FOR USE BY THE DIVISION OF MOTOR VEHICLES

REGISTERED OWNER	AMOUNT – DATE FIRST LIEN	AMOUNT – DATE SECOND LIEN
STREET	LIENHOLDER	LIENHOLDER
CITY, ST, ZIP	STREET	STREET
TITLE NUMBER	CITY, ST, ZIP	CITY, ST, ZIP

☐ Not Registered in North Carolina

Forward this notice to: *NC Division of Motor Vehicles*
License and Theft Bureau
Notice Storage & Theft Unit
3132 Mail Service Center
Raleigh, NC 27699-3132

Set-Off Debt Collection

Chapter 8

Set-Off Debt Collection

1. What is set-off debt collection?

Commonly called debt set-off, this process is an additional collection remedy beyond those found in the Machinery Act. Authorized by Chapter 105A of the General Statutes, debt set-off allows a local government to attach a taxpayer's North Carolina state income tax refund, North Carolina state lottery winnings, or any other amount owed to that taxpayer other than wages to satisfy a debt owed to that local government.[1] The debt could be delinquent taxes or library fines or parking tickets or any obligation owed to a local government. The only limitation is that the debt be at least $50.[2]

For the first thirty or so years of its existence, debt set-off could be used against individuals only. Corporations, partnerships, and similar entities were not covered. This is no longer true.

In 2010 the General Assembly amended the definition of "debtor" in G.S. 105A-2 from "an *individual* who owes a debt" to "a *person* who owes a debt" (emphasis added). This seemingly minor change in terminology resulted in a major substantive change to the program. The General Statutes' rules

---

1. G.S. 105A-2 makes debt set-off applicable to N.C. state income tax refunds of $50 or more. G.S. 18C-134 makes debt set-off applicable to lottery winnings of $600 or more. In 2010 the General Assembly amended G.S. 147-86.25 to make debt set-off applicable to all "payments the State owes to debtors" other than wages. The statute does not explain what these payments include, but presumably they could be payments owed under purchasing and construction contracts. Note that the exclusion of state wages from debt set-off has no impact on the collection of property taxes because local governments already had the authority to attach those wages under G.S. 105-368(h). In addition to local governments, debt set-off is available to water and sewer authorities, regional joint agencies, public health authorities, metropolitan sewer districts, and sanitary districts. G.S. 105A-2(2)(6).

2. G.S. 105A-4.

for statutory construction state that the word "'person' shall extend and be applied to bodies politic and corporate, as well as to individuals, unless the context clearly shows to the contrary."[3] Additional changes to the debt set-off provisions made in the same bill clearly indicate the General Assembly's intent to make corporations, partnerships, and other entities subject to this collection remedy. For example, local governments are encouraged to provide a debtor's federal tax employer identification numbers, which are available to corporations and similar entities. Previously the statute referenced only Social Security numbers, which are available only to individuals.[4]

It remains to be seen how effective debt set-off will be against business entities. As of mid-2011, the N.C. Department of Revenue and the N.C. Local Government Set-off Debt Clearinghouse (see Question 3 below) were still developing the specific procedures to use debt set-off against business entities. Until those procedures are implemented, corporations, partnerships, and other entity taxpayers will not be subject to debt set-off. Even after the process can be used against entities, it seems likely that debt set-off will be less productive for local government tax collectors than it has been when used against individuals. Few corporations receive income tax refunds of any substance because they make partial tax payments throughout the year based on their actual income.

The lack of corporate income tax refunds will be offset somewhat by the General Assembly's expansion of the process to reach other "payments the state owes to debtors."[5] Presumably, this change will allow local governments to attach payments owed by the state to corporations or individuals under construction or procurement contracts. This new option may make debt set-off more productive against business entities who do not normally receive income tax refunds. The statute excludes state employee wages from the reach of debt set-off, but local governments can already attach those wages for delinquent taxes using the Machinery Act attachment and garnishment procedure.[6]

Debt set-off is effective only if the taxpayer is owed an income tax refund or lottery winnings or other payments, of course. That said, many local governments have used the program successfully over the years. In just the

---

3. G.S. 12-3(6).
4. G.S. 105A-3(c).
5. G.S. 147-86.25.
6. See Chapter 6.

first six months of 2011, local governments and agencies across the state collected more than $25 million through debt set-off.[7] Since the program's inception in 1979, thirty-five local governments have each collected more than $1 million in outstanding debts.[8]

2. When can a local government use debt set-off?

Debt set-off is an enforced collection remedy that may be used for the collection of property taxes whenever Machinery Act remedies against personal property are permitted. Such remedies are permitted when:

1. the tax becomes delinquent,[9]
2. the tax collector learns that the property on which taxes are owed has been in a going-out-of-business sale or any other sale outside the normal course of business,[10]
3. the tax collector learns that the property on which taxes are owed is about to be transferred to another taxpayer or removed from the taxing unit's jurisdiction,[11] or
4. the tax collector learns that the taxpayer is or is about to become insolvent.[12]

See Chapter 6 for more details on the timing of enforced collection remedies against personal property.

For taxes other than property taxes, the tax collector may use debt set-off whenever the taxes are past due. The due dates for local taxes for occupancy taxes, privilege license taxes, and other local taxes vary based on state statutes and local ordinances. See Chapter 15 for more details on the collection of these taxes.

---

7. N.C. Local Government Set-off Debt Clearinghouse 2011 statistics, available at www.ncsetoff.org/statistics.htm (last visited July 25, 2011).

8. As of July 2011, according to the N.C. Local Government Set-off Debt Clearinghouse homepage at www.ncsetoff.org/ (last visited July 25, 2011).

9. G.S. 105-366(b). See G.S. 105-365.1 for details on when property taxes become delinquent.

10. G.S. 105-366(d).

11. *Id.* at (c).

12. *Id.*

The clearinghouse that processes local government debt set-off requests requires that debts be delinquent for at least sixty days.[13] While this requirement is not found in the debt set-off statutes, it appears that local governments must honor the clearinghouse's procedures because the governments cannot submit their requests directly to the state. (See the next section for more details on the process.) For the purposes of satisfying the clearinghouse's sixty-day requirement, tax collectors can use the earlier of (i) the actual date of delinquency or (ii) the date on which Machinery Act remedies against personal property became available.

3. How can a local government use debt set-off?

Local governments cannot submit debt set-off claims directly to the N.C. Department of Revenue. Instead, they must work through a third party, the N.C. Local Government Set-off Debt Clearinghouse, a joint effort by the N.C. Association of County Commissioners and the N.C. League of Municipalities.[14] Applications for the debt set-off process are available from the clearinghouse's website at www.ncsetoff.org.

Before submitting a claim through the clearinghouse, the local government must give the taxpayer notice of the intent to use the process as well as the opportunity for a hearing beforehand.[15] Many local governments include the required set-off debt notice in the delinquency letters and notice of advertisement they automatically send to taxpayers with delinquent taxes. This eliminates the need for a separate debt set-off mailing if the tax collector later chooses to use this remedy. The notice must state the basis for the debt and the government's intention to attach the taxpayer's income tax refund, lottery winnings, and/or other payments owed to the debtor by the state and inform the debtor that a $15 collection assistance fee will be added to the debt. This collection fee is retained by the Department of Revenue and has priority over the local government's debt in the situation where the amount collected under debt set-off is not sufficient to pay both the collection assistance fee and the debt owed to the local government.[16]

---

13. See www.ncsetoff.org (last visited Feb. 9, 2011).

14. G.S. 105A-3(b1).

15. G.S. 105A-5(a).

16. G.S. 105A-13(c) and (d). For example, assume that a local government submits a $100 claim for delinquent taxes to debt set-off and that the taxpayer's state income

The notice provided to the taxpayer must also state that the debtor has the right to contest the matter by filing a written request for a hearing within thirty days of the date of the notice.[17]

The debt set-off provisions offer little guidance regarding the hearing process. The statute states only (i) the governing body or a person designated by the governing body must conduct the hearing, (ii) an issue that has been previously litigated in a court proceeding cannot be considered, and (iii) the hearing decision must determine whether a debt is owed to the local agency and the amount of the debt.[18] Clearly, the taxpayer has the right to demonstrate that the tax bill has been paid or that he or she is not personally responsible for the delinquent taxes. But it is unclear whether a taxpayer can contest the assessment that generated the delinquent taxes. Very few assessments will have been "previously litigated in a court proceeding" and therefore explicitly excluded from the scope of the hearing.[19] Nevertheless, it seems unlikely that the General Assembly intended to provide another opportunity to appeal an assessment months or years after the Machinery Act's appeal period closed.[20] When possible, statutes are interpreted to be in harmony with one another.[21] The better interpretation is one that permits a taxpayer to contest issues relating to the collection effort but not those relating to the underlying assessment. For example, a debtor could argue that he or she is not the same individual who owes the delinquent tax or that he or she already paid the delinquent tax. But a debtor should not be permitted to argue that the tax assessment generating the debt is inaccurate.

---

tax refund is only $75. In this situation, the Department of Revenue would retain the full $15 collection fee and remit the remaining $60 to the local government to be credited toward the unpaid taxes.

17. G.S. 105A-5(b) and (c).

18. G.S. 105A-5(c) and (d).

19. Appeals to a county board of equalization and review or the state Property Tax Commission would not constitute "court proceedings."

20. The Machinery Act permits taxpayers to appeal assessments to the Board of Equalization and Review up to the date that board adjourns or up to thirty days after receiving notice of the assessed value of personal property, whichever is later. G.S. 105-322(g)(2)(a); G.S. 105-317.1(c) and G.S. 105-330.2(b).

21. People v. Cone Mills Corp., 316 N.C. 426, 444 (1986) ("A canon of statutory interpretation is that statutes dealing with the same subject matter must be construed together and harmonized, if possible, to give effect to each.").

A taxpayer who disagrees with the hearing decision has thirty days to file an appeal with the state Office of Administrative Hearings pursuant to G.S. Chapter 150, Article 3.[22]

If a local government submits a claim to the debt set-off program without sending the required notice or prior to a hearing decision in favor of the taxpayer, the local government must refund to the taxpayer all amounts recovered through debt set-off as well as the $15 collection assistance fee.[23] The local government must pay the taxpayer interest on such an inappropriate debt set-off collection beginning on the fifth day after the Department of Revenue notifies the taxpayer of the set-off.[24] The rate is the same rate that applies to late state income tax refunds.[25]

4. May a tax collector use debt set-off simultaneous with Machinery Act remedies, such as a wage garnishment or a bank account attachment?

Yes. The debt set-off provisions explicitly state that this remedy is "in addition to and not in substitution for any other remedy allowed by law."[26] The tax collector need not wait until an attachment or a garnishment runs its course before initiating a debt set-off claim.

However, the same is not true concerning foreclosure actions and debt set-off. The Machinery Act prohibits a tax collector from targeting a taxpayer's personal property after a foreclosure action has begun.[27] Technically, this restriction limits only Machinery Act procedures against personal property. The set-off debt collection remedy is created by another chapter of

---

22. G.S. 105A-5(c).

23. G.S. 105A-5(e).

24. *Id.*

25. *Id.* That interest rate, which also applies to property tax overpayments caused by a Property Tax Commission ruling in favor of the taxpayer, is set every six months by the Department of Revenue pursuant to G.S. 105-241.21. It is generally much lower than the roughly 10 percent annual interest applied to late property tax payments under the Machinery Act. As of June 2011, the rate was 5 percent.

26. G.S. 105A-3(a).

27. G.S. 105-366(b) prohibits the use of Machinery Act remedies against personal property after a foreclosure complaint has been filed under G.S. 105-374 or a foreclosure judgment has been docketed under G.S. 105-375.

the General Statutes, meaning that the restriction on the use of Machinery Act remedies may not apply to the use of set-off debt collection. However, seeing as set-off debt collection is simply another method of attaching the taxpayer's personal property, the best practice is to assume that Machinery Act restrictions also apply to set-off debt collection. A tax collector should terminate any existing debt set-off claims and should not initiate any new debt set-off claims for a particular tax obligation if the local government decides to initiate a foreclosure proceeding for that obligation.

A local government cannot collect the same tax twice, of course. Once the tax is collected in full through any method, the tax collector should contact the clearinghouse to terminate an existing debt set-off. If the tax collector receives a payment from debt set-off beyond what is owed by the taxpayer, the tax collector must refund the excess payment to the taxpayer with interest as described above.[28] But the tax collector is not required (or authorized) to repay to the taxpayer the $15 collection assistance fee in this situation.[29]

Because debt set-off is in addition to any remedies provided by the Machinery Act, it might be most helpful to a tax collector in two specific situations in which the Machinery Act requires the use of a civil lawsuit to recover delinquent taxes.

One situation involves the going-out-of-business provisions in G.S. 105-366(d), which hold the buyer of business personal property responsible for taxes owed on that property.[30] If the tax collector wishes to use attachment and garnishment or levy and sale remedies against the buyer, the collection action must begin within six months of the going-out-of-business sale. After six months the only remedy under the Machinery Act is a civil suit against the buyer, which can be expensive and time-consuming. Now that it can be used against corporations, debt set-off might be a good option in such cases.

The second situation is when delinquent taxes are owed by public service companies. G.S. 105-344 states that the only Machinery Act remedy available against such a taxpayer is a civil action. Although public service companies generally pay their taxes on time, debt set-off might the best option if enforced collection is required.

---

28. G.S. 105A-5(e).

29. *Id.*

30. For a detailed discussion of these provisions see Chapter 6.

5. What statute of limitations applies to the use of debt set-off?

The debt set-off provisions do not include any reference to a time limitation on the use of that remedy. However, the Machinery Act's ten-year statute of limitations applies to "any remedy provided by law for the collection of taxes" and not just to Machinery Act remedies.[31] The safest course of action for tax collectors is to assume that the Machinery Act's ten-year limitation applies to debt set-off. The process should not be used for tax obligations that are more than ten years past due.[32]

____

31. G.S. 105-378(a).

32. Taxes on real property and personal property other than registered motor vehicles are due on September 1 of the year in which they are levied. G.S. 105-360(a). Taxes on registered motor vehicles are due the first day of the fourth month after a new registration is applied for or an existing registration expires. G.S. 105-330.4(a)(1).

Advertising Delinquent Property Taxes

Chapter 9

Advertising Delinquent Property Taxes

The Machinery Act sends mixed messages regarding a taxing unit's obligation to advertise tax liens on real property. G.S. 105-369 expressly requires the advertisement of tax liens. The statute uses the terms "must" and "shall" more than a dozen times when describing the duty to advertise, leaving little room to argue that these ads are optional.[1] However, the statute also declares, in two separate provisions, that the failure to advertise or to send advance notice of the advertisement to the taxpayer "does not affect the validity" of the taxes, the tax liens, or a subsequent foreclosure action.[2]

How should a tax collector decipher these seemingly incongruent messages? Despite the understandable desire to avoid the often substantial costs, the safest course of action is to assume that the obligation to advertise is a non-negotiable requirement. North Carolina courts have not yet been asked to opine on the "escape clauses" that apparently excuse the failure to advertise. With this in mind, tax collectors would be wise to assume that these provisions do not excuse the deliberate decision not to advertise real

---

This chapter updates information published as *Property Tax Bulletin* No. 148 (July 2009).

1. These mandates include the following: "the governing body *must* order the tax collector to advertise the tax liens," G.S. 105-369(a); and, "the county tax collector *shall* advertise county tax liens by posting a notice of the liens at the county courthouse and by publishing each lien at least one time in one or more newspapers having general circulation in the taxing unit. The municipal tax collector *shall* advertise municipal tax liens by posting a notice of the liens at the city or town hall and by publishing each lien at least one time in one or more newspapers having general circulation in the taxing unit." G.S. 105-369(c) (emphasis added).

2. G.S. 105-369(b1) and (c).

property tax liens. This is especially true for taxing units that employ the in rem foreclosure process under G.S. 105-375, for which the advertisement of a tax lien is the first step.

1. Which taxes should be advertised?

G.S. 105-369(a) mandates that the tax collector must first inform the governing body of and then advertise the "total amount of unpaid taxes for the current fiscal year that are liens on real property."[3] This amount should include any special service district property taxes but not special assessments, which fall outside of the Machinery Act's definition of "taxes" (G.S. 105-273(17)). The amount advertised should be only the principal amount of taxes owed, not including any interest, costs, or fees (see Question 5 for additional information).

Tax liens on real property represent real property taxes as well as personal property taxes owed by taxpayers who own real property in the taxing unit as of the January 1 listing date.[4] Personal property taxes are a lien on *all* real property parcels owned by the same taxpayer in the taxing unit. If the taxpayer owns personal property and multiple parcels of real property, the tax collector has the options of either (1) adding the personal property taxes to only *one* of the real property liens or (2) adding the personal property taxes to *all* of the real property liens. The personal property taxes may be collected only once, and until they are paid they will constitute a lien on all real property owned by the taxpayer in the taxing unit regardless of how they are advertised.

For example, assume Wanda Wolfpack owns Parcel A, Parcel B, and a boat, all in Carolina County. The tax lien on Parcel A includes the taxes on the real property itself as well as the taxes on the boat. The tax lien on Parcel B includes the taxes on the real property itself and the taxes on the boat.

---

3. A taxing unit has the option of also advertising personal property taxes that are *not* a lien on real property, but the cost of that advertisement may not be passed along to taxpayers as is the cost of the real property tax lien advertisement. G.S. 105-373(a)(1)(b).

4. G.S. 105-355(a) ("the lien for taxes levied on a parcel of real property shall attach to the parcel taxed on the date as of which property is to be listed under G.S. 105-285, and the lien for taxes levied on personal property shall attach to all real property of the taxpayer in the taxing unit on the same date").

Technically, the tax collector should include the taxes on the boat in the advertisement for both Parcel A and Parcel B. However, because of limitations with their tax software, many collectors will include the taxes on the boat in only one of the real property tax liens.

Although the Machinery Act mandates only that the current year's tax liens be advertised, some tax offices advertise liens from prior years as well. While this practice does not violate the Machinery Act, arguably tax collectors may pass along to the advertised taxpayers only the cost of the advertisement for the current year's tax liens. Any increased advertisement costs due to the inclusion of prior years' tax liens in the advertisement should be borne by the tax office and not passed along to the advertised taxpayers.

2. How should subdivided parcels be advertised?

How should a tax lien be advertised if the underlying parcel has been subdivided and transferred since the listing date? The advertising statute itself is silent on this question, but general Machinery Act principles provide some guidance.

If the subdivided parcels have been individually appraised and listed by the assessor by the time the tax collector begins the advertising process, the tax collector should advertise the tax liens that arise from the subdivided parcels' new assessments. This approach is consistent with the opportunity created by G.S. 105-362(b)(2) for the owner of a subdivided parcel to release the lien on the parcel by paying the new assessment, plus a proportionate share of the original owner's personal property taxes that were secured by the parcel, if any such taxes exist.

If the subdivided parcels have not yet been individually appraised by the assessor, best practice is to advertise the full amount of the original tax lien for each subdivided parcel and make the necessary adjustments when the subdivided parcels are appraised by the assessor. In the text of the advertisement, the tax collector should explain this approach and add an indicator such as "(subd.)" next to each subdivided parcel so that the taxpayer is aware that adjustments to the advertised amount will be required when the tax lien is satisfied. This approach is preferable to the tax collector attempting to estimate the values of the subdivided parcels, which is a task the Machinery Act reserves exclusively for the assessor.

3. When should tax liens be advertised?

G.S. 105-369(c) requires that real property tax liens for the current tax year be advertised at any time from March 1 through June 30. Most taxing units prefer to advertise earlier rather than later. Three actions must occur before the advertisement may be published and posted.

First, in February the tax collector must report to the governing body the "total amount of unpaid taxes for the current fiscal year that are liens on real property."[5] Second, the governing body must issue an order to the tax collector to advertise the tax liens; the order will be issued, presumably, immediately upon receipt of the tax collector's report.[6] Third, at least thirty days before the advertisement is published and posted, the tax collector must provide written notice to the affected taxpayers of the intent to publish outstanding current tax liens.[7] In many counties, this notice produces more tax payments than does the actual advertisement.

4. Who should be named in the advertisement?

The advertising statute requires that a tax lien be advertised in the name of the owner as of the date of delinquency. Generally, real property taxes are delinquent on January 6 of the fiscal year in which they are levied; 2009 real property taxes, for example, are delinquent on January 6, 2010.[8] If Parcel A is listed for 2009 taxes in the name of Taxpayer 1 but is owned by Taxpayer 2 on January 6, 2010, the outstanding tax lien on the parcel must be advertised in the name of Taxpayer 2.

G.S. 105-369 originally required that a tax lien be advertised in the name of the listing taxpayer, regardless of subsequent transfers. This requirement changed along with the Machinery Act's enforced collection procedures.

---

5. G.S. 105-369(a). County tax collectors must make their reports by the first Monday in February; municipal tax collectors must do so by the second Monday in February.

6. *Id.*

7. G.S. 105-369(c).

8. Taxes that are not deferred taxes are delinquent on the date they first accrue interest. G.S. 105-365.1(a)(1). Real property taxes are due on September 1 of the fiscal year for which they are levied and first accrue interest on January 6 following the due date. G.S. 105-360(a).

Prior to 2006, the listing taxpayer was the only taxpayer who could be targeted by enforced collections. Beginning with the 2006 tax year, the taxpayers who are subject to enforced collection remedies for real property taxes include not only the record owner on the date of delinquency but also all subsequent owners.[9] When the responsibility for delinquent taxes shifted from the listing taxpayer to the owner as of the date of delinquency, the burden of being named in the tax lien advertisement also shifted.

Suppose a delinquent parcel changes hands between January 6 and the date on which the tax collector sends the required notice of advertisement. Taxpayers who take ownership subsequent to January 6 share responsibility for the delinquent taxes along with the owner prior to January 6. Because the advertising statute makes no mention of post-January 6 owners, a tax collector must still send notice of the intent to advertise to the January 6 owner despite the fact that the parcel has changed hands. In the interest of providing notice to all taxpayers potentially subject to enforced collection remedies, the tax collector also may, and probably should, send notice of the intent to advertise to all post-January 6 owners and advertise in their names as well.

The following example illustrates this approach. Assume Parcel A is listed in the name of Taxpayer 1, is owned by Taxpayer 2 on the following January 6, and is transferred to Taxpayer 3 on February 1. If taxes remain outstanding when the tax collector prepares to advertise tax liens, notice must be sent to Taxpayer 2, the owner on January 6. However, Taxpayer 3 is also responsible for the outstanding taxes, and it is also appropriate to send notice to Taxpayer 3. If the taxes remain unpaid thirty days later, the tax collector must advertise in the name of Taxpayer 2 and may also advertise in the name of Taxpayer 3. However, under no circumstances should the tax collector advertise in the name of Taxpayer 1.

Tax collectors must work closely with assessors to ensure that they have accurate record owner information as of January 6. The longer it takes to compile this information, the later the advertising date. If a taxing unit wishes to advertise in early March, the transfer information needs to be provided to the tax collector by late January so that the required notices can be compiled and mailed in early February.

---

9. G.S. 105-365.1(b)(1).

The Machinery Act provides several layers of protection to tax collectors who advertise in the name of the wrong taxpayer. The advertising statute expressly states that neither the failure to notify the correct taxpayer (G.S. 105-369(b1)) nor the failure to advertise the correct taxpayer (G.S. 105-369(f)) shall affect the validity of a tax lien. Furthermore, the general immaterial irregularity provision, G.S. 105-394, excuses minor defects in any Machinery Act procedure. That said, it is best practice for a tax collector to correct any taxpayer identification errors if a city or county intends to proceed with an in rem foreclosure under G.S. 105-375. Because the advertisement of a tax lien is the first step in an in rem foreclosure process, the tax collector would be wise to send a new notice to the correct taxpayer and publish a new advertisement in the correct taxpayer's name before moving forward. Note that the advertising statute provides for criminal penalties if a tax collector knows that a tax has been paid but willfully advertises the parcel regardless.[10]

5. What information must be included in the advertisement?

G.S. 105-369(c) mandates that the advertisement includes

- the name of the record owner as of the date of delinquency,
- a brief description of the parcel (such as street address or tax map number),
- the principal amount of taxes that are a lien on the parcel,
- a statement that the amounts advertised will be increased by interest and costs,
- the names of the newspapers and the dates on which the advertisements will run (if the list of tax liens has been divided among several newspapers), and
- a statement that the liens may be foreclosed and the properties sold.

Note that the statute (1) directs that only the "principal amount" of taxes be included in advertisement, despite the fact that at least three months of interest will have accrued on these liens by the date of the advertisement and (2) does not permit a tax collector to add to the advertised amounts any fees, penalties, or costs that the taxpayer might have already accumulated. In the

---

10. G.S. 105-369(g).

Figure 9A. Possible Text of Tax Lien Advertisement

NOTICE OF ADVERTISEMENT OF TAX LIENS ON REAL PROPERTY

_______________ COUNTY

TOWN OF _______________

Under the authority vested in me by Section 105-369 of the North Carolina General Statutes and pursuant to an order of the Board of Commissioners/Town Council of __________________ dated, ___________ , I am hereby advertising tax liens for the year _____ upon the real property described below.

The real property parcel subject to the lien, the name of the parcel's owner as of January 6, _____ (and/or the names of subsequent owners), and the amount of taxes due are set out below. The amount advertised represents only the principal taxes for tax year _____ that were unpaid as of ___________ . The actual amount owed by the taxpayer will be increased by all taxes owed for prior tax years and by all applicable interest, costs, and fees. The omission of prior years' taxes and interest, costs, and fees from the amount advertised will not constitute a waiver of the taxing unit's claim for these items.

If the taxes remain unpaid, the tax collector will use all available collection remedies to collect the delinquent taxes, including the levy on personal property, the garnishment of wages, the attachment of bank accounts, rents, debts, or other property and the foreclosure and sale of the real property. These collections procedures do not apply to taxpayers subject to pending federal bankruptcy petitions.

When a parcel was subdivided after January 1, _____ , and the ownership of one or more of the resulting parcels were transferred, the amount of the tax lien on each parcel, as shown in this advertisement, is the amount of the lien on the original parcel as it existed on January 1, _____ , and is subject to adjustment when the taxes are paid or the lien is foreclosed.

This the _____ day of ________ , 20___ .

_______________ County Tax Collector

Town of _______________ Tax Collector

---

interest of providing taxpayers with more accurate information about their tax obligations, some tax collectors include in the advertisement all amounts owed. The better practice, however, is to conform to the statutory requirement and print only the principal taxes along with a prominent warning that these amounts will be increased by interest and costs. See Question 7 for details on how interest and advertising costs are calculated. Possible text for the advertisement is presented in Figure 9A.

6. Where must the advertisement be posted and published?

The tax lien advertisement must appear publicly in at least two locations: posted at the county courthouse or town hall and published in a newspaper having "general circulation" in the taxing unit.[11] In light of the substantial costs involved—Forsyth County spent more than $33,000 on its tax lien advertisement in 2009—the newspaper selection process can be a delicate legal, political, and financial issue.

The sole North Carolina appellate court decision interpreting the "general circulation" requirement in G.S. 105-369 is a 1981 case that approved the advertisement of county tax liens in a weekly paper with fewer than 500 subscribers.[12] In determining that the newspaper used by the county satisfied the advertising statute, the North Carolina Supreme Court identified four standards that still apply today. To meet the "general circulation" requirement a newspaper must

- offer content that is "appealing to the public generally,"
- have more than a *de minimus* number of actual paid subscribers,
- have paid subscribers in more than one community or section of the taxing unit, and
- be available to anyone in the taxing unit that wishes to subscribe.[13]

The fact that a newspaper with only a few hundred paid subscribers can satisfy these standards indicates that a tax collector need not run the advertisement in the newspaper with the largest or most geographically diverse subscriber base in the taxing unit. The chosen newspaper's subscribers are not required to be evenly distributed throughout the city or county, nor does the newspaper need to have subscribers in *every* part of the taxing unit. As long as there are some paid subscribers in more than one community of the city or county, the newspaper could satisfy these standards.

The tax collector must use at least one newspaper that satisfies the "general circulation" requirement, assuming one exists. Although running the advertisement in several small newspapers may be less expensive and may actually reach more local readers than doing so in one larger newspaper, a tax collector cannot rely on this piecemeal approach. However, if no sin-

---

11. G.S. 105-369(c).

12. Great S. Media, Inc. v. McDowell Cnty., 304 N.C. 427, 284 S.E.2d 457 (1981).

13. *Id.* at 442, 284 S.E.2d at 467.

gle newspaper in the taxing unit is able to satisfy the "general circulation" requirement, it might be acceptable to rely on several newspapers with limited circulation.

Beyond the Machinery Act mandates, additional statutory requirements for the chosen newspaper are created by G.S. 1-597, which sets the regulations for the publication of all legal notices and advertisements in the state. The newspaper must

- be admitted to the United States mails as a second-class matter and
- have been regularly and continuously issued in the city or county at least one day in each calendar week for at least twenty-five of the twenty-six weeks preceding the advertisement date.

Read together with the Machinery Act, these provisions eliminate a number of possibly less expensive publication options. A tax collector cannot advertise *exclusively* in the following publications, regardless of how popular they might be among local readers:

- a free newspaper,
- a newspaper available only on the Internet,
- a monthly newspaper or magazine, or
- a newspaper that has been in publication for fewer than six months.

Another inexpensive approach that does not pass muster under the current statute is to advertise by posting tax liens on the county or city website. Although the General Assembly has authorized several localities to forgo traditional newspaper publication in favor of website postings for public meetings,[14] this authority has yet to be extended to cover Machinery Act procedures.

One creative legal solution to the advertising question is for a county to work with a local newspaper to produce a special section (similar to one commonly published for television listings) for the tax lien advertisement.[15]

---

14. For example, S.L. 2003-81 (Cabarrus County); S.L. 2007-86 (towns of Apex, Garner, and Knightdale).

15. However, an insert similar to the traditional Sunday morning coupon and store flyers would likely not satisfy the publication requirement. While such inserts are distributed with the newspaper, they are not actually published as part of the newspaper. A special section avoids this problem because it carries the newspaper banner and is published as part of the regular newspaper.

Often less expensive than a traditional advertisement, a special section may better attract readers' attention and can provide space for the tax office to share with taxpayers details about the county's budget or property tax procedures.[16]

7. How are costs and interest calculated?

G.S. 105-369(d) mandates that each parcel included in the tax lien advertisement be assessed an advertising fee to cover publication costs. The statute allows the tax collector to allocate the cost among the tax liens "on any reasonable basis," and the standard approach is to evenly divide the cost of advertising by the total number of listed parcels. For instance, if the advertisement costs $100, and there are 100 parcels listed in the advertisement, the tax collector will add $1 to each advertised tax lien. Keep in mind that only the original tax lien amount should be advertised, however.

Interest accrues on advertised tax liens in this standard process: 2 percent beginning on the delinquency date (usually January 6) and 0.75 percent on the first day of each subsequent month until paid.[17] The advertising cost is added to the tax liens on the day the advertisement is published, and that cost will accrue interest along with the principal taxes.

For example, assume that $100 of principal taxes are delinquent on Parcel A when the county advertises tax liens on March 15. If the advertising cost allocated to Parcel A is $5, what is the total amount that the parcel's owner must pay to release the tax lien if the owner appears at the tax office prepared to pay the taxes on July 1?

First, calculate the interest owed up to the publication date, which is 3.5 percent of $100, or $3.50. This represents 2 percent for January and 0.75 percent each for February and March, multiplied by the principal tax of $100. The advertising cost is not included in the January, February, and

---

16. Both Forsyth and Guilford counties have used this approach for several years. Pete Rodda, the Forsyth County assessor and collector, reports that the county saves at least 20 percent in publishing costs by relying on a special section rather than a traditional advertisement. Jay Heavner, the Gaston County director of revenue, uses extra space at the back of the county's special section to provide answers and contact information for common property tax questions and to share details about the county's revenues and expenses.

17. G.S. 105-360(a).

March interest calculation because it is not incurred until the publication date in mid-March. Next, calculate the interest owed *after* the publication date, which is $3.15. This represents 3 percent in interest—0.75 percent each for April, May, June, and July, multiplied by $105, the sum of the principal tax plus the allocated advertising cost. Because Machinery Act interest is not compounded, interest is not charged again to the pre-advertisement totals. If the taxpayer satisfies the tax lien on July 1, the total owed is $111.65, which is the sum of the principal tax ($100), the allocated advertisement cost ($5), the pre-publication interest ($3.50), and the post-publication interest ($3.15).

8. Should a tax collector advertise a taxpayer in bankruptcy?

No. When a taxpayer files a bankruptcy petition, an "automatic stay" immediately becomes effective. Essentially this stay bars any effort by a creditor to collect a debt from the debtor in bankruptcy, including "any act to create, perfect, or enforce any lien" on property covered by the bankruptcy filing.[18] Willful violations of the automatic stay—that is, a collection action undertaken with knowledge that the debtor is in bankruptcy—may be punished with contempt of court sanctions as well as punitive damages and the assessment of attorneys fees.[19]

The advertisement of a tax lien arguably qualifies as an act to enforce a tax lien and is therefore barred by the automatic stay.[20] The safest course of action is for the tax collector to exclude from the advertising process any taxpayer who is the subject of a pending bankruptcy petition—taxpayers in bankruptcy should not receive a notice of advertisement nor should their

---

18. 11 U.S.C. § 362(a).

19. *Id.* at 362(h) and 362.11.

20. Although there appear to be no federal bankruptcy court opinions on this specific issue, several have held that the *sale* of a tax lien violates the automatic stay. *In re* Haight, 52 B.R. 104, 105 (Bankr. W.D.N.Y. 1985) (sale of tax lien constitutes a prohibited collection action because it is "a step along the road to the enforcement of the tax lien by attempting to coerce the debtor into paying the delinquent taxes"). Because the motivation behind the notice and advertisement of tax liens under the Machinery Act is to induce payment and to lay the foundation for a foreclosure, it seems reasonable to conclude that the automatic stay would bar the advertisement of tax liens as it does their sale.

names or parcels be included in the published advertisement. Some tax collectors take the additional precaution of including in the text of the advertisement a disclaimer stating that enforced collection actions will not be undertaken against taxpayers involved in pending bankruptcies, just in case such a taxpayer is mistakenly included in the advertisement.

Once a bankruptcy case is terminated through either a discharge or dismissal, a tax collector generally may proceed with advertising and enforced collections for delinquent tax liens that remain.[21]

9. Should a tax collector advertise assessments that are under appeal?

No. G.S. 105-378(d) prohibits any "collection of taxes or enforcement of tax lien" that has been appealed to either a county board of equalization and review or the state Property Tax Commission (PTC), the state board that hears taxpayer appeals from county boards of equalization and review.[22] The only collection step permitted by this statute is the mailing of an initial bill to the taxpayer. As discussed above in reference to bankruptcy, advertising a tax lien could be considered the first step in enforcing a tax lien and would therefore likely violate the prohibition found in G.S. 105-378(d). Advertisement and other collection actions may begin once the assessment appeal has been "finally adjudicated," that is, when a decision is issued by the state supreme court or when the appeal deadline from a lower court or body expires.

Note that the advertising prohibition does not apply to a tax assessment subsequent to an assessment that is still pending before a board of equalization and review or the PTC. For example, assume Tommy Tarheel appeals his 2011 real property tax assessment to the PTC. If that appeal is still pending when the 2012 tax liens are advertised, Tommy's 2012 assessment should be advertised, unless he has formally amended his 2011 appeal to include the 2012 assessment as well.

---

21. For a detailed discussion of how a bankruptcy filing affects the tax collection process, see Chapter 16.

22. For many years this prohibition applied only to assessments on appeal to the PTC or the state courts. In 2011, S.L. 2011-3 extended the prohibition to cover appeals to county boards of equalization and review.

Chapter 10

Foreclosure Myths

Foreclosure is the process of enforcing a lien on real property by selling the property to the highest bidder. The procedural requirements for tax foreclosures have been expertly detailed by former School of Government Professor William A. Campbell in his book *Property Tax Lien Foreclosure Forms and Procedures*.[1] Although the most recent edition of this book was published in 2003, the information therein remains accurate.[2] Therefore this chapter will not delve into the procedural issues Professor Campbell has already covered extensively but instead will attempt to eliminate some of the confusion surrounding tax foreclosures by debunking ten recurring myths about this process.

Only taxing units may pursue tax foreclosures.[3] In North Carolina the Machinery Act provides for two different tax foreclosure procedures. The first is the mortgage-style procedure created by G.S. 105-374, which involves a standard civil action filed in state court. The second is the in rem procedure created by G.S. 105-375, an expedited procedure that permits a taxing

---

This chapter updates information published as *Property Tax Bulletin* No. 158 (Oct. 2010).

1. This publication is available for purchase from the School of Government at http://shopping.netsuite.com/s.nl/c.433425/it.A/id.68/.f. Professor Campbell's recommended forms are also available in CD-ROM format for ease of use by practitioners and can be purchased at http://shopping.netsuite.com/s.nl/c.433425/it.A/id.185/.f.

2. One recent change to the tax foreclosure procedure is worth noting. As of July 1, 2011, the administrative charge that local governments pursuing in rem foreclosures may add to the taxes owed increased from $50 to $250. S.L. 2011-352.

3. Until the early 1980s, foreclosures could be inititated by private parties who had purchased tax liens from taxing units. In 1983 the General Assembly enacted legislation that ended the sale of property tax liens by taxing units. 1983 N.C. Sess. Laws ch. 808.

unit to docket a judgment against the property in state court and proceed with a foreclosure sale three months later.

Neither procedure can begin until after taxes become delinquent. Non-deferred taxes on real property and taxes on personal property other than registered motor vehicles become delinquent when interest begins to accrue on January 6 of the year in which the taxes were levied.[4] Nearly all taxing units advertise their tax liens prior to initiating any foreclosures, but such advertisements are required only for in rem foreclosures.[5]

The tax lien that is the basis for a foreclosure should include taxes on the real property itself and taxes on all personal property other than registered motor vehicles owned by the same taxpayer in the same jurisdiction.[6] The lien may also include special assessments and other obligations—such as nuisance abatement costs—that are collectible as property taxes.[7] The tax lien on real property should not include taxes on other real property owned by the taxpayer.[8]

If the taxpayer does not satisfy the outstanding taxes and the foreclosure continues to a sale, the sale proceeds are applied first to the costs of the foreclosure and then to the taxes, special assessments, and other obligations included in the tax lien. Any surplus funds should be turned over to the court for distribution to junior lienholders or to the taxpayer who owned the property prior to foreclosure.[9]

Ten foreclosure myths that deserve debunking follow.

---

4. G.S. 105-365.1. Deferred taxes become delinquent on the date a disqualifying event occurs. If the disqualifying event is the death of the owner, the deferred tax becomes delinquent on the first day of the ninth month after the death.

5. G.S. 105-375(b) prohibits a tax collector from docketing a judgment against real property for delinquent property taxes until thirty days after the tax lien advertisement runs. For details regarding the advertisement process, see Chapter 9.

6. G.S. 105-355(a). G.S. 105-330.4(c) excludes taxes on registered motor vehicles from the real property tax lien.

7. For a full discussion of property tax liens, see Chapter 5.

8. G.S. 105-355(a).

9. See Chapter 5.

Myth 1: The in rem foreclosure process may violate the U.S. or N.C. constitutions.

The expedited nature of in rem foreclosures has been the source of numerous court challenges to the process in its sixty-plus-year history. Owners and lienholders have repeatedly alleged that the in rem procedure fails to provide constitutionally adequate notice to interested parties before property is sold and their interests terminated.[10] Although none of these legal challenges have managed to invalidate G.S. 105-375, several identified weaknesses in the in rem procedure subsequently remedied by the General Assembly. For example, the statute originally required that notice be provided only to the taxpayer that originally listed the property for taxation even if that taxpayer no longer owned the property. The statute now requires notice be given to the current owner of the property, a more logical and constitutionally sound approach.

Court rulings in other jurisdictions motivated the General Assembly to enact additional amendments to the statute. Most notable was *Mennonite Board of Missions v. Adams*,[11] a 1983 U.S. Supreme Court decision that struck down part of a similar Indiana tax foreclosure statute because it did not require that notice be mailed to lienholders. The Court held that lienholders, like property owners, "are entitled to notice reasonably calculated to apprise [them] of a pending tax sale."[12] After *Mennonite*, lienholders such as mortgagees are entitled to notice of the foreclosure by mail rather than simply by publication if their addresses can be obtained without undue hardship.

The *Mennonite* decision was the basis for a 2010 challenge to an in rem foreclosure sale conducted by the city of Charlotte for unpaid demolition

---

10. *See, e.g.*, Hardy v. Moore Cnty., 133 N.C. App. 321 (1999) (county not required to locate taxpayer's new address by contacting the country club of which the property was a part; acceptable for county to mail notice to taxpayer's last known address in England); Jenkins v. Richmond Cnty., 99 N.C. App. 717 (1990) (due process not satisfied when city did not attempt to mail notice to each individual taxpayer listed on the most recent deed to the property being foreclosed upon); Overstreet v. City of Raleigh, 75 N.C. App. 351 (1985) (both mortgage-style and in rem foreclosures defeat claims of adverse possession without the foreclosing government having to give individual notice to persons who might hold adverse possession claims).

11. 462 U.S. 791 (1983).

12. 462 U.S. at 798.

costs. In *Da Dai Mai v. Carolina Holdings, Inc.,*[13] the plaintiff, Carolina Holdings, held a lien on the property that was sold by the city of Charlotte. As required by G.S. 105-375, the city sent letters to the property owner and to Carolina Holdings prior to docketing a judgment against the property. Months later the city mailed notice of sale to the property owner but not to Carolina Holdings, in accord with the statute's requirements. The city also published notice of the sale in a local newspaper, but Carolina Holdings claimed it didn't learn of the sale to Mai until a full year later. Carolina Holdings then challenged the in rem procedure in court, alleging that failure to provide personal notice to lienholders of record violates the due process clauses of the Unites States and North Carolina constitutions.

Carolina Holding's argument fell on deaf ears. The N.C. Court of Appeals found that the *Mennonite* standard was more than satisfied by the G.S. 105-375 requirement that lienholders receive notice via registered or certified mail of the intent to docket a judgment months before a foreclosure sale. The court based its decision in large part on language from *Henderson County v. Osteen,* a N.C. Supreme Court case that spoke approvingly of the in rem procedure.[14] Building on *Osteen,* the N.C. Court of Appeals concluded that failure to send a second notice to lienholders such as Carolina Holdings prior to the actual foreclosure sale does not render the entire process constitutionally inadequate. Essentially the court found that Carolina Holdings ignored the initial notice of the foreclosure at its peril and could not legitimately complain that it was harmed by its failure to learn of the specific sale date.

The importance of the *Mai* decision lies not only in its substantive holding—it is acceptable to mail only a single notice to lienholders—but also in its unqualified adoption of the N.C. Supreme Court's language in *Osteen,* language previously considered nonbinding *dicta* and now more appropriately viewed as a conclusive blessing of the in rem foreclosure procedure.

---

13. 696 S.E.2d 769 (N.C. Ct. App. 2010).

14. 292 N.C. 692 (1977). In this case, the court held that the Machinery Act's immaterial irregularity provisions do not permit a taxing unit to proceed with an in rem foreclosure sale without first attempting to provide the owner with individual notice. While reaching that decision, the court observed that if the taxing unit had provided such individualized notice, the in rem procedure "would, in our opinion, be sufficient to satisfy the fundamental concept of due process and, therefore, to comply with Article 1, section 19, of the Constitution of North Carolina and the Due Process Clause of the Fourteenth Amendment of the Constitution of the United States." *Id.* at 708.

The *Mai* decision should reassure local governments that rely on the in rem procedure for tax foreclosures. Courts surely will continue to scrutinize in rem foreclosures to ensure that local governments follow the procedural requirements with extreme particularity. And a taxing unit will always be wise to exceed the minimum notice requirements when it can do so without great effort—for example, by sending a second notice to lienholders if addresses are easily obtainable. But in general the *Mai* case demonstrates that the in rem procedure stands on solid constitutional ground.

Myth 2: Foreclosure may be used to collect only property taxes.

Foreclosure is available to collect any obligation owed to a local government that constitutes a lien on real property. As discussed above, all property taxes other than those owed on registered motor vehicles are liens on real property as of January 1 of the year in which they are levied. Other local taxes—such as occupancy, privilege license, and food and beverage levies—do not constitute liens on real property unless the local government sues the taxpayer for nonpayment and obtains a judgment. The same applies to most nontax obligations, such as license and inspection fees and utility and user fees.

However, four types of obligations do create liens on real property without additional government action. Special assessments, public nuisance abatement costs, minimum housing standards enforcement costs, and solid waste fees billed with property taxes all automatically create liens on a taxpayer's real property.[15] Any one of these obligations can be the basis for foreclosure actions even if the taxpayer owes no property taxes.

If property taxes are also involved in a foreclosure related to nonpayment of one of these obligations, questions of priority (that is, who gets paid first) will arise. Liens for public nuisance abatement costs and solid waste fees

---

15. G.S. 153A-200(c) and G.S. 160A-233(c) (special assessments); G.S. 153A-140 and G.S. 160A-193 (nuisance abatement costs); G.S. 160A-443(6)(a) (minimum housing standards enforcement costs); G.S. 153A-293 and G.S. 160A-314.1 (solid waste fees billed with property taxes). For solid waste fees, the governing board must first adopt an ordinance mandating that the fees be billed and collected in the same manner as property taxes. For more details about the collection of other taxes and fees, see Chapter 15. For more details about the priority of local government liens on real property, see Chapter 5.

billed with property taxes share the same priority as property tax liens and are paid at the same time as property taxes after the foreclosure sale.[16] The liens for special assessments and minimum housing standards enforcement costs are junior to tax liens but senior to private liens such as those held by mortgage lenders.[17]

Myth 3: Real property owned by the sole shareholder of a corporation or sole member of a limited liability corporation can be foreclosed upon to satisfy the corporation's tax obligations.

Corporations and their shareholders are distinct and separate taxpayers that must list their respective property separately for taxation.[18] Because the tax obligations of one taxpayer cannot be the basis for enforced collection actions against the property of another taxpayer, generally shareholders and members cannot be held liable for the tax obligations of their corporations.[19] For example, assume Wanda Wolfpack is the sole shareholder of Wolfpack Inc., which owes delinquent property taxes on its business personal property. Wanda owns Parcel A, on which the taxes are current. The tax collector may not foreclose on Parcel A to satisfy the taxes owed by Wolfpack Inc., because Wanda and the corporation are separate taxpayers—even though she owns and controls the corporation. The same would be true if Wanda owed taxes on her personal property and Wolfpack Inc. owned Parcel B. Wolfpack Inc.'s real property could not be subject to foreclosure to satisfy taxes owed by its sole shareholder.

These same principles apply to any situation in which there exist multiple related but distinct taxpayers, including partners and partnerships,[20]

---

16. See Chapter 5.

17. *Id.*

18. G.S. 105-302(c)(2) (real property) and G.S. 105-306(c)(3). The same is true of limited liability corporations and their members.

19. See G.S. 55-6-22 (providing that shareholders are not liable for the acts of the corporation).

20. G.S. 105-366(b)(8) permits a tax collector to proceed against a partner's personal property for a partnership's tax obligation if the tax collector cannot satisfy the partnership's property taxes. But a partner's real property is always immune from collection for a partnership's tax obligation.

trusts and trustees,[21] and spouses.[22] Tax obligations of one of those taxpayers may not be the basis for foreclosure on real property owned by the related taxpayer.

There are two situations in which shareholders can be held liable for the obligations of their corporations, but they rarely arise. The first is when a corporation has formally dissolved without giving proper notice to its creditors. Those creditors may then hold the shareholders liable for the dissolved corporation's debts to the extent that the shareholders received corporate assets when the corporation was dissolved.[23] Unfortunately, when small corporations go out of business often they do not formally dissolve—they simply stop functioning as corporations and thus the dissolution remedies are no help to creditors.

The second situation in which shareholders can be held liable for a corporation's tax obligations is when one or two shareholders have abused the corporate form and used the corporation as an alter ego to avoid personal liability for certain obligations. In such cases a court may permit creditors to "pierce the corporate veil" and hold the shareholder(s) personally liable.[24] Such a remedy is granted only in cases of egregious behavior by shareholders, and it is unclear whether the simple failure to pay corporate property taxes would meet this standard.[25]

---

21. Property owned by a trust is listed in the name of the trustee in his or her fiduciary capacity only and does not subject the trustee's individual property to enforced collection actions for the trust's tax obligations. G.S. 105-302(c)(7) and G.S. 105-306(c)(6).

22. Real property owned by spouses as tenants by the entirety is considered to be owned by a separate taxpayer—the marital unit—from the individual spouses. Taxes owed by an individual spouse cannot be the basis for a foreclosure action against real property owned by the spouses as tenants by the entirety. See G.S. 105-302(c)(10) and Davis v. Bass, 188 N.C. 200 (1924). Similarly, taxes on property owned by one spouse individually may not be the basis for a foreclosure action on property owned by the other spouse individually.

23. G.S. 55-14-08 and G.S. 57C-6-09.

24. *See* State v. Ridgeway Brands Mfg., LLC, 362 N.C. 431 (2008) (permitting state to pierce the corporate veil because of controlling shareholders' efforts to avoid required payments to state tobacco litigation settlement escrow fund).

25. The North Carolina Supreme Court requires the following to justify piercing the corporate veil: the shareholder must exert "complete domination, not only of finances, but of policy and business practice in respect to the transaction attacked so that the corporate entity as to this transaction had at the time no separate mind, will or existence of its own; and such control must have been used by the defendant

Myth 4: Foreclosure cannot be used against property owners who are exempt from property taxes or against taxpayers who have been through bankruptcy.

The only situation in which foreclosure is not available to enforce a valid tax lien on real property is when the property is currently owned by the state, a local, or the federal government.[26] Otherwise, foreclosure remains an option even if the property is owned by a religious or charitable organization, an independent school, or another private party that is exempt from property taxes.

For example, assume that in February 2011 Tom Tarheel sells Parcel A to the Church of the Benevolent Blue Devil, a religious organization that will use the property for religious purposes and will therefore be exempt from property taxes. Because Parcel A was owned by a taxable owner as of January 1, 2011, it should be listed and assessed taxes for the 2011–2012 tax year even though it is now owned by an exempt organization. If the 2011 taxes are not satisfied at closing and become delinquent as of January 6, 2012, the tax collector could enforce the lien against the church through attachment and garnishment, levy and sale, or foreclosure. While there may be political or public relations concerns associated with the use of enforced collection remedies against religious organizations or other exempt entities, the tax collector is obligated to use all methods at his or her disposal to collect taxes for which these parties are responsible.

Foreclosure can also be used against taxpayers dismissed or discharged from bankruptcy proceedings. The automatic stay prohibits foreclosures, attachments, and all other collection actions while a bankruptcy is pending, of course. But after the proceeding ends, tax collectors can resume collec-

---

to commit fraud or wrong, *to perpetrate the violation of a statutory or other positive legal duty,* or a dishonest and unjust act in contravention of plaintiff's legal rights." B-W Acceptance Corp. v. Spencer, 268 N.C. 1, 9 (1966) (emphasis added). While the failure to pay property taxes by itself seemingly constitutes a "violation of a statutory duty," North Carolina courts have not addressed that specific scenario.

26. *See* Vaughn v. Bd. of Comm'rs of Forsyth Cnty., 118 N.C. 636 (1896) (government property exempt from seizure and sale by creditors). When a government purchases real property, it must satisfy all outstanding property tax liens at closing. G.S. 105-385(d). If the government fails to do so, the taxing unit's only option is to sue the offending government in state court. This requirement does not apply if the government obtains the property through a gift or a bequest or any method other than a purchase.

tion of unpaid property taxes. In some circumstances the taxpayer may no longer be personally responsible for property taxes after discharge, meaning the taxpayer's personal property may not be attached or levied upon. However, the taxpayer's real property is still subject to foreclosure if the tax lien survives bankruptcy. Thankfully, most do.[27]

Myth 5: The Machinery Act's statute of limitations requires that the foreclosure sale must be completed within ten years of the original due dates for all delinquent taxes included in the foreclosure action.

The statute of limitations in G.S. 105-378(a) requires only that an enforced collection remedy be instituted within ten years of the tax's original due date. A foreclosure action is instituted either by the filing of a complaint under G.S. 105-374 or by the docketing of a judgment under G.S. 105-375. So long as one of those actions occurs prior to the ten-year cutoff, the statute of limitations will not serve as a defense to a foreclosure action even if the actual sale of the property does not occur until months later.

Taxes on real property and personal property other than registered motor vehicles are due on September 1 of the fiscal year for which they are levied.[28] As a result, a foreclosure action for a tax levied in year 0 must begin on or before August 31 in year 10 to avoid the statute of limitations concerns.

However, a statute of limitations is an affirmative defense that must be raised by a defendant to be effective.[29] The statute does not serve as a prior restraint on local governments' collection actions. If a defendant does not assert the statute of limitations as a defense, a taxing unit may proceed with a foreclosure action regardless of when the taxes originally came due.[30]

The use-it-or-lose-it nature of a statute of limitations defense raises interesting questions for tax collectors and local governments. Is it appropriate to

---

27. For more details on property taxes and bankruptcy, see Chapter 16.

28. G.S. 105-360(a). Taxes on registered motor vehicles are due on the first day of the fourth month following the date a prior registration expires or a new registration is applied for. G.S. 105-330.4. But because taxes on registered motor vehicles are never a lien on real property, the due date for these taxes is irrelevant to foreclosure actions. G.S. 105-330.4(c).

29. G.S. 1A-1, Rule 8(c), of the N.C. Rules of Civil Procedure.

30. Iredell Cnty. v. Crawford, 262 N.C. 720 (1964).

initiate a collection action that can succeed only if the taxpayer is ignorant of his or her defenses under the Machinery Act? Would doing so be considered the equivalent of preying upon uninformed taxpayers or an admirable effort by the local government to collect all validly levied taxes?

Similar questions arise for attorneys who assist local governments with foreclosure actions. Attorneys are forbidden from proceeding with frivolous actions that lack legal merit.[31] But attorneys do not violate this ethical rule by proceeding with an action that could be barred by the statute of limitations because that time limitation does not affect the substantive validity of the underlying claim.[32]

However, the same ethical conclusions probably should not apply to local governments. Local governments almost certainly have greater obligations to protect the interests of their taxpayers than attorneys have to protect the interests of opposing parties. For both ethical and political reasons, local governments are wise to avoid initiating foreclosures or other collection actions based entirely on taxes more than ten years past due.

Including taxes outside the ten-year limitation in a collection action that also involves taxes less than ten years past due should be less problematic. For example, assume a local government is owed taxes from the years 2000 through 2010 on Parcel A. If that local government proceeds with a foreclosure action on Parcel A in 2011, the 2000 taxes would fall outside of the ten-year limitation because they were originally due on September 1, 2000. Regardless, the 2000 taxes should probably be included in the foreclosure action because even if the taxpayer raises the statute of limitations defense, the foreclosure could proceed. Accusations of unfairness or deceptive collection practices would less likely gain traction in that situation as compared to a foreclosure action that included only time-barred taxes.

---

31. N.C. State Bar, Rules of Prof'l Conduct R. 3.1.

32. N.C. State Bar, 2003 Formal Ethics Op. 13 (Jan. 16, 2004) ("Filing suit after the limitations period has expired does not affect the validity of the claim, nor does it divest a court from having jurisdiction to hear the matters raised therein. . . . Because a time-barred claim can be enforced by a court if the defense raises no objection, filing suit under these circumstances would not violate the prohibition against an attorney advancing a frivolous claim under Rule 3.1."). This opinion mirrors those reached by other ethics committees across the country. *See, e.g.,* ABA Comm. on Ethics & Prof'l Responsibility, Formal Op. 387 (1994) (discussing disclosure to opposing party and court that statute of limitations has run).

Myth 6: At a tax foreclosure sale, the minimum bid must be set at the total amount of taxes, interest, fees, and costs owed on the property.

The Machinery Act does not require a minimum bid at a foreclosure sale. Under both mortgage-style and in rem foreclosures, property must be sold to the highest bidder.[33] If the government conducting the foreclosure sale chooses not to enter an opening bid, then any bid from any party—including the taxpayer who owns the property being sold—will be sufficient to purchase the property, even if that bid does not cover the outstanding taxes.[34] In addition, the purchaser will take the property free and clear of all tax liens included in the foreclosure action.[35]

To ensure the property is not sold for less than the amount the government is owed, it must enter its own bid in that amount. This opening bid should include all amounts owed by the taxpayer, including the taxes and special assessments of all local governments party to the action plus interest and the costs of the foreclosure. If no one else bids on the property, the government will become the owner of the property after the upset bid period ends.

Unlike all other winning bidders, when a local government finalizes its purchase of real property at a tax foreclosure sale, it need not pay the entire bid in cash. The purchasing government may elect to pay "only that part of the purchase price that would not be distributed to it and other taxing units on account of taxes, penalties, interest and such costs as accrued prior to the initiation of the foreclosure action."[36] In other words, the purchasing

---

33. G.S. 105-374(m) for mortgage-style foreclosures and G.S. 1-339.51 for in rem foreclosures.

34. Although the Machinery Act does not limit the types of eligible bidders at foreclosure sales, other conflict of interest laws and regulations might. For example, G.S. 14-234.1 prohibits a government official from obtaining property about which he or she possesses "information which was made known to him in his official capacity and which has not been made public." This statute effectively prohibits bids from county employees who have nonpublic insider information about property being sold at foreclosure. Conflict of interest considerations also prohibit an attorney who is prosecuting the foreclosure on behalf of the local government from bidding at the sale, even if that attorney does not have the insider information covered by G.S. 14-234.1. *See* N.C. State Bar, 2006 Formal Ethics Op. 5 (Apr. 21, 2006).

35. G.S. 105-374(k) and G.S. 105-375(i).

36. G.S. 105-376(b).

government must pay only the foreclosure costs owed to third parties, usually the attorney who represented the government in the foreclosure and, for in rem foreclosures, the sheriff who conducted the sale. The purchasing government is not required to pay itself or other local governments for the taxes and other amounts owed on the property. However, if the purchasing government later sells the property, it must use the proceeds to satisfy the tax liens held by itself and other governments after first repaying itself for the out-of-pocket foreclosure expenses.[37] Myth 9 provides more details about a local government's obligations after purchasing property at a foreclosure sale.

Myth 7: If multiple local governments hold property tax liens on the property sold at foreclosure, the oldest taxes have priority and are paid first.

All local government property tax liens are of equal dignity.[38] This means that they all have the same payment priority, regardless of when they arose or which government initiated the foreclosure action. If the sale proceeds are insufficient to satisfy all of the tax liens, then after costs are satisfied the tax liens are paid proportionately.[39] For example, assume that Carolina County has a $1,000 property tax lien from 2005 on Parcel A. Blue Devil City has a $500 lien on the same parcel for 2007 property taxes. The fact that Carolina County's tax lien is older than Blue Devil City's tax lien is irrelevant to the priority of those liens; they both are of equal dignity and are paid at the same time. Nor does it matter which government initiates the foreclosure action. If either Carolina County or Blue Devil City forecloses on Parcel A and the sale produces $600 after costs are paid, then the two jurisdictions would

---

37. *Id.*

38. G.S. 105-356(a)(2). Also paid at the same time as local government property tax liens are liens for solid waste fees authorized to be billed as property taxes and liens for public nuisance abatement costs. For solid waste fees, see G.S. 153A-293 (counties) or G.S. 160A-314.1 (municipalities). For nuisance abatement costs, see G.S. 153A-140 (counties) or G.S. 160A-193 (municipalities). As is true for property tax liens, the priority of solid waste liens and nuisance abatement liens is not affected by the identity of the foreclosing party.

39. This rule also applies to the proceeds from the sale of real property purchased by a local government at a tax foreclosure sale. See G.S. 105-376(b) and Myth 9.

split the proceeds proportionately: $400 (two-thirds) for Carolina County and $200 (one-third) for Blue Devil City.[40]

Myth 8: If the foreclosure sale does not produce enough funds to satisfy the taxes owed, the local government may use enforced collection remedies against the taxpayer's personal property to make up the difference.

Foreclosure is the ultimate Machinery Act collection remedy. Tax collectors may not target a taxpayer's personal property through attachment and garnishment or levy and sale after a foreclosure action is initiated.[41] If the foreclosure sale does not produce enough funds to satisfy all costs and taxes owed, the tax collector no longer has any Machinery Act collection options against the former owner for the deficiency.

Property sold at foreclosure is deeded to the purchaser free and clear of all liens included in the judgment, meaning that the new owner cannot be held responsible for the prior owner's unpaid taxes.[42] The only tax lien that can remain on real property after a foreclosure is the lien for taxes that cannot be determined at the time of the judgment because the tax rate has not yet been set. For example, assume that in late 2010 Carolina County initiates a foreclosure action against Parcel A for unpaid taxes from 2008 and 2009. The property goes to sale in January 2011. The attorney or tax official prosecuting the foreclosure should include the 2010 taxes in the judgment and sale even though those taxes were not delinquent when the action was initiated.[43] The 2011 taxes should not be included because the final amount

---

40. For more details on the priority of tax liens, see Chapter 5.

41. G.S. 105-366(b). This prohibition is triggered by the filing of a foreclosure complaint under G.S. 105-374 or the docketing of a judgment under G.S. 105-375, regardless of whether the foreclosure proceedings are completed.

42. G.S. 105-374(k) and G.S. 105-375(i).

43. The complaint in a mortgage-style foreclosure should include an allegation of "subsequent taxes which are or may become a lien on the same real property." G.S. 105-374(e). Immediately before the sale is ordered by the court, the taxing unit should file a certificate listing all of the taxes, interest, and costs it is owed, including those not yet delinquent. The only exception is a tax lien for which the exact amount of tax owed cannot be determined at the time of judgment. When proceeding with an in rem foreclosure, the certificate of taxes owed should include all taxes that are liens

of those taxes cannot be determined until the county sets its property tax rate for 2011–2012. As a result the 2011 tax lien is the only lien that will survive the foreclosure sale, even if the sale price is not enough to satisfy the 2008, 2009, and 2010 taxes.[44]

Once foreclosure occurs, the tax collector is out of options under the Machinery Act. The only collection remedy that remains after foreclosure is the set-off debt collection procedure under Chapter 105A, which permits a local government to attach a taxpayer's state income tax refund or lottery winnings. But this option is of course only helpful if the taxpayer is entitled to a refund or wins the lottery.

For all of these reasons, plus the fact that foreclosures take several months at a minimum to complete, most tax collectors will first exhaust remedies against a taxpayer's personal property before turning to foreclosure. That said, the Machinery Act does not require a tax collector to exhaust these remedies first. A tax collector may choose among Machinery Act remedies unless (1) the governing board orders the tax collector to first target a taxpayer's personal property or (2) a taxpayer or lienholder requests that the collector first turn to the taxpayer's personal property and gives the tax collector a description and location of that property.[45]

Myth 9: If the county or city purchases real property at a tax foreclosure sale, it cannot subsequently sell the property for less than the total amount of taxes, interest, and costs owed on the property.

Local governments often end up owning foreclosed property because no bidders are willing to top the governments' opening bids set at the amount of taxes, interest, and costs owed on the foreclosed properties. As discussed above, local governments are not required to submit opening bids, but most

---

on the property and that can be determined at the time of foreclosure, even if those taxes are not yet delinquent. G.S. 105-375(b).

44. The 2011 taxes would already be a tax lien on the property as of the time of judgment, because the tax lien on real property arises as a matter of law on the listing date, January 1, regardless of when the actual tax obligation is determined. G.S. 105-355(a).

45. G.S. 105-366(a).

do so to prevent bidders from purchasing the foreclosed property for less than the amounts owed. Once a local government becomes the owner of foreclosed property, it may use or dispose of that property just as it may with any other property it owns.

If the purchasing government wishes to use the property for a public purpose, it may do so. This option will remove the property from the tax rolls and effectively eliminate any possibility of recovering the delinquent taxes on the property owed to that government and other local governments. As a result, the Machinery Act requires a purchasing government wishing to make public use of purchased property to compensate other local governments that are owed taxes on the property. The interested governing bodies (that is, the county commissioners and the city council) should agree on the amount of compensation. If the parties cannot agree, then the superior court is authorized to set the amount.[46] That said, a local government can perhaps best protect its interest in foreclosed property by itself bidding on the property, thus preventing another government from purchasing it and controlling its disposition.

If the local government instead wishes to dispose of the property and get it back on the property tax roll, it may do so pursuant to the property disposal rules in Article 12 of G.S. Chapter 160A, subject to two important restrictions created by the Machinery Act.[47] First, the government that purchased the property at foreclosure holds it for the benefit of all other taxing jurisdictions that were parties to the foreclosure sale.[48] This provision means that if the purchasing government eventually sells the property, it must use the sale proceeds to satisfy all tax liens included in the foreclosure sale, after paying itself back for any costs it previously paid. Second, if the purchasing government sells the property to the taxpayer who owned the property prior to foreclosure, the sales price cannot be lower than the total taxes, interest, penalties, and costs originally owed by that taxpayer.[49]

For example, assume Wanda Wolfpack owes $5,000 in property taxes to Carolina County on Parcel A. The county proceeds with a foreclosure, and

---

46. G.S. 105-376(b).

47. Although on its face G.S. Chapter 160A, Article 12, applies only to municipalities, G.S. 153A-176 makes these provisions applicable to counties as well.

48. G.S. 105-376(b).

49. G.S. 105-376(c). As noted above, this restriction does not apply to the initial foreclosure auction sale and the subsequent upset bid period.

at the time of sale the amount of taxes, interest, and costs totals $6,000. If the county chooses not to enter an opening bid, then any party, including Wanda, could purchase Parcel A for $1. Assume that the county submits an opening bid of $6,000 and no other bids are received. After the upset bid period ends, the county would take ownership of Parcel A. If it later attempts to sell the property, the county could sell it to any party so long as the property disposition rules are followed. But if Wanda is the purchaser, the price cannot be lower than the $6,000 in taxes, interest, and costs she owed on the property at the time of foreclosure.

Regardless of who buys the property or for how much, it will be transferred from the local government to that buyer free and clear of all tax liens with the exception of those for taxes that could not be determined at the time of sale. Foreclosure extinguishes the tax liens and all junior liens on the property, even if the local government is the high bidder at the auction.[50]

Here is another example to illustrate the priority of tax liens and the rules concerning government purchases of foreclosed property. Assume that in 2011 Carolina County forecloses on Parcel B for $4,000 in delinquent property taxes for the years 2008–2010. Parcel B is subject also to Blue Devil City property taxes of $2,000 for the same time period and a 2005 Blue Devil City special assessment of $1,000. Carolina County appropriately names Blue Devil City as a defendant in the action, and the city files a timely answer. Foreclosure costs, including attorneys' fees, amount to $800.

At the foreclosure sale, Carolina County enters an initial bid of $4,800, which would cover its taxes and costs. There are no other bidders at the sale or during the upset bid period. As the winning bidder, Carolina County is required to pay only the $800 in costs relating to the foreclosure. It then holds Parcel B for the benefit of itself and of Blue Devil City. Six months later Carolina County sells Parcel B to a third party for $3,800. Table 10.1 summarizes how the sale proceeds will be distributed.

Note that because the property was sold to a party other than the previous owner, the county was permitted to sell it for less than the taxes owed. Costs are always paid first, meaning the county can reimburse itself for the

---

50. G.S. 105-374(k) and G.S. 105-375(i) require property to be sold at foreclosure free and clear of all tax liens except for taxes not yet determined because the taxing unit has not set its tax rate. *See also* Dixieland Realty Co. v. Wysor, 272 N.C. 172 (1967) (foreclosure of senior mortgage extinguishes junior mortgages and liens) and G.S. 1-339.68 (real property sold at execution subject only to senior liens).

Table 10.1.   Distribution of Proceeds from Sale of Parcel B

First priority: Costs	$ 800 (Carolina County)
Second priority: Property taxes	$ 2,000 (Carolina County) $ 1,000 (Blue Devil City)
Third priority: Special assessments	$ 0
Total	$ 3,800

costs it paid at the initial foreclosure sale. Next in line for payment are the property tax liens, which are all of "equal dignity" and therefore paid at the same time regardless of jurisdiction or year of levy.[51] Because the sale price was not sufficient to satisfy all of the property tax liens in full, the remaining proceeds are shared between the city and county proportionately. The county's tax liens of $4,000 represent two-thirds of the $6,000 total tax liens on the property, so the county receives two-thirds of the remaining proceeds. The city receives one-third. There are no sale proceeds remaining to satisfy the city special assessment lien, which is junior to property tax liens and therefore extinguished by the foreclosure sale. Parcel B is sold free and clear of all tax and special assessment liens included in the foreclosure sale.

Myth 10: A taxpayer can redeem his or her property within one year from the date of the foreclosure sale.

Several states provide for a post-sale redemption period in which a taxpayer may pay the taxes and costs owed on the property and reverse a foreclosure sale.[52] But in North Carolina, the taxpayer has no right of redemption after a foreclosure sale. After a mortgage-style foreclosure is confirmed by the court or the upset bid period ends for an in rem foreclosure sale, a North Carolina taxpayer cannot reverse the sale simply by paying the amounts owed on the property. The taxpayer's only option after the sale of property at

---

51. See Chapter 5 for more details on the priority of tax and special assessment liens.

52. For example, Texas allows a taxpayer two years to reverse a tax foreclosure sale by paying the purchaser the sale amount, the outstanding taxes and costs, and a redemption premium of 25 to 50 percent of the purchase price. Tex. Tax Code § 34.21, available at www.statutes.legis.state.tx.us/Docs/TX/htm/TX.34.htm#34.21.

a tax foreclosure has been confirmed is to initiate a legal action challenging the validity of the process. The Machinery Act requires that any such legal challenge be raised within one year of the date on which the foreclosure deed is recorded.[53]

At any point before a court confirms a mortgage-style foreclosure sale or before the upset bid period ends for an in rem foreclosure, the taxpayer or any other party can redeem the property and stop the foreclosure procedure by paying all of the taxes, costs, and fees owed on the property.[54] For example, assume Billy Blue Devil owns a property being foreclosed upon by Carolina County using the mortgage-style procedure for $10,000 in taxes and costs. The high bid at the initial auction of Billy's property is $50,000. Billy may redeem his property prior to confirmation of sale for $10,000, even though the high bid is $40,000 more than the amount owed on the property. Although this option seems unfair to the foreclosing entity, in reality the county would not lose any money if Billy were to redeem his property after the $50,000 bid was received. All sale proceeds in excess of the $10,000 in taxes and costs owed to the county would be turned over to the court for distribution to junior lienholders or to Billy.

---

53. G.S. 105-377. That said, courts may be willing to ignore this limitation when a plaintiff complains of a constitutionally defective lack of notice. *See* Henderson Cnty. v. Osteen, 292 N.C. 692 (1977) (holding that the one-year limitation did not apply to motion by deceased taxpayer's heirs and administrator to set aside in rem foreclosure sale for lack of notice).

54. G.S. 105-374(e) (mortgage-style foreclosure can be stopped at any point up to confirmation); G.S. 105-375(g) and G.S. 1-339.57 (in rem foreclosure can be stopped at any point prior to the expiration of the upset bid period). For both mortgage-style and in rem foreclosure sales, other bidders can upset the high bid at the initial auction sale by submitting within ten days a bid that exceeds the original high bid by at least 5 percent, with a minimum increase of $750. G.S. 105-374(o) and G.S. 1-339.64. Every upset bid starts a new ten-day upset bid period, meaning foreclosure sales can continue for weeks or months if bidders keep upsetting each others' bids. The sale cannot be confirmed until the ten-day upset bid period ends without a new upset bid being submitted.

Chapter 11

Discovery and Immaterial Irregularities

Discovery and Immaterial Irregularities

How may a tax collector recover taxes on property that was not appropriately listed, assessed, levied, or billed? The Machinery Act provides two different remedies for these situations: the discovery provisions in G.S. 105-312 for listing errors and omissions made by the taxpayer and the "immaterial irregularity" provisions in G.S. 105-394 for errors and omissions made by the tax office. This chapter explains when and how a tax collector can apply these two statutes.[1]

1. What is a discovery?

A discovery occurs when an assessor learns that property was not listed accurately for taxation in a particular year. The Machinery Act defines "discovered property" to include

1. property that was not listed during a listing period,
2. property that was listed at a substantial understatement, and
3. property that was granted an exemption or exclusion for which it was not qualified.[2]

G.S. 105-312 authorizes the tax office to list, assess, and levy taxes on discovered property for the year of the discovery plus the preceding five

---

1. For a more detailed analysis of the differences between the discovery and the immaterial irregularity provisions, including analysis from the perspective of the assessor, see Stan C. Duncan and Christopher B. McLaughlin, "Discovery, Immaterial Irregularity, and the *Morgan* decision," *Property Tax Bulletin* No. 147 (Mar. 2009), available at www.sog.unc.edu/pubs/electronicversions/pdfs/ptb147.pdf.
2. G.S. 105-273(6a).

years. For example, assume that in March 2011 the Carolina County assessor learned that Tom Taxpayer failed to list his boat for taxation during the past ten years. The assessor would apply G.S. 105-312 and list, assess, and levy taxes on Tom's boat for six years: the year of the discovery, 2011, plus the preceding five years, 2010–2006.

2. When do discovery penalties apply?

Taxpayers who fail to list their property for taxation accurately and in a timely fashion are subject to annual penalties of 10 percent, calculated separately for each year the listing error or omission occurred.[3] However, these penalties are triggered only by listing errors and omissions made by the taxpayer, not by the assessor. As of 2004, all North Carolina counties were required to adopt permanent listing systems for real property.[4] Under such systems, assessors rather than taxpayers are responsible for appropriately listing all real property for taxation.[5] Discovery penalties do not apply for the failure to list land for taxation.[6] Similarly, assessors and not taxpayers are responsible for listing registered motor vehicles based on the information provided to assessors by the N.C. Division of Motor Vehicles.[7] If a registered motor vehicle is not listed for taxation, discovery penalties do not apply.[8]

Taxpayers remain responsible for listing improvements to land, separate rights or interests in land, and personal property other than registered motor vehicles.[9] Discovery penalties apply whenever a taxpayer fails to satisfy one of these listing obligations.

Here is how these rules work in practice. Assume that Tina Taxpayer buys unimproved Lot A in 2000 and constructs a house on the lot in 2005, which should have been first listed for the 2006 tax year. Neither the lot nor

---

3. G.S. 105-312(h). Also known as late-listing penalties, these penalties apply to inaccurate or incomplete listings as well as listings not made by the listing date, usually January 31.

4. S.L. 1999-297, sec. 3; G.S. 105-303(b).

5. G.S. 105-303(b)(1).

6. G.S. 105-303(b)(3).

7. G.S. 105-330.3(a)(1).

8. *Id.*

9. G.S. 105-303(b)(2) (improvements to and separate rights in land); G.S. 105-304 (personal property).

Table 11.1.   Calculation of Tina Taxpayer's Taxes and Penalties under G.S. 105-312

Tax Year	Taxes Owed	Penalties	Total Due
2011	Lot: $200	0 % ($0)	$1,300
	House: $1,000	10 % ($100)	
2010	Lot: $200	0 % ($0)	$1,400
	House: $1,000	20 % ($200)	
2009	Lot: $200	0 % ($0)	$1,500
	House: $1,000	30 % ($300)	
2008	Lot: $200	0 % ($0)	$1,600
	House: $1,000	40 % ($400)	
2007	Lot: $200	0 % ($0)	$1,700
	House: $1,000	50 % ($500)	
2006	Lot: $200	0 % ($0)	$1,800
	House: $1,000	60 % ($600)	
Totals	$7,200	$2,100	$9,300

the house is listed or assessed until the assessor discovers the error in May 2011. The property should have been levied $1,200 in taxes annually, $200 for the lot and $1,000 for the house. Table 11.1 demonstrates how the taxes and discovery penalties would normally be calculated.

Note that discovery penalties are applied only to taxes on the house, not the lot. Penalties are calculated separately for each tax year, with a 10 percent penalty applied for the listed period the taxpayer missed. For example, for the 2009 taxes, the penalty is 30 percent because the taxpayer missed three listing periods (2009, 2010, and 2011). Because the discovery provisions limit recapture of taxes to the year of discovery plus the preceding five years, the earliest year for which Tina may be billed for taxes is 2006.

3. When are discovery bills due?

Discovery bills become part of the tax levy for the tax year that opens in the calendar year in which the discovery occurs. In the Tina Taxpayer example above, the discovery was made in May 2011. This means that the entire discovery bill of $7,700 would become part of the 2011 tax levy. That bill would be due on September 1, 2011, and be delinquent and begin accruing interest on January 6, 2012.

This rule means that discoveries made late in the calendar year will be due immediately and may become delinquent in a matter of weeks or even days. For example, assume that the assessor discovers Tina's failure to list her property on December 30, 2011. The resulting discovery bill would be delinquent only one week later, on January 6, 2012. However, if the discovery were made in January 2012, the discovery bill would become part of the 2012 levy, be due on September 1, 2012, and become delinquent and begin accruing interest in January 2013.

4. What tax value and tax rate should be used to calculate discovery bills?

Although a discovery bill is considered part of the tax levy for the year in which the discovery occurred, the tax office should not use the current tax value and tax rate to calculate discovery bills that relate to prior tax years. Instead, the tax office must use the tax value and tax rate in effect for each tax year the discovery bill covers.

For example, assume Billy Blue Devil failed to list his boat for taxation beginning in 2009. If the assessor discovers this listing failure in March 2011, the discovery bill will cover three years, 2009, 2010, and 2011. The discovery calculation for each year must be based on the county's tax rate and the boat's tax value for each of those years. See Table 11.2 for the details of the calculation, which include the discovery penalties that apply to unlisted personal property other than registered motor vehicles.

Note that the tax value of the boat decreased each year, as is true of most personal property. Were this discovery bill one that included improvements to real property, the tax value of the property could increase over time due to renovations or countywide revaluations. The tax rate is set each year by the county's governing board, meaning it too can vary over time. The key point to remember is that the tax office cannot use the current tax value and the current tax rate when creating discovery bills for prior listing periods.

Table 11.2.   Details of the Calculation of Taxes on Billy Blue Devil's Boat

Tax Year	Tax Value	Tax Rate	Taxes Owed	Penalties	Totals
2011	$2,000	.50	$10.00	10% ($1.00)	$11.00
2010	$2,200	.50	$11.00	20% ($2.20)	$13.20
2009	$2,400	.52	$12.48	30% ($3.75)	$16.23
					$40.43

5. Who is responsible for discovery bills?

In general, the discovery bill should be issued in the name of the taxpayer who had the duty to list the discovered property for the year(s) in question. However, the responsible taxpayer—in other words, the taxpayer whose personal property can be targeted with enforced collection actions—will vary depending on the type of property involved. For taxes on real property, including improvements, the responsible taxpayers are both the owner as of the delinquency date and all subsequent owners.[10] For taxes on personal property, the listing taxpayer is the only taxpayer personally responsible for the taxes.[11]

For example, assume that Tom Tarheel bought a boat in 2008 and sold it to Wanda Wolfpack in 2010. If the assessor discovers in 2011 that the boat has never been listed for taxation, Tom should receive the discovery bills for 2009 and 2010 and Wanda should receive the discovery bill for 2011. Tom will be personally responsible for the 2009 and 2010 taxes on the boat, while Wanda will be personally responsible for the 2011 taxes.

Now assume that in 2008 Tom Tarheel built a garage on Parcel A but never listed that improvement with the assessor. In 2010 Tom sells Parcel A, including the garage, to Wanda Wolfpack. The garage remains unlisted until the assessor discovers the improvement in 2011. As with the boat, Tom should receive the initial discovery bills for 2009 and 2010, the years in which he had the responsibility for listing the improvement, and Wanda should receive the initial discovery bill for 2011.

However, if the discovery bills are not paid Wanda will be responsible for all three years of discovery bills. Tom will not be personally responsible for any of the discovery bills, despite the fact that he was the taxpayer that

---

10. G.S. 105-365.1(b)(1).
11. G.S. 105-365.1(b)(2).

created the listing problem. Why? Because the discovery bill is considered part of the 2011–2012 levy and will not become delinquent until January 6, 2012. For improvements to real property, the responsible taxpayer is the record owner as of the delinquency date. Assuming Wanda still owns the property on January 6, 2012, she will be the responsible taxpayer for all three years of the discovery bill.

As a result, when dealing with discovery bills for taxes on real property the best practice is to send the bills to both the original listing taxpayer *and* the current owner of the property. Doing so will give the current owner notice of his or her potential tax liability. Not surprisingly, the current owner will likely be furious that he or she may have responsibility for a tax that should have been levied on the previous owner. However angry that taxpayer may be, his or her claim lies against the previous owner of the property and not with the tax office. The current owner may be able to seek reimbursement of the discovery bill taxes from the prior owner, but that possibility has no relevance to the tax office's right and duty to collect the discovery bill from the current owner.

6. May discovery bills be waived or compromised?

Yes. G.S. 105-312(k) is the *only* provision in the Machinery Act that grants a local governing board the discretion to waive, negotiate, or compromise a validly levied tax. This provision permits a governing board to waive some or all of a discovery bill, which includes the principle taxes, discovery penalties, and interest if the discovery bill is not paid before its delinquency date. G.S. 105-312 places no limitations on the board's discretion, neither does it mandate waiver or compromise in certain circumstances.[12] The only limitation on this authority is the generally accepted view espoused by the N.C. Department of Revenue that a governing board cannot compromise a dis-

---

12. See *In re* Popkin Bros. Enters., Inc., 90 P.T.C. 82 (Aug. 23, 1991). In this case, the Property Tax Commission rejected a taxpayer's appeal of discovery penalties for property that was listed only two days after listing period closed. The PTC observed, "The decision to compromise pursuant to GS 105-312(k) is purely a discretionary matter; where the board acts in good faith, its decision must stand."

covery bill that has already been paid by the taxpayer.[13] Compare that broad authority to the limited release and refund authority created by G.S. 105-381. Discussed in detail in Chapter 12, these provisions permit the board to forgive only those taxes that were levied illegally or imposed due to a clerical error by the tax office.

Municipalities are not bound by a board of county commissioners' decision to compromise a discovery bill. Despite the fact that county officials control the listing and assessing process, municipal governing boards are free to make their own decisions on these matters. That a county board agrees to waive a discovery bill under G.S. 105-312(k) does not require the municipality to do likewise.

7. When do the immaterial irregularity provisions apply?

The immaterial irregularity provisions of G.S. 105-394 permit a tax office to list, assess, levy, and collect property taxes despite defects in the process. Tax collectors may rely on this statute whenever taxes were not collected due to errors or omissions by the tax office. In essence, G.S. 105-394 prevents a taxpayer from relying on a taxing authority's failure to satisfy a particular Machinery Act requirement as an excuse not to pay an otherwise valid tax.

In contrast to its relatively limited definition of "discovered property," the Machinery Act provides an expansive and nonexclusive explanation of the phrase "immaterial irregularity." G.S. 105-394 offers ten different specific examples of immaterial irregularities, including the failure of tax officials to take the required oaths, the failure to list, appraise, or assess property, and the failure to advertise tax liens appropriately, plus a seemingly unlimited catch-all provision.

North Carolina courts have relied upon G.S. 105-394 to excuse a wide variety of procedural failures, including a transposed number in an assessment value,[14] the lack of notice in a discovery proceeding,[15] the inadvertent

---

13. Conversation with David Baker, director, Local Government Division, N.C. Department of Revenue, May 17, 2011. Taxpayers seeking relief from paid discovery bills must petition for refunds under G.S. 105-381.

14. *In re* Notice of Attachment & Garnishment Issued by Catawba Cnty. Tax Collector against Nuzum-Cross Chevrolet, Inc., 59 N.C. App. 332, 296 S.E.2d 499 (1982).

15. Appeal of Pilot Freight Carriers, Inc., 28 N.C. App. 400, 221 S.E.2d 378 (1976).

destruction of a listing form,[16] a drainage district's failure to levy special assessments in a timely fashion,[17] and the unexplained failure to assess a property that was properly listed by the taxpayer.[18]

Left unanswered by these cases and by the statute itself is the question of when, if ever, a defect in the property tax process could be substantial enough that it would invalidate a property tax procedure. Only once has a court identified a tax procedure that was "indispensable" and therefore outside the scope of the immaterial irregularity provisions. In *Henderson County v. Osteen*,[19] the North Carolina Supreme Court found that the in rem foreclosure notice provisions in G.S. 105-375 were constitutionally necessary to satisfy due process concerns. The court invalidated a foreclosure sale that lacked the required notice, concluding that it would be unconstitutional for G.S. 105-394 to excuse the lack of notice.

It appears that unless a procedural defect interferes with a taxpayer's constitutional right to due process, G.S. 105-394 will excuse any and all defects in the administration of the property tax. In the author's view, tax officials should not be timid when applying this statute. All valid taxes should be assessed, levied, and collected, regardless of the type or duration of procedural errors or omissions made by a taxing unit. The only caveat is for taxing units to consider providing the taxpayer with similar notice and appeal procedures as required under G.S. 105-312 when billing for back taxes under G.S. 105-394.

When remedying procedural failures, local officials should keep in mind both the broad scope of G.S. 105-394 and the well-established legal principle that local governments do not waive their rights to appropriately enforce Machinery Act provisions simply due to past practices of inappropriate enforcement. For example, assume that for years a county only assessed new improvements to property when those improvements were 100 percent complete. This approach would violate the requirement in G.S. 105-309 to list and tax all improvements over $100 in value "that have been acquired, begun, erected, damaged or destroyed since the time of the last appraisal." If the county realizes the error of its ways and begins to fully enforce the

---

16. *In re* Dickey, 110 N.C. App. 823, 431 S.E.2d 203 (1993).

17. Northampton Cnty. Drainage Dist. No. One v. Bailey, 92 N.C. App. 68, 373 S.E.2d 560 (1988).

18. *In re* Morgan, 362 N.C. 339, 661 S.E.2d 733 (2008).

19. 292 N.C. 692, 235 S.E.2d 166 (1977).

listing requirement both retroactively and prospectively, could a taxpayer rely on the county's past practice to avoid collection efforts? The answer is no. The concept of waiver or estoppel can be raised against private parties who fail to exercise their rights but not against a government, which always maintains the right to enforce a valid law.[20] A tax jurisdiction should never hesitate to enforce the Machinery Act correctly, regardless of how long it may have followed an erroneous approach.

Following are a few common situations in which a tax collector may rely on G.S. 105-394 to recover taxes that were not appropriately listed, assessed, levied, or billed due to errors or omissions by the tax office.

Failure to Assess

Consider a situation in which a homeowner appropriately lists a house he or she has built on a lot but for some reason the county does not assess the new house and continues to bill the taxpayer only for the value of the lot. This is an assessment error, not a failure to list, meaning that the discovery provisions in G.S. 105-312 do not apply. It should be remedied under G.S. 105-394 by preparing and distributing a retroactive tax bill for each year the property was not assessed.

Failure to Levy Annexed Property

Assume that in 2000, Blue Devil City annexed ten parcels previously situated in an unincorporated area of Carolina County. If in 2009 the Blue Devil City tax collector learns that only county taxes have been levied on the annexed parcels for the past nine years, how should the problem be resolved?

Many municipalities have resolved this situation by creating discovery bills under G.S. 105-312 for the current year plus the previous five years, without interest or penalties. Other municipalities conclude that this situation may not be corrected retroactively and may only be resolved for 2009 and subsequent tax years under G.S. 105-287.

---

20. *See* Henderson v. Gill, 229 N.C. 313, 49 S.E.2d 754 (1948) (state not estopped from collecting sales taxes despite incorrect advice given to taxpayers by state revenue agents). Although the Small Business Protection Act, S.L. 2008-107 (H 2436), provided limited relief for retailers who incorrectly collect certain sales taxes in reliance on past audit advice from the Department of Revenue, the *Henderson* case still stands for the proposition that a local government never waives its right to enforce a valid law.

However, this common situation is not a failure to list subject to the discovery provisions in G.S. 105-312 or an appraisal issue subject to the forward-looking remedies in G.S. 105-287. The property in question was listed and assessed by the county as intended. Instead, this situation involves a levying and billing failure caused most often by a failure to update the annexed parcels' tax situs codes. Such a situation must be resolved using the immaterial irregularity provisions of G.S. 105-394. The municipality should prepare and distribute retroactive tax bills for each year since the annexation that municipal taxes were not levied on the properties in question.

Failure to Bill

Assume that a taxpayer lists his or her property, receives an accurate assessment, but is mistakenly billed for only half of the appropriate tax levy. This continues for ten years before the tax collector notices the mistake. How can the assessor resolve the property that escaped taxation? Because this was not the result of a failure to list, the G.S. 105-312 discovery provisions cannot apply. The omitted taxes should be billed retroactively under G.S. 105-394.

8. When do taxes billed under G.S. 105-394 become due and delinquent?

Once a tax collector determines that an error has occurred and that the immaterial irregularity provisions apply, he or she should prepare new or corrected bills for each of the tax years in question. These tax bills will be due and delinquent as if they had been listed, assessed, levied, and billed correctly in their original year of levy. Interest will accrue on these taxes from their original date of delinquency, which means that some of these bills may immediately be subject to multiple years' worth of interest charges.

This approach was approved by the North Carolina Supreme Court in *In re Morgan*, a 2008 case from Henderson County.[21] In *Morgan*, the taxpayer had listed her home for taxation, but for nine years the county inexplicably had failed to assess the home or levy taxes on it. The court permitted the county to rely on G.S. 105-394 to collect all nine years of back taxes, plus interest, despite the fact that the taxpayer was not at fault for the omission.

---

21. 362 N.C. 339 (2008).

Because the taxpayer had satisfied her listing obligation, the discovery provisions of G.S. 105-312 could not apply. The county therefore could recover all of the back taxes without regard to the six-year limitation for discovered property. Interest for each of the nine years of taxes accrued from the original delinquency date for that tax year.

9. Is there a time limitation on retroactive tax bills issued under G.S. 105-394?

No. Tax collectors are obligated to bill and collect all taxes with which they have been charged.[22] That said, most taxing units usually choose to issue retroactive bills only for the most recent ten years of omitted taxes in light of the Machinery Act's ten-year statute of limitations.[23] However, the statute of limitations only affects the collection of taxes, not their levy. That a tax is not collectible does not mean it should not be levied and billed. In the author's view, the tax collector should levy and bill all omitted taxes, regardless of how old they are. While the collector will not be permitted to use enforced collection actions for taxes more than ten years past due, they nevertheless might be paid at closing if the affected property is transferred so that the new owner can take clear title.

10. Can G.S. 105-394 apply to an assessor's failure to list real property?

Possibly. Although the courts have yet to resolve this question, the relevant statutory language appears to permit a tax collector to rely on the immaterial irregularity provisions instead of the discovery provisions for real property that was not listed due to an error or omission by the assessor. This approach may increase the amount that can be collected.

As discussed above, the definition of "discovered property" includes all property, both real and personal, regardless of whether the assessor (for land) or the taxpayer (for personal property and improvements to real property) had the obligation to list the property. That definition implies that the

---

22. G.S. 105-350(1).
23. G.S. 105-378(a).

only method to recover taxes on property that was not listed accurately is the discovery provisions in G.S. 105-312.

However, the definition of an immaterial irregularity in G.S. 105-394 also includes the failure to list property, without regard for who had the obligation to list the property. Further, permanent listing systems having been introduced across the state, discovery penalties no longer apply to listing errors and omissions made by the assessor.[24] These two provisions suggest that perhaps a tax collector can rely on G.S. 105-394 rather than G.S. 105-312 to bill taxes on property that the assessor failed to list. Neither the General Assembly nor the courts have provided guidance on this apparent overlap between G.S. 105-312 and G.S. 105-394.

The *Morgan* case discussed above highlights two important reasons why a tax collector might prefer to rely on the immaterial irregularity provisions rather than the discovery provisions. The first is time. G.S. 105-312 limits discovery bills to six years: the current tax year plus the preceding five. No such limitation exists for taxes billed retroactively under G.S. 105-394. In *Morgan*, the tax collector billed the taxpayer for nine years of back taxes. Had the discovery provisions applied, the county would have been limited to six years.[25] The second reason is interest. *Morgan* approved the addition of interest to all nine years of back taxes. In contrast, when the discovery provisions are used to recover back taxes on real property not listed by the assessor, neither interest nor discovery penalties apply.

Table 11.3 returns to the Tina Taxpayer example from Question 2 above to demonstrate how using G.S. 105-394 in addition to G.S. 105-312 affects the recovery of back taxes. Recall that Tina Taxpayer buys unimproved Lot A in 2000 and constructs a house on the lot in 2006, which should have been first listed for the 2007 tax year. Neither the lot nor the house are listed or assessed until the assessor discovers the error in May 2011. Annual

---

24. G.S. 105-303(b)(3).

25. It is unclear whether the ten-year statute of limitations for enforced collection actions found in G.S. 105-378(a) would limit back taxes billed under G.S. 105-394. In the author's view, it should not. The statute of limitations affects collection remedies, not the validity of the underlying tax. Even if a tax is more than ten years old and therefore not subject to enforced collection actions, a tax official should assess, levy, and bill that tax as permitted under G.S. 105-394 without regard for the statute of limitations.

Table 11.3. Calculation of Tina Taxpayer's Taxes and Penalties under G.S. 105-312 and G.S. 105-394

Tax Year	Taxes Owed	Penalties	Interest	Total Due
2011	Lot: $200	0 % ($0)	$ 0	$ 1,300
	House: $1,000	10 % ($100)	$ 0	
2010	Lot: $200	0 % ($0)	$ 10	$ 1,410
	House: $1,000	20 % ($200)	$ 0	
2009	Lot: $200	0 % ($0)	$ 28	$ 1,528
	House: $1,000	30 % ($300)	$ 0	
2008	Lot: $200	0 % ($0)	$ 46	$ 1,646
	House: $1,000	40 % ($400)	$ 0	
2007	Lot: $200	0 % ($0)	$ 64	$ 1,764
	House: $1,000	50 % ($500)	$ 0	
2006	Lot: $200	0 % ($0)	$ 82	$ 1,882
	House: $1,000	60 % ($600)	$ 0	
2005	Lot: $200	0 % ($0)	$100	$ 300
2004	Lot: $200	0 % ($0)	$118	$ 318
2003	Lot: $200	0 % ($0)	$136	$ 336
2002	Lot: $200	0 % ($0)	$154	$ 354
2001	Lot: $200	0 % ($0)	$172	$ 372
Totals	$8,200	$2,100	$910	$11,210

taxes of $1,200 should have been levied on the property, $200 for the lot and $1,000 for the house.

As Table 11.1 indicated, if the tax collector relies only on G.S. 105-312 to recover the missed taxes on her property, Tina would be responsible for $9,300 in back taxes and penalties. However, as shown in Table 11.3, if the tax collector relies on both G.S. 105-312 *and* G.S. 105-394—discovery for the house and immaterial irregularity for the lot—Tina will owe $11,210 in back taxes, interest, and penalties. The roughly $2,000 difference is due to the fact that G.S. 105-394 permits the tax collector to collect all eleven years of back taxes on the lot, plus interest.

11. May taxes billed under
G.S. 105-394 be waived or compromised?

Generally, no. Chapter 12 explores the Machinery Act's refund and release provisions in detail, but basically releases and refunds are permitted only when a tax is illegal or was imposed due to clerical error.[26] These rules apply to the release and refund of interest just as they do for principle taxes.[27] That a taxing unit did not levy a tax or interest in a timely fashion does not render that tax illegal.[28] Similarly, although a clerical error by the taxing unit may have delayed the imposition of the taxes that are being billed retroactively under G.S. 105-394, that fact does not mean that the retroactive taxes are being *imposed* due to clerical error. As a result, a release or refund generally would not be justified for retroactive taxes billed under G.S. 105-394.

The only situation in which a release of retroactive tax bills may be justified is when a municipality fails to levy taxes for several years on annexed property and the owner of the annexed property had no notice of the annexation, either formally as part of the annexation or informally through the receipt of municipal services. When the municipality learns of the error, it should retroactively bill the omitted taxes for every year the property has been part of the taxing unit. To comply with the *Morgan* decision, those bills should carry interest from their original date of delinquency.[29] While the principal taxes cannot be released, this author believes that the municipality's governing board could legally waive the interest on the bills on the theory that the interest was imposed due to the tax office's clerical error: but for the error by the tax office, the taxpayer would have paid the municipal tax bills in the same timely fashion as he or she paid the county tax bills every year. Tax collectors must remember that the decision to release taxes under G.S. 105-381 must be made by the board and not by the collector's office.[30]

---

26. G.S. 105-380 and -381.

27. The Machinery Act defines the terms "tax" and "taxes" to include the principle amount of taxes as well as all interest and penalties. G.S. 105-373(15). As a result, the limitations on the refund and release of taxes also apply to interest and penalties.

28. G.S. 105-348 charges all taxpayers with notice of the taxes on their property regardless of whether they receive actual notice of those taxes.

29. 362 N.C. 339 (2008). See the previous question for a detailed discussion of this case.

30. G.S. 105-381(b) permits the governing board to delegate responsibility for approving refund and release requests of less than $100 to the finance officer, manager, or attorney of the taxing unit. Note that this responsibility may never be delegated to the tax collector or his or her deputies.

Chapter 12

Refunds and Releases

Refunds and Releases

Few issues carry a greater potential for conflict between taxpayers and tax offices than do requests for refunds or waivers of property taxes. This is true in large part because the Machinery Act allows refunds and waivers only under two very limited circumstances. Unless the disputed tax is imposed due to clerical error or is illegal, the Machinery Act prohibits the refund of a tax payment or the waiver—called a release in the Machinery Act—of an unpaid tax obligation. Contrary to what many taxpayers believe, the refund and release process is not the venue for a re-examination of a property's value or taxable status. Although some governing boards desire to be more forgiving on these issues, they do so at their peril: board members who approve refunds or releases that violate the Machinery Act can be held personally responsible for the lost taxes.[1]

1. Who may approve refunds and releases?

The governing board, always. The local government's manager, attorney, or finance officer, sometimes. But the tax collector, never.

G.S. 105-381(b) gives the governing board primary responsibility for approving refund and release requests. For refunds and releases of less than $100, the board may delegate this responsibility to the manager, attorney, or finance officer, who must then report monthly to the board on the actions taken. Conspicuously absent from this list is the tax collector. In practice many tax collectors approve small, noncontroversial refunds and releases

---

This chapter updates information published as *Property Tax Bulletin* No. 153 (Apr. 2010).

1. G.S. 105-380(c).

and later seek approval from the governing board. This approach carries some risks, however, and is not recommended for more substantial requests.

Once a refund or release is approved by the board or its delegate, the tax collector should be credited with that amount in the next annual settlement.[2]

2. When are refunds and releases authorized?

Technically, refunds and releases are authorized in three situations: when a tax is (1) imposed through clerical error, (2) illegal, or (3) levied for an illegal purpose.[3] However, because reasons 2 and 3 overlap substantially, if not entirely, in practice there are only two situations that justify a refund: when a tax is imposed due to clerical error or is illegal.

Clerical Error

The General Assembly has not defined the term "clerical error," but state courts have. In 1997, the North Carolina Court of Appeals tackled this issue in *Ammons v. Wake County.*[4] In this case, the taxpayer asked the assessor if his forest land qualified for present-use value (PUV) tax deferrals for the 1993 tax year. The assessor answered no and the taxpayer did not apply for the PUV program. One year later, the taxpayer ignored the assessor's opinion and applied for a PUV deferral. The assessor denied the application, but the taxpayer won his appeal to the board of equalization and review and was granted PUV status for the 1994 tax year. The taxpayer then requested a refund for the 1993 taxes he would have been able to defer had the assessor provided accurate advice about the property's eligibility for the PUV program. After the board of county commissioners denied the refund request, the taxpayer turned to the courts. The superior court ruled that the assessor's incorrect advice did not constitute a clerical error under G.S. 105-381 and dismissed the taxpayer's claim. The court of appeals affirmed this decision, which became final when the North Carolina Supreme Court declined to hear the taxpayer's appeal.

---

2. G.S. 105-381(b).

3. G.S. 105-381(a)(1).

4. 490 S.E.2d 569, 127 N.C. App. 426 (1997), *cert. denied,* 500 S.E.2d 84, 347 N.C. 670 (1998).

According to the court of appeals, to qualify as a clerical error under G.S. 105-381 the tax office's error "must ordinarily be apparent on the face of the instrument," "must be capable of being corrected by reference to the record only," and must produce an unintended result. Prime examples are transcription errors, such as when an additional zero is added to tax valuation or when two numbers are transposed on a tax bill.

The definition of clerical error adopted in *Ammons* excludes a factual or judgment error by an appraiser, which must be addressed during the assessment appeal period and not in a refund and release request. For example, assume that in 2007 an appraiser values a lakefront lot with the understanding that it is buildable. Three years later, the taxpayer applies for a building permit and is denied based on the size and slope of the lot. The taxpayer immediately asks the tax office for a retroactive decrease in the tax value of the lot and a tax refund, based on the fact that the lot was never buildable. Applying the *Ammons* test, this error does not justify a refund under G.S. 105-381 because it is a judgment error and not a clerical error. First, the error is apparent and correctable only through an examination of the property and a decision by the county inspections department, not by reference to the appraisal documents. Second, the error has not caused an unintended result. In 2007, the appraiser intended to value the house as a buildable lot, and it was so valued. The judgment error by the appraiser can be corrected under G.S. 105-287(a)(2) for current and future tax years, but it does not justify a retroactive change to the tax value or a refund for past years under G.S. 105-381.

For a terrific analysis of the *Ammons* case and its definition of clerical error, see William A. Campbell's *Property Tax Bulletin* No. 111.[5]

Can a clerical error by the taxpayer ever justify a refund or a release? No. Based on the language in G.S. 105-381, a refund or release is justified only if the tax is "imposed through clerical error." Because only the government can impose a tax, only a clerical error by the government can justify a refund or release under G.S. 105-381.

Consider the situation in which Tina Taxpayer forgets that her mortgage company is escrowing her property tax payments and makes a payment to

---

5. William A. Campbell, "*Ammons v. Wake County*: Some Light on Clerical Errors," *Property Tax Bulletin* No. 111 (Oct. 1997), available at www.sog.unc.edu/pubs/electronicversions/pdfs/ptb111.pdf.

the tax office. Can Tina's payment be refunded based on the fact that her mortgage company will pay the tax bill later in the year with the escrowed funds? No. Even though Tina's error may be a clerical one, it does not satisfy G.S. 105-381 because the tax on her home was not imposed due to her error. Tina's refund request should be directed to her mortgage company, not to the tax office.

Similarly, a refund is not justified if a taxpayer mistakenly pays the taxes on property that he or she sold to another taxpayer at some point after the listing period. The taxpayer may have made a clerical error when he or she wrote the wrong parcel number on the payment check, but that does not mean the taxes on that parcel were imposed due to clerical error. The same is true when a mortgage company indicates the wrong parcel number on a tax payment. In both situations the tax office appropriately applied the payment to the parcel indicated by the taxpayer. The taxpayer's remedy, if any, would be from the owner of the property that benefited from the taxpayer's mistake.[6]

Illegal Taxes

Taxes that are either *illegal* or *levied for an illegal purpose* may be released or refunded under G.S. 105-181. Situations in which refunds may occur include:

1. double taxation, when the same property is taxed more than once;
2. situs mistakes, when a taxing unit taxes property that has no situs in the unit's jurisdiction;
3. procedural defects, when a taxing unit levies a tax without a required ordinance or referendum;[7]
4. excess taxation, when a taxing unit levies a tax in excess of the applicable cap on that tax;[8] and

---

6. A refund *is* justified, however, if the tax office mistakenly applies a tax payment to the wrong parcel in contradiction of instructions from the taxpayer.

7. For example, county and municipal property taxes must be included in the government's annual budget ordinance. G.S. 159-13. Rural fire district taxes require a petition signed by 35 percent of the affected landowners and voter referendum in the proposed district. G.S. 69-25.1.

8. For example, with some exceptions general county and municipal property tax rates are capped at $1.50. G.S. 153A-149; G.S. 160A-209. Rural fire district tax rates

5. improper purposes, when a taxing unit levies a tax for a purpose not permitted by the General Assembly.[9]

This author believes some local governments inappropriately shoehorn valuation errors and/or judgment errors into the illegal tax category and authorize refunds for matters that should be resolved during the valuation appeal process.

For example, consider the situation in which the assessor's office incorrectly assumes during a reappraisal that Tom Taxpayer's house has a finished third floor. Two years later, Tom demonstrates to the assessor that his house has never had a finished third floor. Tom asks that his assessment be reduced retroactively and that his excess tax payment for the past two years be refunded. The error at issue clearly is not a clerical error under the *Ammons* test. Nevertheless, is a refund justified because the resulting tax is illegal, in that the county taxed Tom for property (a finished third floor) that Tom has never owned?

Many counties would answer yes, but this author disagrees. If valuation errors such as the one involving Tom's third floor are refundable under the illegal tax category, then the deadline for valuation appeals becomes irrelevant. Local governments would lose all certainty about the value of their tax bases and find it impossible to budget accurately. For this reason, the best interpretation of the illegal tax category is one that excludes valuation judgment errors. If a taxpayer wishes to contest the valuation of his or her property, he or she must do so through the board of equalization and review appeal process, not through the refund and release process.[10]

---

are capped at either 10 cents or 15 cents, depending on the language of the authorizing referendum. G.S. 69-25.4.

9. G.S. 153A-149 and G.S. 160A-209 list the approved purposes for general county and municipal property taxes. Special service district taxes may be used only for the provision of additional services in those districts such as beach erosion control, sewer systems, fire protection (counties only), and downtown revitalization projects (municipalities only). G.S. 153A-301; G.S. 160A-536. Rural fire district taxes may be used only for the provision of fire protection services in these districts. G.S. 69-25.4.

10. The same is true of taxability errors. As the *Ammons* case demonstrates, incorrect decisions by the assessor regarding applications for exemptions or exclusions do not justify refunds or releases. If a taxpayer believes that he or she is entitled to an exemption or exclusion, the taxpayer must take advantage of the application and appeal process in G.S. 105-282.1. The taxpayer cannot retroactively raise these issues using the refund and release process under G.S. 105-381.

Listing errors must also be resolved during the initial appeal period to the board of equalization and review rather than through the refund and release process. For example, assume that Tom Taxpayer has listed a boat in Carolina County for several years. In November 2009 he sells the boat to his neighbor, Tina Taxpayer. In January 2010 Carolina County sends Tom a listing form that includes the boat. Tom signs and returns the form without carefully reading it. The county subsequently assesses the boat for taxation under Tom's name. When Tom receives the tax bill for the boat, he promptly pays it. Six months later he realizes he has paid taxes on a boat he no longer owns and demands a refund from Carolina County. Tom is not entitled to a refund under G.S. 105-381 because the tax on the boat is not illegal: Carolina County is authorized to tax the boat because it still has situs in Carolina County on January 1, 2010. Nor is Tom entitled to a refund under the clerical error category because the listing error does not satisfy the *Ammons* test. Tom's opportunity to contest the listing of the boat in his name ended when the valuation appeal period ended thirty days after he received notice of the boat's tax valuation.[11]

That said, refunds and releases *are* justified under G.S. 105-381's illegal tax category for taxes levied on property that does not exist or does not have situs in the taxing unit as of the listing date. Consider the example above, but assume instead that in mid-2009 Tom sold the boat to a resident of another county who promptly removed it from Carolina County. If Tom mistakenly listed his boat for taxation in Carolina County for 2010, he would be entitled to a refund or a release of those taxes after providing evidence that the boat did not have situs in Carolina County on January 1, 2010. The same would be true if Tom's boat was destroyed by hurricane in mid-2009 and he mistakenly listed it for taxation for 2010. Tom would be entitled to a refund or release of the taxes on the boat if he could provide evidence that the boat no longer existed as of January 1, 2010.[12]

---

11. G.S. 105-317.1(c). Under G.S. 105-306, the county is permitted to correct the listing error and proceed as if it had been listed in Tina's name all along. This means that if Tom had never paid the taxes, he would no longer be considered the responsible taxpayer and could not be subject to enforced collection remedies. The same conclusions would be reached under G.S. 105-302 if the listing error concerned real property.

12. In contrast, this author believes that a refund or release is *not* justified under G.S. 105-381 when a business taxpayer lists a certain dollar amount of personal property for taxation and then later seeks a refund or release of the related taxes on the grounds that the taxpayer included in that amount some personal property that was

3. Which taxes must be released or refunded under G.S. 105-381?

The Machinery Act defines the term "tax" as "the principal amount of any property tax or dog license tax and costs, penalties, and interest."[13] This definition means that G.S. 105-381 controls the refund or release of all property taxes, including special service district taxes and rural fire district taxes. G.S. 105-381 does not control the refund or release of other local taxes, such as privilege license taxes and occupancy taxes, nor does it control the refund or release of costs and fees, such as special assessments and nuisance abatement costs, that by statute are collectible as property taxes.[14] See Question 8 for details on the refund and release of other taxes and fees.

4. Does G.S. 105-381 govern the refund or release of interest?

Yes. Because the term "taxes" as used in GS 105-381 includes interest, any refund or release of interest must conform to the restrictions in that statute. Only when interest is levied illegally or added due to a clerical error can it be released or refunded. For example, if the tax office miscalculates the interest owed by a taxpayer, that interest charge could be refunded or released under G.S. 105-381.

What if the taxpayer claims that he or she was charged interest only because the tax office failed to send a tax bill in a timely fashion or sent an inaccurate tax bill? The North Carolina Supreme Court answered this question in the negative when it decided *In re Morgan* two years ago.[15] In this case, the taxpayer listed her house with the Henderson County assessor but the house was never assessed or taxed due to tax office error. Eight years later the tax office learned of its mistake and sent retroactive tax bills, plus interest, for each year the house had escaped taxation. The taxpayer contested both the principal taxes and the interest. The Supreme Court

---

disposed of prior to January 1. This relatively common situation involves a dispute over the *valuation* of the taxpayer's aggregate personal property as opposed to a dispute over the *existence* of taxable property. Accordingly, the taxpayer's opportunity to contest the issue should be through the listing and appraisal appeal period, not through the refund and release process.

13. G.S. 105-273(15).

14. See Chapter 17 for more details regarding special service districts and rural fire districts.

15. 362 N.C. 339, 661 S.E.2d 733 (2008).

ruled in favor of the county, approving not only the principal taxes but also the addition of interest to the tardy tax bills. The court's decision relied on G.S. 105-348, which provides taxpayers with notice of their taxes regardless of when or if they receive tax bills, and G.S. 105-394, which forgives minor defects—"immaterial irregularities" in the language of the statute—during the taxation process.[16] Although the taxpayer in *Morgan* did not seek a release under G.S. 105-381, the result would be the same had she done so. *Morgan* makes clear that it is legal for interest to accrue on taxes billed after the delinquency date due to tax office error. A release is, therefore, not justified under G.S. 105-381.

The release of interest may be justified under G.S. 105-381 in one common situation involving municipal annexations. Assume that Blue Devil City annexed Parcel A in 2000 but for some reason failed to levy city property taxes on the property. In 2010 the city learns of the omission and sends Parcel A's owner retroactive tax bills for 2001 through 2010, plus interest from each year's original due date as permitted under the *Morgan* decision.[17] If the owner of Parcel A seeks a release of these retroactive bills under G.S. 105-381, the city would not be permitted to authorize a release of the principal taxes for the same reasons that the principal taxes could not be released in the *Morgan* case. The tax office's error did not cause the back taxes to be imposed, as is required to justify a release. Quite the opposite, in fact: the tax office's error *prevented* the city's taxes from being imposed in a timely fashion.

But the taxpayer may have a reasonable argument for the release of the *interest* on those retroactive tax bills. If the taxpayer paid the county taxes on Parcel A in a timely fashion each year, it seems reasonable to assume that the taxpayer would also have paid the city taxes each year before they became delinquent and accrued interest. The taxpayer could argue that the

---

16. For more on *Morgan* and the immaterial irregularity provisions, see Stan C. Duncan and Christopher B. McLaughlin, "Discovery, Immaterial Irregularity, and the *Morgan* Decision," *Property Tax Bulletin* No. 147 (Mar. 2009), available at www.sog.unc.edu/pubs/electronicversions/pdfs/ptb147.pdf.

17. This failure to levy city taxes is not a discovery because the property in question was listed by the county for taxation. As a result, the discovery provisions of G.S. 105-312 do not apply and the city's recovery is not limited to the current year plus the most recent five years, as is the case for discoveries. Instead the city is permitted (and in fact required) to bill all omitted taxes retroactively under the immaterial irregularity provisions of G.S. 105-394. For more details on the interplay between the discovery provisions and the immaterial irregularity provisions, see Chapter 11.

only reason he or she is being charged interest is due to the tax office's mistake: but for the tax office's error, interest would not have been imposed. If true, then a release could be justified under G.S. 105-381. In part, the decision should turn on how much notice the taxpayer had of the annexation. The justification for a release would be much weaker if the taxpayer was properly notified originally of the annexation or if the taxpayer has been receiving city services since the annexation. A release seems most justified when the taxpayer received no notice, actual or implicit, of the fact that his or her property had been annexed by the city.

5. How many years of taxes can be released or refunded?

Different rules apply depending on whether the taxpayer seeks a refund of paid taxes or a release of unpaid taxes. Refunds are limited to the later of (1) five years from the tax's original due date and (2) six months from the date the taxes are paid. Releases of unpaid taxes may be granted at any time.

For example, assume that Carolina County improperly levies taxes for 2005–2009 on a boat that Tina Taxpayer keeps permanently moored in Ocean County. These taxes are illegal and justify relief under G.S. 105-381. If Tina has never paid the boat taxes to Carolina County, she can obtain a release of the taxes and interest at any time. She can ask for a release immediately upon discovering the mistake in 2010 or wait years to submit her request; either way, Tina will be entitled to a full release as long as the taxes have not been paid.

If Tina has been paying the Carolina County taxes punctually each year, then the refund rules apply. Tina can obtain a refund for all taxes that were originally due within five years of her refund request. Her 2005 taxes were due on September 1, 2005; as long as she requests a refund before September 2, 2010, she is entitled to a refund of the 2005 taxes and all subsequent taxes. If Tina submits her request after September 1, 2010, she cannot obtain a refund of the 2005 taxes.

The *six months from payment* provision will apply if Tina learns of the Carolina County taxes in 2010 and pays in full for the years 2005–2009 on June 1, 2010. In this case, six months from the date of payment (Dec. 1, 2010) will be later than five years from the tax's original due date (Sept. 1, 2010). Tina will, therefore, have until December 1, 2010, to request a refund of the 2005 taxes.

6. Must a local government pay interest on refunds?

No. Local governments are neither required nor permitted to pay interest on refunds that are approved by the governing board under G.S. 105-381. In contrast, interest must be paid on refunds on overpayments that result from rulings of county boards of equalization and review and the state Property Tax Commission. See Chapter 3 for more details on this issue.

7. If the governing board denies a request for a refund or release, does the taxpayer have the right to appeal that decision?

Yes. If the governing board denies the taxpayer's request or fails to act on the request within ninety days, the taxpayer has the right to bring a civil action in state court within three years.[18] The taxpayer must pay the disputed taxes before initiating a lawsuit if the request is for a release. If the taxpayer prevails, the taxing jurisdiction must refund the disputed taxes plus six percent interest, as well as all costs and attorneys' fees incurred by the taxpayer.

Note that the governing board of each taxing unit levying taxes on a particular property has the authority (and the responsibility) to rule on a refund and release request for the property independently of the decision on that request made by the governing board of any other taxing unit. For example, assume Parcel A sits in Blue Devil City, the largest municipality in Carolina County. Both Blue Devil City and Carolina County levy property taxes on Parcel A. If the owner of Parcel A requests a release of both city and county taxes on Parcel A for 2010, the governing board of the county and the governing board of the city must each act on that request. The Blue Devil City Council will not be bound by the decision of the Carolina County Commissioners or vice-versa. This independence exists even if the county collects property taxes for the city.

---

18. G.S. 105-381(c).

8. Does G.S. 105-381 govern the refund or release of other taxes or fees collected by a local government?

No. In addition to property taxes, local governments are authorized to levy a variety of taxes on activities ranging from owning a pet to selling alcohol to renting cars.[19] All of these taxes may be collected using Machinery Act remedies of attachment, garnishment, and levy.[20] However, none of the authorizing statutes for these various taxes specifically incorporates the Machinery Act refund and release provisions. Local governments are, therefore, free to develop their own refund and release policies for taxes other than property taxes or can choose to adopt the Machinery Act approach. Regardless of the chosen method, local governments would be wise to adopt formal refund and release policies for all of their various taxes in order to avoid controversy.

The same approach holds true for local government costs and fees that may be collected using Machinery Act enforced collection remedies for delinquent property taxes.[21] These include special assessments, public nuisance abatement costs, and solid waste fees.[22] Like the taxes discussed above, the authorizing statutes for these fees and costs do not specifically incorporate the Machinery Act refund and release provisions. As a result, local governments are free to craft their own refund and release provisions for most of the fees and costs they collect. The only exceptions are special assessments, which are governed by their own amendment procedures.[23]

---

19. See Chapter 15 for more details on local taxes beyond the property tax.

20. G.S. 153A-147 (counties) and G.S. 160A-207 (municipalities).

21. See Chapter 15 for more details on the levy and collection of local government costs and fees.

22. For special assessments for the cost of public works projects such as water and sewer system extensions, see G.S. 153A-195 (counties) and G.S. 160A-228 (municipalities). For mowing, trash collection, or other costs incurred abating public nuisances on private property, see G.S. 153A-140 (counties) and G.S. 160A-193 (municipalities). For solid waste fees included on property tax bills, see G.S. 153A-293 (counties) and G.S. 160A-314.1(b) (municipalities).

23. G.S. 153A-198 (counties) and G.S. 160A-231 (municipalities) permit special assessments to be modified only in cases of "irregularity, omission, error or lack of jurisdiction."

Mobile Homes

Chapter 13

Mobile Homes

Mobile homes—or manufactured homes, trailers, single-wides, or double-wides, as they are variously known—are constant problems for tax officials. These problems often arise during the listing process, because mobile homes can be reclassified from real property to personal property and back again. Problems also arise during the collection process, in part because mobile homes and their owners sometimes disappear from the taxing unit without notice. This chapter is intended to reduce the confusion related to this type of property for tax collectors and taxpayers alike.

Although the terms "manufactured home" and "mobile home" are often used interchangeably, they carry distinct technical meanings under the Machinery Act. "Mobile home" is defined as any type of structure that can be moved by attaching wheels to its frame and that is used as an office, dwelling, or similar "place of habitation."[1] A "manufactured home" is a mobile home that satisfies additional criteria: it must be at least 8 feet wide and 40 feet long when in "traveling mode," is 320 or more square feet when erected on site, is built on a permanent chassis, and is to be used as a dwelling.[2] Neither definition turns on whether the structure is a single- or double-wide.

All mobile homes—and therefore all manufactured homes—are subject to the moving permit requirement described in Question 3. But only manufactured homes—that is, mobile homes of a certain size that are to be used as residences and not offices—can be listed as real property, and only if they satisfy the requirements described in Question 1.

This chapter updates information published as *Property Tax Bulletin* No. 157 (Sept. 2010).

1. G.S. 105-316.7. Presumably, the only type of movable structure that would *not* constitute a mobile home would be one used for storage and not "habitation."

2. G.S. 105-273(13) adopts the definition of "manufactured home" used in G.S. 143-143.9(6), one of the statutes concerning manufactured home warranties.

1. Should manufactured homes be listed as real property or personal property?

It depends on the home's physical characteristics, use, and location. A manufactured home must be listed as real property if it satisfies the criteria included in G.S. 105-273(13), the Machinery Act's definition of real property:

a. it is a residential structure;
b. it has the moving hitch, wheels, and axles removed;
c. it is placed on a permanent foundation; and
d. it is sited on land owned by the owner of the manufactured home or on land in which the owner of the manufactured home has a leasehold interest with a term of at least twenty years and the lease provides for the disposition of the home upon the lease's termination.

The four requirements are presented in visual format in Figure 13A.

Before these requirements were clarified in 2001, many counties listed all double-wide manufactured homes as leasehold improvements, a type of real property, even if they did not satisfy all of the requirements in G.S. 105-273(13).[3] Since the 2001 changes, the fact that a manufactured home is a single-wide or a double-wide should have no bearing on whether it is listed as real or personal property. If all four requirements are met, the manufactured home must be listed as real property. If the manufactured home fails to meet even one of the requirements, it must be listed as personal property.

To be a residential structure, the manufactured home must be intended to be used as a place for someone to live, not just a place for someone to conduct business. The home need not be someone's permanent residence nor must it be the owner's residence. For example, a manufactured home owned by the owner of a mobile home park and rented to families on a monthly basis could qualify as real property. The fact that business might be conducted out of the home would not disqualify it so long as it was also used for residential purposes. For example, if Tom Tarheel lives in a manufactured home but also runs his landscaping business from the home, that home could still qualify as real property.

---

3. S.L. 2001-506 eliminated the requirement that a manufactured home be "multi-section" to qualify as real property and clarified that all manufactured homes that failed to satisfy all of the requirements in G.S. 105-273(13) must be listed as personal property.

Figure 13A. Classification of Manufactured Homes as Real or Personal Property (G.S. 105-273(13))

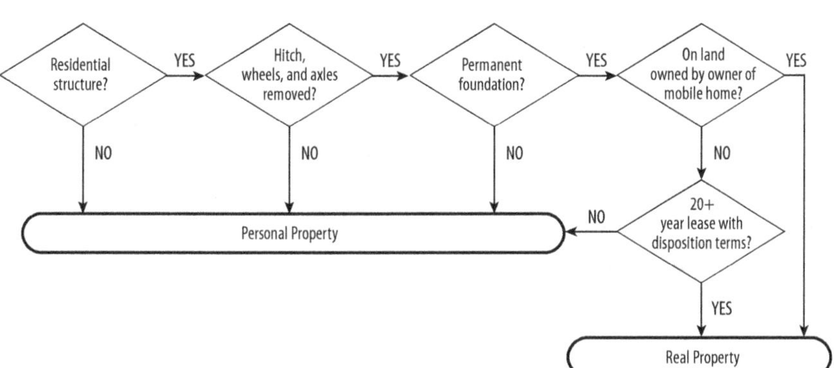

The requirement that the home's hitch, wheels, and axles be removed is self-explanatory. But the same cannot be said for the requirement that the home be on a "permanent foundation." Exactly what does this mean? The statute provides no explanation, but the Department of Revenue advises that, to be "permanent," a manufactured home's foundation must satisfy the applicable building code requirements, which can vary from county to county.[4] If the foundation has been inspected by the appropriate local government and found to satisfy the building code, then it is permanent. If not, the foundation is not permanent and the manufactured home that sits thereon is personal property, not real property.

The fourth requirement is the one that prevents many manufactured homes from being classified as real property. If the manufactured home sits on land not owned by the owner of the manufactured home, it cannot be listed as real property unless the homeowner has a long-term lease on the land. For example, if Wanda Wolfpack owns a manufactured home that sits on land she owns, the home must be listed as real property if it satisfies the other three requirements. If Wanda's home sits on land owned by her sister, Wilma Wolfpack, the home must be listed as personal property

---

4. Letter from John C. Bailey, director, Property Tax Division, N.C. Dept. of Revenue, to county assessors (Feb. 1, 2002), referencing building codes for manufactured homes issued by the N.C. Department of Insurance that require piers and footings, the depth of which can vary by county based on the frost line.

unless Wanda is leasing Wilma's land for a term of at least twenty years and the lease has specific provisions for what happens to the mobile home when the lease ends. If Wanda's home sits on land owned jointly by Wanda and Wilma, the home must be listed as real property if it satisfies the other three requirements. That Wanda owns a joint interest and not an exclusive interest in the property does not disqualify the home from having real property status. But if Wanda's home sits on land owned jointly by Wanda and her husband Walter as tenants by the entirety, the manufactured home could not be listed as real property absent a long-term lease because the owner of the home (Wanda) is different from the owner of the land (the marital couple of Wanda and Walter). Similarly, if Wanda's manufactured home sits on land owned by WW, Inc., a corporation of which Wanda is the only shareholder, the home could not be listed as real property without a long-term lease on the land because Wanda and her corporation are different taxpayers.

Record ownership of mobile homes should be based on documents filed with the N.C. Department of Motor Vehicles (DMV) or the county register of deeds. Mobile homes are titled and registered by the DMV unless and until they satisfy the Machinery Act's definition of real property.[5] Record ownership of a mobile home properly classified as personal property should be based on the DMV title and registration documents. Once a mobile home is properly classified as real property and no longer registered with the DMV, record ownership should be based on the recorded deeds for the land on which the home sits.

2. What remedies are available to collect taxes on mobile homes?

The remedies available depend in large part on whether the mobile home is classified as real or personal property.

---

5. All vehicles "intended to be operated on the highways of this state" must be registered with the DMV. G.S. 20-50. A mobile home with its hitch, wheels, and axles attached is considered a vehicle because it is a "device in, upon, or by which any person or property is or may be transported or drawn upon a highway." G.S. 20-4.01(49). The obligation to register a mobile home can be terminated by filing with the DMV form MVR-46G, an affidavit that the home now satisfies the real property requirements found in G.S. 105-273(13).

If the mobile home is properly classified as real property, the taxes on the mobile home are a lien upon the land on which the home sits. The collector may use the foreclosure remedy against the land as well as attachment, garnishment, and levy remedies against the responsible taxpayer's personal property. The responsible taxpayer for taxes on real property is the owner as of the delinquency date, which is January 6 of the fiscal year for which the taxes are levied, plus all subsequent owners.[6]

If the mobile home is properly classified as personal property, the tax collector will be limited to remedies against the responsible taxpayer's personal property. The responsible taxpayer for taxes on personal property is the owner of record on the listing date, which is the previous January 1.[7] If that listing taxpayer also owned real property in the taxing unit, then the tax collector could pursue foreclosure on that real property.[8]

For example, assume that Billy Blue Devil owns a manufactured home that sits on land owned by Suze Seahawk. The home must be listed as personal property in Billy's name and the taxes on the home will not be a lien on Suze's land. The tax collector could not pursue any collection remedies against Suze if the taxes on Billy's home become delinquent. Instead, the tax collector could pursue remedies against Billy's personal property such as a wage garnishment, a bank account attachment, or the seizure and sale of the mobile home or Billy's car. If Billy owned real property elsewhere in the county, the taxes on Billy's manufactured home would be a lien on that property and the tax collector could initiate a foreclosure action against it.

Assume Billy sells the mobile home to Suze in February 2011, when the 2010 taxes on the home are delinquent. Can the tax collector now proceed against Suze's property to collect the delinquent 2010 taxes on the mobile home? No. Billy remains the only responsible taxpayer for the 2010 taxes because he was the listing taxpayer. Billy will also be responsible for the 2011 taxes on the home, because as of January 1, 2011, the home was still properly classified as personal property and Billy was the listing owner. The home will finally be listed in Suze's name for 2012 taxes, assuming she still owns it as of January 1, 2012, when it should be listed as real property if it

---

6. G.S. 105-365.1(b)(1). For example, the delinquency date for 2011 real property taxes is January 6, 2012.

7. G.S. 105-365.1(b)(2).

8. Taxes on personal property are a lien on all real property owned by the same taxpayer in the same taxing unit. G.S. 105-355(a).

satisfies the three other requirements. If the 2012 taxes remain unpaid on January 6, 2013, while Suze still owns the land, then Suze will be personally responsible for those taxes. But Suze will never be responsible for the taxes from prior years.

3. When is a moving permit required?

To help with tax collection, the Machinery Act requires a person who wishes to move a mobile home to a different property to first obtain a moving permit from the tax collector.[9] If the mobile home is moved to a different site on the same property, no permit is required. But if the mobile home is moved to any other property, even property owned by the same taxpayer, a permit is required.

Manufacturers and retailers of mobile homes are exempt from the permit requirement, except when they are repossessing a previously sold home. (Repossession is discussed in more detail in Question 5.) Thus, when a newly purchased mobile home is moved by the retailer to the buyer's property, no moving permit is required. Also exempt from the moving permit requirement are licensed carriers, the trucking companies that actually transport the homes. Although not required to obtain permits themselves, these carriers are responsible for ensuring that the owners obtain the required permits and can be subject to criminal penalties if the owners fail to do so.[10]

4. What must an applicant do to obtain a moving permit?

An applicant must first do one of three things to obtain a moving permit:

- pay all property taxes due to be paid by the owner to the county, city, and special districts;
- provide proof that no taxes are due to be paid;
- demonstrate that the removal of the mobile home will not jeopardize the collection of any property taxes due or to become due.[11]

---

9. G.S. 105-316.1(a).
10. G.S. 105-316.1(b).
11. G.S. 105-316.2(a).

Read literally, the first requirement suggests that the only taxes at issue are those owed by the current owner of the mobile home. But this interpretation could allow buyers of mobile homes to obtain moving permits even if many years of taxes remain outstanding on those homes, clearly not the result intended by the Machinery Act or desired by tax collectors.

For example, assume that in February 2011 Mitch Mountaineer buys a mobile home from Fred Fortyniner. Fred owes 2010 taxes on the mobile home and on his boat. Mitch owns no real property and the only taxable personal property he owns is a car, on which no taxes are outstanding. If Mitch wants to move the mobile home, what taxes, if any, must he pay to obtain the necessary moving permit?

If the moving permit statutes were interpreted to require payment only of taxes owed by the current owner of the mobile home, then Mitch could obtain the permit without paying any additional taxes because, as of the date on which the permit is requested, Mitch is the current owner and owes no taxes. The mobile home is not listed in Mitch's name and will not be listed in his name until 2012, meaning as of February 2011 Fred is the responsible taxpayer for the taxes owed on the mobile home.[12]

Most tax collectors would instead require Mitch to pay both 2010 and 2011 taxes on the mobile home, despite the fact that the home was listed in Fred's name for those years. And many tax collectors would require Mitch also to pay the taxes on Fred's boat, because the statute refers to "*all* taxes due to be paid" by the (presumably former) owner.

Also subject to varying interpretations is the option of demonstrating that the removal of the mobile home will not "jeopardize" the collection of outstanding property taxes. The statute provides no guidance as to when or how a tax collector can make this determination. Most tax collectors err on the side of caution and very rarely, if ever, conclude that removal of a mobile home creates no risk to tax collection.

After paying the taxes, proving that the taxes have been paid, or demonstrating that the removal will not affect the collection of taxes, the applicant must provide his or her name and address, the addresses from which and to which the mobile home is to be moved, and the name and address of the carrier who will transport the home.[13]

---

12. G.S. 105-365.1(b)(2).
13. G.S. 105-316.2(b).

5. What are the moving permit requirements when a mobile home is repossessed?

A North Carolina resident taking possession of a mobile home through the enforcement of a lien on that home and planning to move the home to another location in North Carolina can obtain a moving permit without initially paying any taxes.[14] The repossessing party must notify the tax collector of the intent to move the home when applying for the required permit and within seven days must pay all taxes due on the mobile home itself. The repossessing party is not required to pay any other taxes owed by the mobile home's former owner. If the repossessing party is not a resident of North Carolina, the party is subject to the same obligations described in Question 4 and must pay the taxes prior to obtaining a permit. The same applies to North Carolina repossessors who intend to move the mobile home out of state.

6. How can the tax collector enforce the moving permit requirement?

Not very well, unfortunately. The moving permit statutes do not make a party who moves a mobile home without a moving permit personally liable for the taxes owed on the mobile home. Nor do they make a repossessor liable for the unpaid taxes if it fails to pay them within seven days of the move. As a result, tax collectors may not use Machinery Act collection remedies against new owners or repossessors based solely on their failure to obtain a permit. The statutes do provide for criminal misdemeanor liability for parties that fail to satisfy the moving permit requirements, but it is unclear if anyone has ever been prosecuted for a moving permit violation anywhere in the state.[15] Even if a local district attorney is willing to attempt such a prosecution, the penalties are extremely light: the harshest sentence a first-time offender can receive is a ten-day suspended jail sentence and a $200 fine.[16]

---

14. G.S. 105-316.4. This exception applies whether the repossessor is acting in reliance on a court order or on the terms of a financing agreement.

15. G.S. 105-316.6 makes it a Class 3 misdemeanor to move a mobile home without a permit.

16. G.S. 15A-1340.23.

The most frequent violators of the moving permit requirement are mobile home retailers and financing companies that repossess and move homes on which they have liens without providing notice or payment of outstanding taxes. Often these companies do not have offices in the taxing unit, making it extremely difficult for tax collectors to enforce the companies' Machinery Act obligations. Regardless, it is good practice for tax collectors to seek out these companies and remind them of the criminal sanctions they could face for violating the moving permit requirement.

Chapter 14

Registered Motor Vehicles

Since Article 22A was added to the Machinery Act in 1993, the assessment and collection of property taxes on registered motor vehicles has been governed by very different rules from those that apply to taxes on real property and other types of personal property.[1] This chapter examines these rules in detail, employing a question-and-answer format. A table summarizing the rules also is provided.

In 2005 the General Assembly enacted House Bill (H.B.) 1779, which once again dramatically changed the motor vehicle tax assessment and collection process.[2] H.B. 1779 was originally scheduled to take effect in 2009 but has been delayed repeatedly by substantive changes to the law and by concerns over development of the necessary computer software.[3] As of this writing, it remains unclear when or if the proposed changes will become effective. For that reason, this chapter focuses primarily on the property tax provisions for registered motor vehicles that were effective for the 2010–2011 tax year. The last section offers a brief overview of how the process would work if H.B. 1779 becomes effective.

This chapter updates information published as *Property Tax Bulletin* No. 160 (Dec. 2010).

1. Article 22A of the North Carolina General Statutes, which contains the special provisions for the taxation of motor vehicles, was added to G.S. Chapter 105 effective 1993 by 1991 N.C. Sess. Laws ch. 624.

2. S.L. 2005-294.

3. See, e.g., S.L. 2008-134, S.L. 2009-445, and S.B. 1177 (2009), repeatedly extending the effective date of H.B. 1779. Several members of the General Assembly have introduced bills that would repeal H.B. 1779 entirely and keep the current taxation system for registered motor vehicles in place. See, e.g., H.B. 1434 (2009).

1. What vehicles are subject to Article 22A?

Article 22A of the Machinery Act applies only to classified motor vehicles. For both property tax and Division of Motor Vehicles (DMV) purposes, a motor vehicle is (i) a self-propelled vehicle or (ii) a vehicle that is designed to be run upon the highways which is pulled by a self-propelled vehicle.[4] The term specifically excludes mopeds but otherwise includes all cars, trucks, motorcycles, golf carts, and trailers.

The Machinery Act considers all motor vehicles *classified* except these four categories: (i) vehicles exempt from the registration requirement, such as farm equipment; (ii) manufactured homes and mobile offices or classrooms; (iii) trailers registered on a multiyear basis; and (iv) vehicles owned or leased by public service companies.[5] If a motor vehicle is not classified, it is not covered by Article 22A and should be taxed as "regular" personal property.[6]

The bulk of Article 22A concerns *registered* classified motor vehicles (RMVs), meaning those that have been registered with the DMV to operate upon the state's highways.[7] These registrations must be renewed annually.[8] A few types of vehicles must be registered annually each January 1.[9] But the

---

4. In G.S. 105-330(2), the Machinery Act adopts the definition of motor vehicle used in G.S. 20-4.01(23), from the chapter that creates the Division of Motor Vehicles and establishes procedures for registration, driver's licenses, and the like.

5. G.S. 105-330.1.

6. G.S. 105-275(16) exempts from taxation most nonbusiness personal property, including household furnishings, clothing, pets, and lawn equipment. However, this exclusion does not include motor vehicles, mobile homes, planes, and boats, meaning these types of personal property are taxable.

7. G.S. 20-50(a). G.S. 20-51 provides a list of vehicles that are exempt from the registration requirement, including farm equipment, cars owned by the federal government, and motorized wheelchairs. These vehicles are not classified by the Machinery Act and therefore not subject to Article 22A's special tax provisions.

8. G.S. 20-66.

9. The following types of owners and vehicles operate under the "annual" registration system that requires renewals every January 1: Civil Air Patrol members, Consular Corps members, N.C. district attorneys, N.C. House members, N.C. senators, judges and magistrates, clerks of superior court, National Guard members, state government vehicles, registers of deeds, sheriffs and retired sheriffs, U.S. House members, U.S. senators, U.S. attorneys, and U.S. marshals. See N.C. Department of Transportation, Division of Motor Vehicles, "Frequently Asked Questions for Staggered Renewals,"

vast majority of vehicles are registered on a staggered basis throughout the calendar year. As discussed in detail below, property taxes on a registered classified motor vehicle are tied to the vehicle's registration date, which could fall in any month of the year. As a result, there are no fixed dates on which property taxes on RMVs become due or delinquent as there are for property taxes on real property and other types of personal property. Table 14.1 summarizes these floating dates and deadlines for property taxes on RMVs.

Only two of the special tax provisions in Article 22A apply to *unregistered* classified motor vehicles: the notice requirement discussed in Question 2, below, and the appeal process discussed in Question 7. Outside of those two issues, unregistered classified motor vehicles should be listed, assessed, and taxed as is other taxable personal property such as boats and planes.[10]

For example, assume Wanda Wolfpack owns two cars, a Honda Civic and a Ford Explorer. To save money, Wanda decides she will drive only the Civic for the coming year and lets the registration on the Explorer expire in November 2010. Wanda should list the unregistered Explorer as taxable personal property for 2011 taxes during the January 2011 listing period. Those taxes will be due on September 1, 2011, and delinquent on January 6, 2012, just like property taxes on Wanda's real property and other taxable personal property.

2. What are the special tax notice requirements for classified motor vehicles?

For most property taxes, the Machinery Act does not require any type of tax notice or tax bill.[11] For taxes on classified motor vehicles, both registered and unregistered, the assessor is required to provide tax notices that include the appraised value of the vehicle, the tax rate of the tax units included on the notice, and a statement informing taxpayers that appeals of the appraised

---

available at www.ncdot.org/dmv/vehicle_services/registrationtitling/faq.html#faq11 (last visited June 14, 2010).

10. See note 6.

11. G.S. 105-348 puts all taxpayers on notice of the taxes owed on their property regardless of whether they receive tax bills.

Table 14.1. Controlling Dates for the Assessment and Collection of Taxes on Registered Motor Vehicles (RMVs)

New Registrations	Value G.S. 105-330.2(a)	Tax Rate G.S. 105-330.5(a)	Tax Year G.S. 105-330.6(a)	Levy Year G.S. 105-330.5(d)
Staggered Registrations	January 1 of the year taxes are due	Rate in effect first day of month in which registration applied for	Begins first day of first month that follows the date the new registration is applied for Ends on the last day of the month in which new registration expires	Included in levy for fiscal year in which taxes become due unless tax notice is prepared after due date—then include taxes in levy for current fiscal year
Annual Registrations			Begins first day of first month following the date new registration applied for and ends Dec. 31	

Renewed Registrations	Value G.S. 105-330.2(a)	Tax Rate G.S. 105-330.5(a)	Tax Year G.S. 105-330.6(a)	Levy Year G.S. 105-330.5(d)
Staggered Registrations	January 1 of the year taxes are due	Rate in effect first day of month in which former registration expired	Begins first day of first month following date registration expires Ends on the last day of the month in which the current registration expires	Included in levy for fiscal year in which taxes become due *UNLESS tax notice is prepared after due date—then include taxes in levy for current fiscal year*
Annual Registrations			Begins first day of first month following the date the registration expires Ends Dec. 31	

Note: The bulk of this table was originally compiled by my School of Government colleague Shea Riggsbee Denning.

Ownership, Situs, Taxability G.S. 105-330.2(a)	Due Date G.S. 105-330.4(a)	Interest G.S. 105-330.4(b)	Block Date G.S. 105-330.7
Date registration applied for	First day of fourth month following last day of month in which new registration applied for	5% accrues first month following date taxes due *UNLESS notice prepared after due date—then 5% accrues the first day of the second month after notice* .75% each month thereafter	Tenth day of fourth month after month taxes become due

Ownership, Situs, Taxability G.S. 105-330.2(a)	Due Date G.S. 105-330.4(a)	Interest G.S. 105-330.4(b)	Block Date G.S. 105-330.7
Date of renewal (even if renewed after license expires)	First day of fourth month following date former registration expires	5% accrues first month following date taxes due *UNLESS notice prepared after due date—then 5% accrues the first day of the second month after notice* .75% each month thereafter	Tenth day of fourth month after month taxes become due
	May 1 following date former registration expires		

value must be filed with the assessor within thirty days of the date of the notice.[12] This notice must also include all county and special district taxes. It may also include municipal taxes, depending on whether the vehicle is registered or unregistered.

For registered vehicles, the notice must include municipal taxes even if the county does not normally collect municipal property taxes.[13] The county may retain up to 1.5 percent of all taxes on registered motor vehicles that it collects on behalf of municipalities and special districts.[14]

For unregistered vehicles, the assessor's notice should not include municipal taxes unless the county normally collects municipal taxes under an interlocal agreement. In such cases, the collection fee that the county charges the municipality for the collection of taxes on unregistered motor vehicles is governed by the terms of the agreement and not by the statutory 1.5 percent fee that applies to the collection of municipal taxes on registered motor vehicles.

3. What are municipal privilege taxes on motor vehicles and how are they collected?

All municipalities are authorized to levy taxes on the privilege of operating a motor vehicle within their borders of up to $5 per vehicle, plus an additional $5 per vehicle if the municipality operates a public transportation system.[15]

---

12. G.S. 105-330.5(a) and (c).

13. G.S. 105-330.5(a).

14. G.S. 105-330.5(b).

15. G.S. 20-97(b) and (c). At least one county (Caswell) has received local authority to levy these taxes as well. See S.L. 1979-450 and S.L. 1987-334. The statute incorporates the definition of "public transportation system" provided by G.S. 105-550(5): "Any combination of real and personal property established for purposes of public transportation. The systems may include one or more of the following: structures, improvements, buildings, equipment, vehicle parking or passenger transfer facilities, railroads and railroad rights-of-way, rights-of-way, bus services, shared-ride services, high-occupancy vehicle facilities, carpool and vanpool programs, voucher programs, telecommunications and information systems, integrated fare systems, bus lanes, and busways. The term does not include, however, streets, roads, or highways except to the extent they are dedicated to public transportation vehicles or to the extent they are necessary for access to vehicle parking or passenger transfer facilities." This is

The General Assembly has granted a number of municipalities the authority to levy additional motor vehicle privilege taxes, but in no case may these exceed $30 per vehicle.[16]

Assessors generally treat municipal privilege taxes on motor vehicles the same as municipal property taxes for both tax notice and collection purposes.[17] This occurs despite the fact that Article 22A and the rest of the Machinery Act technically cover only property taxes and not privilege taxes.[18]

4. What are county vehicle registration taxes and how are they collected?

In 2009, the General Assembly granted counties the authority to levy a registration tax of up to $7 per year.[19] However, this tax is permitted only if the county or one of the local governments in the county operates a public

---

nearly identical to the definition of "public transportation system" provided in G.S. 105-506.1 that is the basis for the county vehicle registration taxes discussed in the next question.

16. See, e.g., S.L. 2007-108, authorizing the towns of Apex and Morrisville to levy privilege taxes of up to $15 per vehicle. G.S. 20-97(c) limits the total amount of municipal privilege taxes on motor vehicles, including those authorized by local bills, to $30.

17. Although municipal privilege license taxes are included on the tax notice for motor vehicles, the option to block the taxpayer's registration does not exist for delinquent municipal privilege taxes. That remedy can be used only for delinquent property taxes on motor vehicles. See Question 12 for more on this remedy. For a detailed discussion of the collection remedies for privilege license taxes, see Chapter 15.

18. G.S. 105-273(15) defines "taxes" for the purposes of the Machinery Act as "the principal amount of any property tax or dog license tax and costs, penalties, and interest." Noticeably absent from that definition are privilege license taxes on motor vehicles.

19. G.S. 105-570, effective August 27, 2009, as per S.L. 2009-527, sec. 7.

transportation system.[20] The tax proceeds may be used solely for the creation or operation of a public transportation system.[21]

Unlike a municipal privilege tax discussed in the previous question, a county registration tax is collected by the DMV when the motor vehicle is registered. The county has no collection responsibilities for the tax.

After receiving the tax proceeds from the DMV, the county must distribute the funds pro rata to itself, if it operates a public transportation system, and to each local government in the county that operates a public transportation system. If the county does not operate a public transportation system, then the county does not keep any of the tax proceeds. Similarly, if a particular local government does not operate a public transportation system, then that local government does not receive any of the tax proceeds.

The pro rata distribution to those governments operating public transportation systems is based on population. For the county, it is based only on the portion of the county's population that resides in the unincorporated areas of the county. For a municipality, it is based only on the portion of the municipality's population that resides in the county that levied the tax.

---

20. G.S. 105-570(b). The statute incorporates the definition of "public transportation system" provided in G.S. 105-506.1(3), which is nearly identical to the definition in G.S. 105-550 that is referenced in the municipal motor vehicle privilege tax provision. *See supra* note 15. G.S. 105-506.1(3) defines "public transportation system" as "[a]ny combination of real and personal property established for purposes of public transportation. The systems may include one or more of the following: structures, improvements, buildings, equipment, vehicle parking or passenger transfer facilities, railroads and railroad rights-of-way, rights-of-way, bus services, shared-ride services, high-occupancy vehicle facilities, car-pool and vanpool programs, voucher programs, telecommunications and information systems, integrated fare systems, *and the interconnected bicycle and pedestrian infrastructure that supports public transportation,* bus lanes, and busways. The term does not include, however, streets, roads, or highways except to the extent they are dedicated to public transportation vehicles or to the extent they are necessary for access to vehicle parking or passenger transfer facilities" (emphasis added). The italicized words are the only difference between this definition and that provided in G.S. 105-550.

21. G.S. 105-570(d).

5. When must the assessor create tax notices for motor vehicles?

Tax notices for unregistered motor vehicles that are listed by the taxpayer directly with the assessor must be prepared by September 1.[22] Tax notices for registered motor vehicles cannot be prepared until the DMV informs the assessor that a motor vehicle registration has been applied for or renewed. For registered motor vehicles on the staggered system, the DMV should provide this information by the tenth day of the second month after registration or renewal.[23] For example, in December the assessor will be notified of registrations that were renewed or applied for in October.

Occasionally registration information is sent to the wrong county or a similar mistake is made, resulting in delayed notification to the assessor and therefore a delayed tax notice. As discussed in Question 10, a delayed tax notice can affect the tax's delinquency date.

6. When are ownership, situs, and taxability of RMVs determined?

The ownership, situs, and taxability of RMVs are determined as of the date on which a new registration is applied for or on which an existing registration is renewed.[24] Taxpayers who wish to contest these decisions may do so through the release and refund process in G.S. 105-381.

7. When is the value of a motor vehicle determined and how can it be appealed?

The assessor must value RMVs for tax purposes as of January 1 of the year in which the property taxes become due.[25] (See Question 10 for details on the due date for taxes on RMVs.) Unregistered motor vehicles are valued for tax purposes as of January 1 of the year in which the property is listed, the same date that real property and other taxable personal property is valued.[26]

---

22. G.S. 105-330.5(c).

23. G.S. 20-50.3. For the few types of vehicles on the fixed calendar year registration process, the DMV informs assessors of new or renewed registrations by March 10.

24. G.S. 105-330.2(a).

25. *Id.*

26. *Id.*

Owners of both registered and unregistered motor vehicles must appeal the assessed value of their vehicles within thirty days of the date of the required tax notice described in Question 2.[27] The assessor's office must process motor vehicle valuation appeals in the same way it processes discovery appeals.[28] The assessor should first arrange an informal conference with the taxpayer to discuss the matter and then give the taxpayer notice of the assessor's final decision within fifteen days of that conference (or fifteen days from when the taxpayer provides any additional information requested or promised at that conference).[29] The taxpayer then has fifteen days from that final notice to appeal the assessor's valuation to the board of equalization and review, if that board is still in session, or to the board of county commissioners.[30] If the taxpayer is unhappy with the decision by either of those boards, the taxpayer can appeal the valuation to the state Property Tax Commission and then to the state appellate courts.

Taxpayers appealing the value of their vehicles must still pay the taxes on the vehicles when due.[31] If the taxpayer wins the appeal, the tax office must refund the excess taxes paid plus interest. This requirement is unique to motor vehicle valuation appeals.[32]

8. What is the tax year for RMVs?

The tax year for an RMV begins on the first day of the month following the date on which either (i) a new registration is applied for or (ii) an existing registration expires.[33] The tax year runs for the twelve-month registration period.

---

27. G.S. 330.2(b).

28. G.S. 105-330.2(b) requires that appeals of classified motor vehicle valuations proceed "in the manner provided by G.S. 105-312(d) for appeals in the case of discovered property." That said, the power to compromise discovery bills created by G.S. 105-312(k) does *not* apply to motor vehicle tax bills.

29. G.S. 105-312(d).

30. *Id.*

31. G.S. 105-330.2(b).

32. In contrast, taxpayers who appeal the value of their real property or other types of personal property are not required to pay the taxes on the property in question and are not subject to enforced collection remedies while their appeals are pending. G.S. 105-378(d).

33. G.S. 105-330.6(a).

For example, assume that the registration on Fred Fortyniner's Volvo expires in July 2010. His motor vehicle tax year will run from August 2010 to July 2011 regardless of when he actually renews the registration. If Fred chooses not to renew the registration, then he must list the Volvo as personal property in January 2011 for 2011 property taxes, and the tax year will be the same as that for all other personal property taxes—July 2011 through June 2012.

If an unregistered vehicle is listed for "regular" taxation in January but is later registered with the DMV, it should still be taxed as regular personal property for the full tax year.[34] Continuing with the example above, assume that Fred's Volvo is unregistered as of January 2011 and he lists it for "regular" taxation. If Fred changes his mind and registers his Volvo in May 2011, the car should still be taxed as "regular" personal property for the 2011–2012 fiscal year. The registered motor vehicle tax bill triggered by the May 2011 registration should be disregarded by the tax office. Fred would not list the Volvo for "regular" taxation in January 2012, however, because at that point the car would be registered. When the registration expires in May 2012, the Volvo will then be switched back to the registered motor vehicle tax process and will be subject to a tax year of June 2012 to May 2013. Fred would be entitled to a prorated tax credit, in the form of a release, for the taxes owed on the Volvo for its new tax year. The credit would be for one-twelfth of the 2011–2012 taxes he paid on the unregistered Volvo and would be applied to the new tax bill on the registered Volvo. Otherwise, Fred would be double-taxed for June 2012.[35] See Question 13 for details about prorated tax refunds.

9. What tax rate applies to RMVs?

RMVs are subject to the property tax rate in effect for all other property in the taxing unit on the first day of the month in which a new registration is applied for or in which the old registration expires.[36] For example, assume that the registration for Donald Duke's Toyota Camry expires on June 30, 2011. Regardless of when Donald renews his registration, the tax rate applicable to his Camry will be the rate in place for all other property

---

34. G.S. 105-330.3(a)(2).
35. G.S. 105-330.6(a1).
36. G.S. 105-330.5(a).

in the county as of June 1, 2011—meaning the property tax rate set by the county as of July 1, 2010. Although Donald's tax year will coincide with the 2011–2012 fiscal year, he will be assessed taxes on the Camry based on the rate applicable during the 2010–2011 fiscal year.

10. When are taxes on RMVs due and delinquent?

Taxes on RMVs are due on the first day of the fourth month following the month in which the old registration expired or a new registration is applied for.[37] As is true for all property taxes, the due date for RMV taxes serves as the end date for early-payment discounts[38] and the start date for the five-year limitation on refunds[39] and the ten-year statute of limitations on enforced collections.[40] However, the due date has added significance for property taxes on RMVs.

The due date determines when the RMV will be valued for tax purposes, because the assessor must value the RMV as of January 1 in the calendar year the taxes become due.[41] The due date also determines the levy in which the taxes will be included for the purposes of the tax collector's annual settlement. Assuming that the required tax notice is prepared before the due date, RMV taxes are included in the levy for the fiscal year in which the taxes become due.[42] If the notice is prepared after the due date, then the taxes are included in the levy for the fiscal year in which the notice is prepared.

Finally, the due date determines the date on which interest begins to accrue and enforced collection remedies may begin.[43] If the tax notice is prepared prior to the due date, then interest begins on the first day of the first month after the due date.[44] If the tax notice is prepared after the due date, then interest begins on the first day of the second month after the notice is prepared.[45] Interest on delinquent RMV taxes is greater than that for other

---

37. G.S. 105-330.4(a)(1).
38. G.S. 105-360(c).
39. G.S. 105-381(a)(3).
40. G.S. 105-378(a).
41. G.S. 105-330.2(a).
42. G.S. 105-330.5(d).
43. G.S. 105-365.1(a)(1), -330.4(c).
44. G.S. 105-330.4(b).
45. *Id.*

delinquent property taxes: taxes on RMVs accrue interest of 5 percent the first month, then .75 percent each month thereafter.[46]

Note that the interest provision for RMV taxes expressly incorporates the weekend-and-holiday rule[47] and the postmark rule applicable to interest that accrues on non-RMV taxes.[48] The weekend-and-holiday rule requires that taxpayers be given until the next business day to meet a deadline when such deadline falls on a weekend or holiday. For example, assume that Wanda Wolfpack's RMV taxes are to accrue interest beginning on September 1 but that September 1 falls on a Sunday. Because Wanda's deadline to pay the RMV taxes without interest falls on a Saturday (Aug. 31), the weekend-and-holiday rule would move that deadline to Monday, September 2. Interest would not begin to accrue on Wanda's RMV taxes until Tuesday, September 3. The postmark rule that applies to non-RMV taxes paid by mail apparently also applies to RMV taxes. If Wanda mails her RMV tax payment on Friday, August 30, and the payment is postmarked that same day, her RMV taxes will not accrue interest regardless of when the payment is received by the tax office.

Here is an example of how these rules are applied. Assume that Tom Tarheel registers his new Chevy pickup truck in November 2010 and that Tom's tax notice is prepared by the due date. The applicable property tax dates would be as follows:

Registration Date:	November 12, 2010
Ownership, Situs, and Taxability Date:	November 12, 2010
Valuation Date:	January 1, 2011
Tax Year:	December 2010 to November 2011
Tax Rate:	Rate in effect for the 2010–2011 fiscal year
Due Date:	March 1, 2011
Interest Begins:	April 1, 2011
Tax Levy:	2010–2011 fiscal year

46. *Id.*
47. G.S. 105-395.1.
48. G.S. 105-360(d) and G.S. 105-330.4(d).

Now assume that the DMV initially sends Tom's registration information to the wrong county, which delays Tom's tax notice until July 15, 2011, well after the due date. This delay would change both the interest date and the tax levy in which Tom's taxes will be included:

Registration Date:	November 12, 2010
Ownership, Situs, and Taxability Date:	November 12, 2010
Valuation Date:	January 1, 2011
Tax Year:	December 2010 to November 2011
Tax Rate:	Rate in effect for the 2010–2011 fiscal year
Due Date:	March 1, 2011
Interest Begins:	September 1, 2011
Tax Levy:	2011–2012 fiscal year

11. What enforced collection remedies are available for taxes on RMVs, when can they begin, and against whom can they be used?

Taxes on RMVs can be collected using attachment and garnishment of intangible property such as bank accounts and wages[49] or by levy and sale of any personal property owned by the responsible taxpayer, including but not limited to the vehicle that generated the delinquent taxes.[50] As discussed in the next question, a tax collector also may ask the DMV to block the taxpayer from renewing the registration for a vehicle on which property taxes are outstanding. Unlike taxes on other types of personal property, taxes on RMVs are not a lien on real property owned by the same taxpayer.[51] As a result, foreclosure on real property is never an option to collect taxes on RMVs.

As with other property taxes, enforced collections of taxes on RMVs can begin on the delinquency date, which is the date on which they accrue

---

49. G.S. 105-368.
50. G.S. 105-366 and -367.
51. G.S. 105-330.4(c).

interest.[52] Enforced collection remedies can be aimed only at the taxpayer who was the owner of record as of the date on which a new registration is applied for or on which an existing registration is renewed.[53]

Here is how these rules work in practice. Assume that Dave Deacon registers a Cadillac Escalade on May 15, 2010. In June 2010, he sells the Escalade to Peter Pirate. On October 1, 2010, the unpaid property taxes on the Escalade become delinquent and start accruing interest. Dave is the only responsible taxpayer for the delinquent taxes, despite the fact that he sold the vehicle to Peter before the taxes were due, much less delinquent. The tax collector may seize and levy any property owned by Dave or may attach Dave's bank account or wages. The tax collector may not seize and sell the Escalade or any other personal property owned by Peter, nor may the collector foreclose on anyone's real property.

12. When can the tax collector put a block on the taxpayer's motor vehicle registration?

This remedy, unique to RMV taxes, can be requested on the tenth day of the fourth month after taxes become due.[54] Unlike the interest date, the block date does not change even if the tax notice is prepared late.

For example, assume the registration on Billy Blue Devil's Mazda Miata expires in January 2010 and he renews the registration the next month. Regardless of when the tax notice is prepared, Billy's taxes will be due on May 1, 2010. If Billy fails to pay the taxes, the tax collector will be able to request that the DMV place a block on his registration on September 10, 2010. But that block will not affect Billy until he needs to renew his registration again in early 2011, nine months after the taxes were due. This disconnect between the tax dates and the registration dates is one reason the General Assembly has proposed an overhaul of the entire process.

---

52. G.S. 105-365.1(a)(1), -330.4(c). In certain circumstances, enforced collection remedies may begin before the delinquency date. See G.S. 105-366(c) and (d) and Chapter 6.

53. G.S. 105-365.1(b)(3).

54. G.S. 105-330.7. This date will also always be the tenth day of the eighth month after an existing registration expired or a new registration is applied for.

At present, the authority to block a registration extends only to the motor vehicle on which the taxes are owed.[55] A block cannot be used for taxes owed on other property or for outstanding municipal privilege license taxes on an RMV. For example, if Billy Blue Devil owns a Nissan Pathfinder in addition to his Mazda Miata, the fact that Billy is delinquent on his Miata taxes cannot affect the registration of his Pathfinder, or vice-versa. The Pathfinder could be levied upon and sold to satisfy taxes on the Miata, but its registration could not be blocked on account of those taxes.[56]

13. What happens if the taxpayer sells an RMV in the middle of the tax year?

A taxpayer who sells a registered motor vehicle in the middle of its tax year has two taxation options: (i) surrender the license plates from the sold vehicle and receive a prorated tax release or refund for the months remaining on the sold vehicle's tax year or (ii) transfer the license plates from the sold vehicle to a different vehicle and not pay taxes on the second vehicle until the existing registration expires.

Under the first option, the taxpayer can obtain a partial tax release or refund by surrendering the license plates to the DMV and presenting two documents to the county tax office: (i) a form FS20, the receipt provided by the DMV for the surrendered license plates, and (ii) a bill of sale or other proof of ownership transfer.[57] These documents must be provided to the county tax office within one year of the date on the form FS20. The tax collector must then determine the number of full months remaining in the

---

55. G.S. 20-50.4(a). However, if the new registered motor vehicle property tax system described in Question 14 becomes reality, then a new version of G.S. 20-50.4 will become effective and permit the DMV to deny registration for the failure to pay municipal vehicle fees.

56. G.S. 105-366 and -330.4(c) permit the tax collector to levy upon and sell any tangible personal property of a taxpayer personally responsible for delinquent property taxes.

57. G.S. 105-330.6(c). A prorated refund is also available to a taxpayer who moves out of North Carolina and registers a vehicle in another state. In that situation, the taxpayer must provide a form FS20 and proof that the vehicle has been registered in another state.

vehicle's tax year after the date on the form FS20 and provide a prorated tax release or refund for those months.

For example, assume Suze Seahawk owns a Ford Focus with a tax year that runs from September 2010 to August 2011. She pays her motor vehicles taxes of $100 in November 2010. If Suze sells the Focus in January 2011, surrenders her plates to the DMV in February 2011, and provides a form FS20 and proof of sale to the tax office in March 2011, she will be entitled to a partial refund of the taxes she paid on the Focus. The refund will be $50, representing the six full months (March to August) remaining in the tax year for the Focus after she surrendered her plates in February. Note that the proration is based on the date of the form FS20, not the date of sale or the date on which the taxpayer requests the refund.

Under the second option, a taxpayer may transfer the license plates from a sold vehicle to a newly purchased vehicle. In that situation, the newly purchased vehicle will not be listed or taxed until the registration from the sold vehicle expires and the owner renews the plates on the newly purchased car.[58]

Consider the Suze Seahawk example again, but assume that instead of surrendering the license plates from the Ford Focus after she sells that car she transfers those plates to a newly purchased Dodge Ram pickup truck. Suze will not be required to register or pay taxes on her new pickup truck until the registration for the Ford Focus expires in August 2011. She will be taxed on the value of her new pickup truck when she registers it for September 2011 through August 2012.

14. How will the taxation of RMVs change if H.B. 1779 takes effect?

Quite a bit. H.B. 1779 would fully integrate the registration and taxation of RMVs so that taxes must be paid at the time of vehicle registration. Doing this would eliminate the existing lag time between the registration of a vehicle and the billing of taxes on that vehicle. It would also eliminate the long delay before a registration block affects a taxpayer under the existing system.

------

58. G.S. 105-330.6(b).

Under the future system, the Property Tax Division of the Department of Revenue (DOR) would be responsible for creating combined registration and tax notices for all RMVs. The DOR would be responsible for valuing all motor vehicles based on statewide valuation standards it develops. Assessors would assist the DOR by providing tax rates for all taxing units in their counties as well as mileage and condition information on individual vehicles when available.

Local government tax collectors would no longer be responsible for collecting taxes on RMVs because both taxes and registration fees would be collected at the time of registration or renewal by the DMV or its agents. If an owner refuses to pay taxes on a vehicle, the DMV will not register that vehicle or renew an existing registration for that vehicle. Exceptions would apply for automobile dealers, where new car buyers would be able to obtain two-month registrations on newly purchased vehicles without paying the property taxes on those vehicles. Once the new owner paid the taxes owed on the newly sold vehicles, the limited registrations would become valid for the entire year.

Chapter 15

Collecting Other Taxes and Fees

Collecting Other Taxes and Fees

For decades, most local tax collectors were responsible for a single revenue source, the property tax. Today, county and municipal tax collectors oversee multiple revenue sources with varied collection remedies. This chapter provides two quick-reference tables summarizing the unique collection features of the most common local taxes, costs, and fees followed by a detailed examination of each. It concludes with a discussion of a local government's authority to refund or release these taxes, costs, and fees.

Local Government Revenue Sources beyond the Property Tax

Counties and municipalities receive the majority of their revenues from sources other than the property tax.[1] This chapter focuses on twelve revenue streams that local governments collect directly.[2] Seven revenue streams are tax-based:

This chapter updates information published as *Property Tax Bulletin* No. 162 (Feb. 2011).

1. Property taxes account for 40 percent of county revenue and 20 percent of municipal revenue. The North Carolina Department of State Treasurer provides this data at www.nctreasurer.com/lgc/units/D_AG.htm (municipalities) and www.nctreasurer.com/lgc/units/D_E.htm (counties) (each last visited January 25, 2010).

2. This chapter excludes other major revenue sources for local governments that are collected by the state, such as sales and use taxes. For a detailed analysis of those taxes, see Kara A. Millonzi and William C. Rivenbark, "Phased Implementation of the 2007 and 2008 Medicaid Funding Reform Legislation in North Carolina," *Local Finance Bulletin* No. 38 (Sept. 2008), www.sog.unc.edu/pubs/electronicversions/pdfs/lfb38.pdf. Also excluded are taxes and fees collected before a service is provided, such as county land transfer taxes that must be paid before a deed is recorded by the register of deeds, because enforced collection efforts generally are not needed.

1. privilege license taxes
2. occupancy taxes
3. animal taxes
4. prepared food or meal taxes
5. beer and wine license taxes
6. motor vehicle and heavy equipment rental gross receipts taxes
7. municipal motor vehicle and taxicab taxes.

Fees and costs create the other five revenue streams:

1. solid waste, water, sewer, and stormwater service fees[3]
2. ambulance service fees
3. special assessments
4. nuisance abatement costs
5. minimum housing standards enforcement costs.

Table 15.1 and Table 15.2 summarize the important collection features of each tax, cost, and fee covered herein. A few explanatory notes may help to interpret this information.

Statutory Liens on Real Property

A *lien* is the right of a creditor to satisfy an obligation from the property of the debtor.[4] Liens allow a creditor to seize and sell a debtor's property to satisfy an obligation owed to the creditor. A creditor typically obtains a lien through a contract, such as a financing agreement between a lender and a homebuyer, or through a court judgment, such as when the creditor wins a civil lawsuit against the debtor. Other liens arise automatically as a matter of law because a statute mandates that a lien is created upon the occurrence of a particular event. For example, as a matter of law, property tax liens on real property arise each January 1.[5]

---

3. All of these fees arise under the "public enterprise" provisions for counties, G.S. 105, Article 16, and municipalities, G.S. Chapter 160A, Article 15. The collection remedies discussed herein for water, sewer, and stormwater service fees would also apply to other fees authorized by the public enterprise provisions.

4. Thigpen v. Leigh, 93 N.C. 47 (1885).

5. G.S. 105-355(a). For a detailed examination of tax liens, including a discussion of the priority of competing liens on the same property, see Chapter 5.

In Table 15.1 and Table 15.2, the "statutory liens" column indicates if a lien on a taxpayer's real property arises as a matter of law when a local government provides services or incurs costs. Special assessments,[6] nuisance abatement costs,[7] and housing demolition costs[8] are the only taxes or fees discussed in this chapter that create a lien automatically on the taxpayer's real property without additional action by the local government. Two other fees, solid waste fees and ambulance service fees, can create liens on the taxpayer's property after the local government takes additional action. For solid waste fees the local government must adopt an ordinance requiring that the fees be included on the property tax bill and collected as property taxes.[9] For ambulance service fees the local government must file the lien with the clerk of the superior court.[10]

Interest or Penalties

This column in Table 15.1 and Table 15.2 indicates whether a local government may charge interest or penalties for late payment of each fee and tax. With the exception of solid waste fees, all taxes and fees discussed herein fall into one of two categories: (1) those for which the penalties in G.S. 105-236 for the nonpayment of state taxes apply or (2) those for which interest or penalties apply only if the local government adopts such measures in an authorizing ordinance or resolution.

In contrast, the statute for solid waste fees incorporates the Machinery Act's interest provisions, assuming that the local government has adopted an ordinance requiring that the solid waste fees be billed and collected as property taxes.[11]

---

6. G.S. 153A-195 (counties); G.S. 160A-228 (municipalities).

7. G.S. 153A-140 (counties); G.S. 160A-193 (municipalities).

8. G.S. 160A-443 (covers both counties and municipalities).

9. G.S. 153A-293 (counties); G.S. 160A-314.1 (municipalities).

10. G.S. 44-51.2 (requiring filing within 90 days after provision of services); G.S. 44-51.6 (requiring filing between 90 days and 180 days after provision of services for certain counties).

11. G.S. 105-360(a). Under the Machinery Act interest begins on January 6 of the fiscal year in which the taxes are billed, with 2 percent interest that first month and 0.75 percent interest each month thereafter.

Table 15.1. Taxes

Authorization for Taxes	Statutory Lien on Real Property?	Interest or Penalties?	Collection Remedies
Privilege license taxes *G.S. 153A-152 (counties)* *G.S. 160A-211 (municipalities)*	No	5% penalty for every thirty days that business is conducted without license, up to 25% (G.S. 105-236(a)(2))	• Attachment, garnishment, and levy • Set-off debt collection • Civil suit • Criminal misdemeanor prosecution
Occupancy taxes *G.S. 153A-155 (counties)* *G.S. 160A-215 (municipalities)* *By local bills*	No	5% penalty every thirty days for failure to file return when due, up to 25% (G.S. 105-236(a)(3)) 10% penalty for failure to pay tax when due (G.S. 105-236(a)(4)) Or other penalties specified in local bill	• Attachment, garnishment, and levy • Set-off debt collection • Civil suit • Criminal misdemeanor prosecution
Animal taxes *G.S. 153A-153 (counties)* *G.S. 160A-212 (municipalities)*	No	Yes, if included in the ordinance authorizing the tax	• Attachment, garnishment, and levy • Set-off debt collection • Civil suit • Criminal misdemeanor prosecution, if adopted by ordinance that does not provide otherwise

Tax		Penalty	Collection remedies
Beer and wine license taxes *G.S. 105-113.77 (municipalities)* *G.S. 105-113.78 (counties)* *G.S. 105-113.79 (municipal wholesalers)*	No	5% penalty for every thirty days that business is conducted without license, up to 25% (G.S. 105-236(a)(2))	• Attachment, garnishment, and levy • Set-off debt collection • Civil suit • Criminal misdemeanor prosecution
Prepared food/meal taxes *G.S. 153A-154.1 (counties)* *G.S. 160A-214.1 (municipalities)* *By local bills*	No	5% penalty every thirty days for failure to file return when due, up to 25% (G.S. 105-236(a)(3)) 10% penalty for failure to pay tax when due (G.S. 105-236(a)(4))	• Attachment, garnishment, and levy • Set-off debt collection • Civil suit • Criminal misdemeanor prosecution
Motor vehicle taxes and heavy equipment rental gross receipts taxes *G.S. 153A-156 and -156.1 (counties)* *G.S. 160A-215.1 and -215.2 (municipalities)*	No	5% penalty every thirty days for failure to file return when due, up to 25% (G.S. 105-236(a)(3)) 10% penalty for failure to pay tax when due (G.S. 105-236(a)(4))	• Attachment, garnishment, and levy • Set-off debt collection • Civil suit • Criminal misdemeanor prosecution
Municipal motor vehicle taxes and taxicab privilege license taxes *G.S. 20-97* *By local bills*	No	Yes, if included in the ordinance authorizing the tax	• Attachment, garnishment, and levy • Set-off debt collection • Civil suit • Criminal misdemeanor prosecution, if adopted by ordinance that does not provide otherwise

Table 15.2. Fees and Costs

Authorization for Fees and Costs	Statutory Lien on Real Property?	Interest or Penalties	Collection Remedies
Solid waste fees *G.S. 153A-292 and -293* *G.S. 160A-314 and -314.1*	Yes, if board adopts ordinance requiring fees to be billed with and collected as property taxes	Yes, at Machinery Act rates, if billed with property taxes If not billed with property taxes, penalties may be included in the schedule of fees for the service	• Discontinuation of services • Foreclosure, attachment, garnishment and levy, if billed with property taxes • Set-off debt collection • Civil suit • Criminal misdemeanor prosecution, if adopted by ordinance that does not provide otherwise
Water, sewer, stormwater fees *G.S. 153A-274 and -277* *G.S. 160A-311 and -314*	No	Yes, if included in the schedule of fees for the service	• Discontinuation of services • Set-off debt collection • Civil suit • Criminal misdemeanor prosecution, if adopted by ordinance that does not provide otherwise
Ambulance services fees *G.S. Ch. 44, Art. 9A and Art. 9B*	Yes, must file lien with clerk of superior court	Yes, if included in the schedule of fees for the service	• Foreclosure • Attachment and garnishment, only for Article 9B counties and their municipalities • Set-off debt collection • Civil suit • Criminal misdemeanor prosecution, if adopted by ordinance that does not provide otherwise

Special assessments *G.S. Ch. 153A, Art. 9 and Art. 9A* *G.S. Ch. 160A, Art. 10 and Art. 10A*	Yes	Yes, up to 8% per year if included in the assessment resolution	• Foreclosure, attachment, garnishment, and levy • Set-off debt collection • Civil suit • Criminal misdemeanor prosecution, if adopted by ordinance that does not provide otherwise
Nuisance abatement costs *G.S. 153A-140 and* *G.S. 160A-193 or* *G.S. 153A-123 and* *G.S. 160A-175*	Yes, if proceeding under G.S. 153A-123 or G.S. 160A-175, must file lien with clerk of superior court	Yes, if mandated by the local governing board	• Foreclosure, attachment, garnishment, and levy • Set-off debt collection • Civil suit • Criminal misdemeanor prosecution, if adopted by ordinance that does not provide otherwise
Minimum housing standards enforcement costs *G.S. 160A-443*	Yes, should file lien with clerk of superior court and county register of deeds	Yes, if mandated by the local governing board	• Foreclosure, attachment, garnishment, and levy • Set-off debt collection • Civil suit • Criminal misdemeanor prosecution, if adopted by ordinance that does not provide otherwise

Collection Remedies

Not all local taxes and fees share the same collection remedies. To recover a debt, a local government may employ the following remedies:

1. foreclosure of a lien on real property;[12]
2. attachment and garnishment of intangible property, such as bank accounts and wages;[13]
3. levy and sale of tangible personal property;[14]
4. set-off debt collection;[15]
5. civil lawsuit;
6. prosecution for a criminal misdemeanor;[16]
7. civil penalties.[17]

The availability of these seven remedies varies from tax to tax and fee to fee.

Foreclosure—the right to sell real property to satisfy a debt—is available only to recoup those fees and costs that can create a lien on the debtor's real property: solid waste fees, ambulance service fees, special assessments, nuisance abatement costs, and minimum housing standards enforcement costs.

In contrast, attachment and garnishment—the process by which a tax collector may demand that wages, bank accounts, or other funds owed to a taxpayer be paid to the local government to satisfy a debt—is available for all local taxes and for the fees and costs described in this chapter other than water, sewer, and stormwater fees. The same is true for the levy and sale of the debtor's personal property.

---

12. All but one of the liens covered herein can be foreclosed through the Machinery Act process described in G.S. 105-374. The only exception is the lien for ambulance services, which requires a standard civil foreclosure action.

13. Through the Machinery Act process described in G.S. 105-368, as applied to local taxes by G.S. 153A-147 (counties) and G.S. 160A-207 (municipalities).

14. Through the Machinery Act process described in G.S. 105-366 and -367, as applied to local taxes by G.S. 153A-147 (counties) and G.S. 160A-207 (municipalities).

15. G.S. 105A-5.

16. G.S. 105-236(a)(8) and (9), for those taxes subject to the penalties for nonpayment of state taxes. For all others, see G.S. 153A-123(b) and G.S. 160A-175(b), which authorize criminal misdemeanor prosecution for the violation of any ordinance unless the local government opts out of such a remedy to avoid the requirement that funds collected as late payment penalties be remitted to the public schools pursuant to N.C. CONST. art. IX, § 7.

17. G.S. 153A-123(c) (counties) and G.S. 160A-175(c) (municipalities).

Set-off debt collection, commonly known as debt set-off, is discussed in detail in Chapter 8. The process permits a local government to attach an individual or corporate taxpayer's North Carolina state income tax refund, lottery winnings, or other money owed to the taxpayer by the state to satisfy a debt of $50 or more owed to that local government. Local governments must submit their requests for set-off debt collection to the N.C. Department of Revenue through a third-party clearinghouse. The clearinghouse that processes these requests for local governments requires that debts be delinquent for at least sixty days before submission.[18]

A civil lawsuit is also an option for any debt owed to a local government. This remedy is rarely used, though, because of the costs involved and because winning a civil judgment against a debtor generally provides no better collection options than the local government already possessed through its statutory remedies. However, because civil judgments can be enforced through foreclosures, a civil lawsuit could be helpful to collect a tax or fee for which foreclosure is not a statutory remedy.

Equally rare are criminal misdemeanor prosecutions, which are authorized for local taxes and fees under two different statutes. The first statute is the state sales tax collection remedies provision,[19] which applies to privilege license taxes, occupancy taxes, beer and wine taxes, prepared food/meal taxes, car rental taxes, and heavy equipment rental taxes. The second statute contains the general criminal enforcement provisions available for violations of local ordinances.[20] Any tax or fee that is enacted through an ordinance that is not subject to the sales tax criminal provisions can be enforced using the general criminal provisions. Punishment for a misdemeanor conviction is generally limited to a fine set at the discretion of the sentencing judge.

Finally, civil penalties can be used to punish violations of local ordinances.[21] But if the statutory provisions for a tax or fee provide for specific penalties, then the general civil penalties for ordinance violations are not available. For example, the privilege license statutes incorporate the specific penalties that apply to violations of state sales tax law. As a result, local governments are limited to those specific penalties and cannot create their own civil penalties for privilege license tax violations. In contrast, animal

---

18. The clearinghouse's website is www.ncsetoff.org.

19. G.S. 105-236(a)(8) and (9).

20. G.S. 153A-123(b) and G.S. 160A-175(b).

21. G.S. 153A-123(c) (counties) and G.S. 160A-175(c) (municipalities).

taxes and municipal motor vehicle and taxicab fees lack specific penalty provisions in their authorizing statutes. As a result, local governments levying such taxes are free to develop their own civil penalties for nonpayment. Note that these penalties must be specific in the tax ordinance and cannot be collected through attachment and garnishment or levy and sale, as can the principal taxes.

Taxes

This section describes seven different local taxes and the collection remedies available for each.

Privilege License Taxes

Although their name suggests otherwise, privilege license taxes are not regulatory in nature. They are taxes on the privilege of conducting business within a particular jurisdiction.

Cities have broad authority to levy privilege license taxes on all businesses within their jurisdictions, subject to a long list of exemptions and caps commonly called Schedule B exemptions.[22] If a business is *not* covered by one of those exemptions and caps then a municipality may tax that business in any reasonable manner it chooses.

Cities and towns have several taxation options for businesses not covered by Schedule B exemptions. Many apply a flat-rate tax. For example, the city of Dunn charges a flat tax of $50 for department stores and $35 for grocery stores.[23] Other municipalities levy a gross receipts tax on such businesses, charging each business a certain percentage of its annual income. For example, the city of Durham charges retailers a tax of $50 for the first $15,000 in gross receipts plus $0.50 per each additional $1,000 in gross receipts.[24] The gross receipts approach generally produces significantly more revenue than does a flat-rate tax.[25] Privilege license taxes could also be based on a business's total employment or its square footage.

---

22. G.S. 160A-211.

23. City of Dunn privilege license application, www.dunn-nc.org/finance/downloads/pdf%20-%20PL%20&%20Fire%20Application.pdf (last visited July 14, 2011).

24. City of Durham privilege license tax schedule, www.durhamnc.gov/forms/finance_gm_tax_sched.pdf (last visited Jan. 28, 2010).

25. Consider a big-box "supercenter" store that sells both groceries and general merchandise and that has annual revenue of $20 million. In Dunn that business would

Counties have a narrower authority to levy privilege license taxes. They may tax only certain businesses, and even then, they may only tax them up to limited amounts.[26] For this reason counties do not employ a gross receipts approach and generally collect much less privilege license tax revenue than do municipalities.

G.S. 105-236 includes penalties for the failure to pay state privilege license taxes. These penalties are made applicable to local privilege licenses by G.S. 105-109(a). Operating a business without the required privilege license triggers a monthly penalty of 5 percent of the applicable privilege license tax, up to a total of 25 percent. For example, if a business is required to pay a privilege license tax of $100, the first day that business operates without a privilege license triggers a $5 penalty. If the business is still operating without a license thirty days later, the business would owe another $5. The penalties could continue for five months, up to a total of $25. Although such a penalty seems insignificant based on a $100 flat tax, the maximum penalty could be substantial if it applies to a large business that is subject to a gross receipts tax. In addition, G.S. 105-236(a)(9) makes the failure to pay the privilege license tax a Class 1 misdemeanor.

Tax collectors should read their local privilege license ordinances before proceeding with any collection efforts. Often these ordinances include helpful tools for tax collectors engaged in the collection process, such as the authority to demand access to a taxpayer's financial records.

A common question from municipal tax collectors is whether they may refuse to issue a privilege license based on the applicant's failure to pay another tax or obligation owed to the city. The answer is no because otherwise the municipality risks turning the privilege license tax system into a regulatory scheme rather than a revenue scheme. State courts have ruled that regulatory fees must be limited to the actual cost of the regulatory program.[27] Not surprisingly, most cities rely on their privilege license systems to generate more revenue than they cost to operate. Turning those revenue schemes into regulatory schemes would be very costly to those cities. As a result, a city should issue privilege licenses to applicants who pay

---

likely pay about $200 in privilege license taxes, including the $50 department store tax, the $35 grocery store tax, and a few additional flat-fee taxes. In Durham the store would owe about $10,000 in gross-receipts privilege license taxes.

26. G.S. 153A-152.

27. Homebuilders Ass'n v. City of Charlotte, 336 N.C. 37, 42 (1994).

the applicable privilege license taxes regardless of whether those applicants owe property taxes or other debts to the city.

The only regulatory provision that courts have permitted cities to tie to their privilege license systems has been zoning requirements.[28] If a city's privilege license ordinance requires applicants to demonstrate compliance with applicable zoning regulations before obtaining a privilege license, then the tax collector may refuse to issue a privilege license even upon payment of the applicable tax if the applicant cannot demonstrate that he or she has zoning approval to operate the business that is the subject of the application.

Occupancy Taxes

More than 150 counties and municipalities are the subject of local bills that grant them authority to levy taxes on the rental of rooms or similar accommodations furnished by hotels, motels, and other businesses that are subject to state sales tax under G.S. 105-164.4(a)(3).[29] Details of occupancy taxes vary by locality, but most are limited to a rate of either 3 or 6 percent. The tax revenue must be distributed to the local tourism development authority for use promoting travel and tourism in the area.[30]

The penalties for the failure to pay occupancy taxes are either specified in the local bill that authorized the tax[31] or tied to the penalties for delinquent state sales taxes found in G.S. 105-236.[32] These include a 5 percent-per-month penalty for failure to file the required monthly return, up to a maximum of 25 percent, and a one-time 10 percent penalty for failure to pay the tax along with the monthly return. Both penalties are based on the

---

28. Fantasy World, Inc. v. Greensboro Bd. of Adjustment, 162 N.C. App. 603, 611–12 (2004).

29. Many, but not all, of these counties and municipalities are listed in the general occupancy tax provisions for counties, G.S. 153A-155, and municipalities, G.S. 160A-215. Because no master list of all local government authorizations exists, the best method of determining whether and how a local government is authorized to levy such a tax is to search the "Session Laws" section of the General Assembly's website, www.ncga.state.nc.us/gascripts/EnactedLegislation/ELTOC.pl?sType=Law, using the government's name and "occupancy tax" as search terms.

30. See, e.g., S.L. 2009-429, www.ncga.state.nc.us/enactedlegislation/sessionlaws/html/2009-2010/sl2009-429.html, authorizing 3 percent occupancy taxes for the municipalities of Jacksonville, Lenoir, Lowell, Mount Holly, Cramerton, McAdenville, and Ranlo.

31. See, for example, 1991 N.C. Sess. Laws ch. 392, specifying penalties for the failure to pay Orange County occupancy taxes.

32. G.S. 153A-155(e) (counties) and G.S. 160A-215(e) (municipalities).

amount of tax owed. For example, if a hotel owed $1,000 in occupancy tax for a particular month and did not file a return or pay the tax, the total penalty for the first month would be $150: $50 for the failure to file and $100 for the failure to pay. G.S. 105-236(a)(9) also makes the failure to file a return or pay the tax a Class 1 misdemeanor.

Animal Taxes

All counties and municipalities are authorized to levy a license tax on the privilege of keeping animals.[33] Rates and covered animals vary across the state. For example, residents of Charlotte and Mecklenburg County must pay $30 per year for "unaltered" dogs, cats, and ferrets and $10 per year for neutered or spayed pets.[34] Asheville's $10 annual tax covers only dogs.[35]

The penalties in G.S. 105-236 do not automatically apply to animal taxes. However, a local government may create late-payment penalties for these taxes in its authorizing ordinance.[36]

Prepared Foods/Meals Taxes

Only fourteen local governments have authority to levy taxes on prepared foods.[37] Five of those are counties (Cumberland, Dare, Durham, Mecklenburg, and Wake), and nine are municipalities (Charlotte, Cornelius, Davidson, Hillsborough, Huntersville, Matthews, Mint Hill, Monroe, and Pineville). Although the details of the local authorizing bills vary, these taxes generally are limited to 1 percent and apply to "prepared foods" as defined in the state sales tax provisions, G.S. 105-164.3(28):

---

33. G.S. 153A-153 (limiting county animal taxes to the keeping of "pets"); G.S. 160A-212 (authorizing municipalities to tax the keeping of "any domestic animal").

34. See www.petdata.com/cs/chr/fees.htm (last visited Jan. 28, 2010).

35. See www.buncombecounty.org/governing/depts/sheriff/animalControl.asp (last visited Jan. 28, 2010).

36. G.S. 153A-123(a) and (c) (counties); G.S. 160A-175(a) and (c) (municipalities).

37. S.L. 93-413, as amended by S.L. 2001-347 (Cumberland County); S.L. 91-177, as amended by S.L. 2001-347 and S.L. 2002-141 (Dare County); S.L. 2008-116 (Durham County); S.L. 89-821, as amended by S.L. 2001-347 and S.L. 2001-402 (Mecklenburg County and Charlotte); S.L. 91-594, as amended by S.L. 95-458 and S.L. 2001-347 (Wake County); S.L. 2001-402 (Cornelius); S.L. 2001-403 (Davidson); S.L. 93-449, as amended by S.L. 99-304 and S.L. 2001-341 (Hillsborough); S.L. 2001-405 (Huntersville); S.L. 2001-406 (Matthews); S.L. 2001-407 (Mint Hill); S.L. 2005-261 (Monroe); S.L. 2001-409 (Pineville).

> **Prepared food:** Food that meets at least one of the conditions of this subdivision. Prepared food does not include food the retailer sliced, repackaged, or pasteurized but did not heat, mix, or sell with eating utensils.
>   a. It is sold in a heated state or it is heated by the retailer.
>   b. It consists of two or more foods mixed or combined by the retailer for sale as a single item. This sub-subdivision does not include foods containing raw eggs, fish, meat, or poultry that require cooking by the consumer as recommended by the Food and Drug Administration to prevent food borne illnesses.
>   c. It is sold with eating utensils provided by the retailer, such as plates, knives, forks, spoons, glasses, cups, napkins, and straws.

In 2001 and 2002 the General Assembly made the penalties for unpaid meal taxes uniform by subjecting the taxes to the penalty provisions in G.S. 105-236 and repealing all additional or higher local penalties.[38] These uniform penalties include a 5 percent per-month penalty for failure to file the required monthly return, up to a maximum of 25 percent, and a one-time 10 percent penalty for failure to pay the tax along with the monthly return. Both penalties are based on the amount of tax owed. G.S. 105-236(a)(9) also makes the failure to file a return or pay the tax a Class 1 misdemeanor.

Beer and Wine License Taxes

In counties and municipalities that permit the sale of beer and wine, retailers of such beverages are required to obtain local licenses and pay a privilege tax mandated by statute. These taxes are in addition to the excise taxes imposed by the state, a portion of which is shared on a per-capita basis with the local governments that permit alcohol sales.[39] Note that local governments are not authorized to charge local license taxes for the sale of liquor or mixed alcoholic drinks.

Businesses must pay a tax for each of the taxable activities they conduct. See Table 15.3. If a bar sells beer and wine for take-out and for on-site consumption, it would be required to pay all four local beer and wine license taxes. What about a wine shop that holds tastings for its customers—does that activity require an on-premises license in addition to the shop's off-premises license? Yes, but only if the shop charges for the tastings. If the tastings are free, then there is no retail activity to be taxed.

---

38. S.L. 2001-264 and S.L. 2002-72.
39. G.S. 105-113.82.

Table 15.3. Local Beer and Wine License Taxes

Condition of Sale	County-Imposed Tax[a]	Municipality-Imposed Tax[b] ($)
Beer, on-premises	25	15
Beer, off-premises	5	5
Wine, on-premises	25	15
Wine, off-premises	25	10

[a] G.S. 105-113.78
[b] G.S. 105-113.77

In contrast to retail license taxes, wholesale license taxes are not permitted for counties and are optional for municipalities. Cities and towns may levy a license tax up to $37.50 per year on beer and wine wholesalers.

The penalties in G.S. 105-236 apply to local beer and wine license taxes. Operating a business without the required privilege license triggers a monthly penalty of 5 percent of the applicable privilege license tax, up to a total of 25 percent. G.S. 105-236(a)(9) also makes the failure to pay the tax a Class 1 misdemeanor.

Motor Vehicle and Heavy Equipment Rental Gross Receipts Taxes

Local governments are not permitted to levy property taxes on cars, trucks, or mobile heavy equipment that are held for short-term rental.[40] Instead, counties and municipalities may tax the gross receipts from the rental of these vehicles and equipment as indicated in Table 15.4, below.

Vehicles are defined by G.S. 160A-215.1 as any of the following:

a. A motor vehicle of the passenger type, including a passenger van, minivan, or sport utility vehicle.
b. A motor vehicle of the cargo type, including cargo van, pickup truck, or truck with a gross vehicle weight rating of 26,000 pounds or less used predominantly in the transportation of property for other than commercial freight and that does not require the operator to posses[s] a commercial drivers license.
c. A trailer or semitrailer with a gross vehicle weight of 6,000 pounds or less.

---

40. G.S. 105-275(42) and (42a) exempts these types of property from local property taxes. An annual application is required for the heavy equipment exemption under G.S. 105-275(42a). No application is required for the short-term vehicle rental exemption in G.S. 105-275(42). See G.S. 105-282.1.

Table 15.4. Taxes on Receipts from Rentals

Type of Rental	County-Imposed Tax (%)	Municipality-Imposed Tax (%)
Vehicle	1.5[a]	1.5[b]
Heavy Equipment	1.2[c]	0.8[d]

[a] G.S. 153A-156
[b] G.S. 160A-215.1
[c] G.S. 153A-156.1
[d] G.S. 160A-215.2

Heavy equipment is defined by G.S. 153A-156.1 as "earthmoving, construction, or industrial equipment that is mobile, weighs at least 1,500 pounds," and meets any of these descriptions:

a. It is a self-propelled vehicle that is not designed to be driven on a highway.
b. It is industrial lift equipment, industrial material handling equipment, industrial electrical generation equipment, or a similar piece of industrial equipment.

The jurisdiction from which a rental originates collects the tax on the motor vehicle or equipment rental, even if the vehicle or equipment is delivered and used in another jurisdiction. For example, if a New Hanover County business rents a bulldozer to a Brunswick County business for use in Brunswick County, the rental tax would be owed to New Hanover County.

The penalties for the failure to pay state taxes in G.S. 105-236 apply to vehicle and heavy equipment gross receipt taxes.[41] These include a 5 percent-per-month penalty for failure to file the required monthly return, up to a maximum of 25 percent, and a one-time 10 percent penalty for failure to pay the tax along with the monthly return. Both penalties are based on the amount of tax owed. G.S. 105-236(a)(9) also makes the failure to file a return or pay the tax a Class 1 misdemeanor.

Municipal Motor Vehicle and Taxicab Privilege License Taxes

Municipalities may levy annual taxes of up to $5 on motor vehicles and of up to $15 on taxicabs "for the use and privileges of the public highways."[42] Municipalities that operate public transportation systems may levy an addi-

---

41. G.S. 153A-156(f); G.S. 160A-215.1(f); G.S. 153A-156.1(d); G.S. 160A-215.2(d).
42. G.S. 20-97.

tional tax of up to $5 per year, the proceeds of which must be used to support those systems.[43] These limits have been raised for many municipalities through local bills.[44]

The municipal motor vehicle and taxicab privilege license tax may be collected through levy or attachment and garnishment under G.S. 160A-207. Criminal misdemeanor prosecution and injunctive relief may also be available under G.S. 160A-175 to help with collection efforts. That same statute authorizes a municipality to charge a financial penalty for late or nonpayment of these taxes. To do so, the municipality must include that penalty in the ordinance that adopts the tax.

The penalties in G.S. 105-236 do not automatically apply to municipal motor vehicle and taxicab privilege license taxes. However, a local government may include penalties or interest charges for late tax payments in its authorizing ordinance.[45]

Most often, county assessors include municipal motor vehicle privilege taxes on the property tax notices they are required to send to owners of registered motor vehicles despite the fact that the taxes are actually privilege taxes and not property taxes.[46] As a result, most municipal privilege taxes are collected by county tax collectors along with property taxes assessed by the county and municipality on registered motor vehicles.

At least one town levies and collects the privilege tax itself through a creative automotive decal program. Carolina Beach requires residents who register their cars with the state Department of Motor Vehicles at town addresses to obtain Vehicle Identification Decals (VIDs) each year for display

---

43. G.S. 105-550 defines "public transportation system" as "any combination of real and personal property established for purposes of public transportation. The systems may include one or more of the following: structures, improvements, buildings, equipment, vehicle parking or passenger transfer facilities, railroads and railroad rights-of-way, rights-of-way, bus services, shared-ride services, high-occupancy vehicle facilities, carpool and vanpool programs, voucher programs, telecommunications and information systems, integrated fare systems, bus lanes, and busways. The term does not include, however, streets, roads, or highways except to the extent they are dedicated to public transportation vehicles or to the extent they are necessary for access to vehicle parking or passenger transfer facilities."

44. See, e.g., S.L. 2009-160 (authorizing the city of Raleigh to levy an annual license tax on vehicles of up to $25, $15 of which may be spent for any purpose and the rest to be spent on transportation-related purposes including sidewalks).

45. G.S. 153A-123(a) and (c) (counties); G.S. 160A-175(a) and (c) (municipalities).

46. See Chapter 14 for more on the taxation of registered motor vehicles.

on their windshields. The decals cost \$5, which is in reality the town's privilege tax on motor vehicles. According to the town, "The VID also assists in identifying residents of the town during times of natural disaster and other emergencies. With the purchase of a VID, permanent residents and property owners receive a parking permit at no additional cost."[47] Residents who do not purchase the VID and pay the \$5 tax by March 31 must pay an additional \$10, which apparently is the town's late payment penalty authorized by the privilege tax statute.

Fees and Costs

Tax collectors increasingly are tasked with the collection of fees and costs associated with the provision of specific services by local governments. Details of each fee and cost are discussed below.

Public Enterprise Fees: Water, Sewer, Solid Waste, and Stormwater

Under the public enterprise provisions applicable to counties and municipalities, all local governments are permitted to provide and charge for services such as water distribution, wastewater collection and treatment, solid waste collection and disposal, and stormwater management.[48] For each service that it offers, a local government may set its own fees and late-payment charges.[49]

The primary remedy for collecting unpaid utility fees is to discontinue utility service at the property where the delinquency occurred. City- and county-operated utilities must wait at least ten days after an account becomes delinquent before cutting off services.[50] A local government may also specify in its ordinance how partial payments will be allocated among multiple fees included on the same bill.[51] Most local governments put this

---

47. Town of Carolina Beach website: www.carolinabeach.org/site_new/pages/vehicle_id.html (last visited May 25, 2011).

48. G.S. Chapter 153A, Article 15 (counties), and G.S. Chapter 160A, Article 16 (municipalities). These provisions also authorize other services, but the four listed above are most relevant to local tax collectors.

49. G.S. 153A-277(a) (counties) and G.S. 160A-314(a) (municipalities).

50. G.S. 153A-277(b) (counties) and G.S. 160A-314(b) (counties). In contrast, water and sewer authorities must wait at least thirty days before cutting off services. G.S. 162A-9(c). Note that if a customer has filed for bankruptcy, a utility may be limited in its ability to cut off services. 11 U.S.C. § 366.

51. G.S. 153A-277(a) (counties) and G.S. 160A-314(a) (municipalities).

authority to use by specifying that water service, the one easiest to discontinue and considered most vital by property owners, is paid last.

Beyond discontinuation of services and set-off debt collection, the final collection remedy available for most public enterprise fees is a civil lawsuit to enforce the debt.[52] Outside of a few towns and counties that have been granted special collection authority via local bills,[53] Machinery Act remedies generally are not available for the collection of public utility fees. The one exception to that rule is for the collection of solid waste fees.

If a local government adopts an ordinance requiring solid waste fees be billed and collected as property taxes, then these fees may be included on the property tax bill, will create a lien on the property owner's real property, and may be collected using the Machinery Act remedies of foreclosure, attachment and garnishment, and levy.[54] Without such an ordinance, or if after adopting such an ordinance the local government does not include these fees on property tax bills, then Machinery Act remedies are not available for the collection of solid waste fees.

Generally, collection efforts for unpaid utility bills may only be aimed at the contracting party, that is, the party that established the utility account. For example, if a tenant establishes a utility account, then generally only the tenant, not the property owner, may be held responsible for those bills. The reverse is also generally true: if the property owner establishes the utility account but directs that the bills be sent to a tenant, the property owner remains responsible for those bills.

In two situations collection efforts may be aimed at someone other than the contracting party. The first situation concerns property owners who are landlords. Regardless of who established the utility account, a landlord property owner can be held responsible for unpaid bills if the utility services for multiple tenants are measured on one meter or if the local government

---

52. G.S. 153A-277(b) (counties) and G.S. 160A-314(b) (municipalities).

53. For example, see S.L. 2011-109 and S.L. 2005-441, authorizing Clemmons, Durham, Garner, Kernersville, Knightdale, Morrisville, Wendell, Winston-Salem, and Zebulon to use Machinery Act remedies to collect stormwater utility fees. Similarly, S.L. 2002-127, S.L. 1999-127, S.L. 1998-84, and S.L. 1989-1070 authorize Chadbourn, Locust, Mount Gilead, Norwood, Stanfield, Richfield, and Montgomery County to use the Machinery Act remedy of levy and sale of tangible personal property (G.S. 105-366 and -367) to collect water and sewer bills.

54. G.S. 153A-293 (counties) and G.S. 160A-314.1(b) (municipalities).

bills sewer service fees separately from water service fees.[55] The second situation concerns other members of the contracting party's household. Under certain scenarios unpaid utility bills incurred by one member of a household may justify the discontinuation of utility services to another household member.[56] However, a local government may never subject one household member to set-off debt collection or a civil suit for the unpaid utility bills of another household member.

Ambulance Service Fees

When a local government provides ambulance service to a person, that local government can obtain a lien on all real property owned by that person within the local government's jurisdiction to recover service fees. This is true regardless of whether the local government directly provides the ambulance services or pays a third-party to provide the services. These liens arise under either G.S. Chapter 44, Article 9A or G.S. Chapter 44, Article 9B.

Article 9A requires the local government to file the lien with the clerk of superior court within ninety days of the date it provided the ambulance services. To enforce a lien under Article 9A, the local government must initiate a civil action and obtain a judgment ordering the sale of the property subject to the lien; Machinery Act foreclosure, attachment, and levy remedies are not available.[57]

Eighty-nine counties possess additional enforcement remedies under Article 9B.[58] This article allows the covered counties to treat the ambulance

---

55. G.S. 153A-277(d) and G.S. 160A-314(d).

56. G.S. 153A-277(b1) and G.S. 160A-314(b1).

57. G.S. 44-51.1. The local government must initiate this action before the earlier of (i) ten years from the date on which ambulance services were provided or (ii) three years from the date of the recipient's death.

58. As of the 2009 legislative session, those counties are: Alamance, Alexander, Alleghany, Anson, Ashe, Beaufort, Bladen, Brunswick, Buncombe, Burke, Cabarrus, Caldwell, Camden, Carteret, Caswell, Catawba, Chatham, Cherokee, Chowan, Cleveland, Columbus, Craven, Cumberland, Dare, Davidson, Davie, Duplin, Durham, Edgecombe, Forsyth, Franklin, Gaston, Graham, Granville, Greene, Guilford, Halifax, Harnett, Haywood, Henderson, Hertford, Hoke, Hyde, Iredell, Johnston, Jones, Lee, Lenoir, Lincoln, McDowell, Macon, Madison, Mecklenburg, Mitchell, Montgomery, Moore, Nash, New Hanover, Onslow, Orange, Pasquotank, Pender, Person, Pitt, Polk, Randolph, Richmond, Robeson, Rockingham, Rowan, Rutherford, Sampson, Scotland, Stanly, Stokes, Surry, Swain, Transylvania, Tyrrell, Union, Vance, Wake, Warren, Washington, Watauga, Wilkes, Wilson, Yadkin, and Yancey. G.S. 44-51.8. It is unclear whether these eighty-nine counties have the option of proceeding under either Article

service fees as a tax owed to the county and use Machinery Act remedies of attachment and garnishment to assist with their collection.[59] These counties also obtain a lien on real property if they file the lien with the clerk of superior court after 90 days but within 180 days of the date the ambulance services were provided.[60] The lien under Article 9B covers not only real property owned by the individual that received the ambulance services but also real property owned by people legally responsible for the support of the individual who received the services.[61] For example, if ambulance services are provided to a child by an Article 9B county, then that county would have a lien on real property owned by that child's parents. Similarly, this provision should permit an Article 9B county to attach the wages of the spouse of the person who received the ambulance services to satisfy the debt for those services.[62]

Neither Article 9A nor Article 9B provides for interest or penalties on late payments. However, a local government could adopt one charge or both in its schedule of fees for ambulance services.

Special Assessments

Special assessments are essentially additional property taxes levied to pay for the construction or improvement of particular public works such as streets, sidewalks, or water, sewer, and stormwater systems.[63] Special assessments target particular property owners whose properties benefit from these projects. Some special assessments require approval from a majority of the affected property owners; others may be levied unilaterally by the governing board.[64]

9A or Article 9B. In the author's view the safest course of action is to assume that these counties may proceed only under Article 9B.

59. G.S. 44-51.4. This provision does not include a statute of limitations on such collection actions. Presumably, the ten-year limitation in the Machinery Act would apply to attachments for ambulance service fees. See G.S. 105-378(a).

60. G.S. 44-51.6.

61. G.S. 44-51.5.

62. See N.C. Baptist Hosp., Inc. v. Harris, 319 N.C. 347 (1987) (applying the "doctrine of necessaries" to hold a wife responsible for her husband's medical debt).

63. G.S. Chapter 153A, Article 9 and Article 9A; G.S. Chapter 160A, Article 10 and Article 10A.

64. All special assessments levied under the "critical infrastructure needs" provisions of G.S. Chapter 153A, Article 9A and G.S. Chapter 160A, Article 10A, require petitions signed by the owners of at least 66 percent of the assessed value of real

The cost of a public works project to be paid for by a special assessment is allocated among the properties that will benefit from the project. Several different allocation methods are permitted, including those based on the frontage abutting the project, the acreage served by the project, or the number of lots benefitting from the extension of an existing service.[65]

Special assessments are generally payable in ten annual installments, although those levied under the "critical infrastructure needs" provisions may be paid over thirty years.[66] Most often installments are billed with property taxes and due on September 1 each year, the same day property taxes are due.[67] Interest of up to 8 percent annually may apply to these installments if the governing board so provides in the resolution that authorizes the assessment.[68] Special assessments that are billed with property taxes accrue interest on the due date, September 1, not on the delinquency date for property taxes, January 6.

Once the governing board confirms the final assessment roll—that is, the list of properties responsible for paying the costs—the special assessments are a lien on the properties included in the roll.[69] This lien is senior to all other liens on the property except for federal, state, and local tax liens.[70] Notice of the final assessment roll must be published at least twenty days after confirmation by the governing board.

---

property and 50 percent of the owners that will be subject to the levy. Special assessments for the construction of sidewalks and streets under "traditional" process in G.S. Chapter 153A, Article 9 and G.S. Chapter 160A, Article 10, require petitions signed by owners of at least 50 percent of the lineal feel of frontage of the affected properties. Other special assessments under the "traditional" process, such as those for the extension of water and sewer service, may be levied by resolution of the governing board without input from the property owners. However, local governments generally prefer to confirm that the affected property owners desire water and sewer services before spending the money to extend those lines.

65. G.S. 153A-186 and G.S. 160A-218. In the case of special assessments levied under the new "critical infrastructure needs" provisions, the costs may also be allocated by "any other methods designed to allocate the costs in accordance with the benefits conferred." G.S. 153A-210.2 and G.S. 160A-239.2.

66. G.S. 153A-210.5 and G.S. 160A-239.5. These provisions became law in 2008 and are scheduled to expire in 2013.

67. G.S. 153A-199 and G.S. 160A-232. Alternately, the first installment may be due with applicable interest sixty days after the assessment roll is confirmed, with subsequent installments due on the same date each year.

68. G.S. 153A-200(a) and G.S. 160A-233(a).

69. G.S. 153A-195 and G.S. 160A-228.

70. G.S. 153A-200(c) and G.S. 160A-233(c).

Tax collectors are responsible for collecting special assessments "in the same manner as property taxes," meaning that the Machinery Act remedies of levy, attachment, garnishment, and foreclosure are available for help collecting delinquent payments.[71] If an installment payment is not paid by the due date, the entire special assessment immediately becomes due and delinquent, unless the governing board waives this right of "acceleration."[72] For example, consider a $1,000 special assessment that is payable in ten annual installments of $100. If the property owner fails to pay the first installment when due, the entire $1,000 becomes due and subject to enforced collection remedies. If the board waives its right to accelerate the installment payments, then only the first $100 installment payment could be the subject of Machinery Act collection remedies. Enforcement actions must begin within ten years of the due date of the earliest installment payment included in the action.[73]

Unlike the other taxes and fees discussed in this chapter, special assessments are subject to their own unique amendment provisions. Once confirmed, a special assessment may be modified only through "reassessment" in cases of "irregularity, omission, error, or lack of jurisdiction."[74] This provision appears to eliminate the opportunity for a local government to negotiate or compromise a special assessment once it has been confirmed.

---

71. City of Durham v. Herndon, 61 N.C. App. 275, 300 S.E.2d 460 (1983) (authorizing use of Machinery Act remedies for collection of special assessment liens).

72. G.S. 153A-200(b) and G.S. 160A-233(b).

73. G.S. 153A-200(d) and G.S. 160A-233(d). However, if installment payments are accelerated, the ten-year limitation on enforcement for each installment payment begins to run from the date the installment payment would have been due without acceleration. For example, consider a $1,000 special assessment payable in ten annual installments, with the first installment due on September 1, 2010. If the taxpayer fails to pay the first installment payment by that date, all ten installment payments can become immediately due and payable. However, the ten-year limitation for collecting each installment payment runs from its original due date: enforcement actions to collect the second $100 installment payment could begin as late as August 31, 2021, which would be within ten years of September 1, 2011, the original due date of the second installment before acceleration.

74. G.S. 153A-198 (counties) and G.S. 160A-231 (municipalities).

Nuisance Abatement Costs and Minimum Housing Enforcement Costs

Although authorized by different statutes, both types of costs concern local governments' efforts to remedy dangerous conditions on private property. These costs become a lien on the property that created the need for government action.

Nuisance abatement occurs when a local government takes action "to remove, abate, or remedy [any]thing that is dangerous or prejudicial to the public health or safety," such as overgrown vegetation or trash-filled lots.[75] Municipalities may take abatement actions "summarily," meaning without notice or hearing, but counties must provide the taxpayer with notice, the right to a hearing, and the right to appeal to the courts. Nuisance abatement liens arising under G.S. 153A-140 and G.S. 160A-193, the "traditional" abatement provisions, can be enforced using all Machinery Act remedies and have the same priority as liens for property taxes.[76] These liens do not need to be filed.

Alternately, local governments may take action to abate nuisances under the statutes that provide for general enforcement of their ordinances, which require a court order before the local government may proceed.[77] Some local governments prefer this alternate approach because it may provide additional defenses to trespass allegations or other objections from the landowner. Nuisance abatement liens arising under this approach are equivalent to mechanics' liens arising under G.S. Chapter 44A, Article 2. These liens must be filed with the clerk of superior court and can be enforced only through a civil action. They do not have "super-priority" as do property tax liens.[78]

Minimum housing standards enforcement actions are aimed at dwellings that are "unfit for human habitation" and require repair, closing, or demolition.[79] Before taking action to enforce minimum housing standards, a local government must (1) pass an ordinance finding that unfit dwelling

---

75. G.S. 153A-140 (counties) and G.S. 160A-193 (municipalities).

76. Priority refers to the order in which liens are paid if a property is subject to multiple liens. Generally, property tax liens have the highest priority, followed by special assessment liens, and then by other liens, such as mechanics' liens and mortgage liens. For a detailed discussion of lien priority, see Chapter 5.

77. G.S. 153A-123(e) (counties) and G.S. 160A-175(e) (municipalities).

78. G.S. 44A-13.

79. G.S. 160A-441 (applies to both counties and municipalities).

conditions exist and (2) satisfy certain notice and hearing requirements.[80] Minimum housing standards enforcement liens are the equivalent of liens for special assessments. These liens are senior to all liens except tax liens and may be enforced through Machinery Act foreclosure, attachment, and levy procedures.[81]

Refund and Release

The Machinery Act permits the refund or release of property taxes only in two very limited circumstances: when the taxes (1) were illegal or (2) were imposed due to clerical error.[82] This provision effectively prohibits the negotiation, waiver, or compromise of property taxes.

However, this restrictive provision does *not* apply to other taxes or fees collected by local governments, even for those that may be collected using Machinery Act remedies. None of the authorizing statutes for those taxes and fees specifically incorporate the Machinery Act's refund and release provisions.[83] As a result, local governments are generally free to develop

---

80. G.S. 160A-443.

81. This statute also suggests that housing standards enforcement liens must be filed in the same manner as are special assessment liens. However, there is no requirement that special assessment liens be filed, which calls in to question exactly what filing requirement, if any, applies to housing standard enforcement liens. To protect their interests, local governments that incur housing standard enforcement costs should consider filing their liens both with the clerk of superior court in their county and with the county register of deeds. Even if these filings are not required, they should put prospective buyers of the property on notice of the lien and increase the likelihood that the lien will be satisfied without additional enforcement actions.

82. G.S. 105-381. For a detailed examination of this provision, see Chapter 12.

83. For example, the special assessment provisions state that they may be "delivered to the tax collector for collection in the same manner . . . as property taxes." G.S. 153A-195 (counties); G.S. 160A-228 (municipalities). G.S. 105-381, which governs the refund and release of property taxes, is *not* a collection provision. It is a provision for the elimination of a tax that should never have been levied. Therefore, special assessments (and minimum housing standards enforcement costs, which are collected as special assessments) are not subject to G.S. 105-381. The same argument applies to nuisance abatement costs, the authorizing statutes for which state that they shall be "collected as property taxes." See G.S. 153A-140 (counties); G.S. 160A-193 (municipalities). The statutes authorizing the use of Machinery Act remedies for the collection of solid waste fees use slightly different language. Solid waste fees "may be billed with property taxes, may be payable in the same manner as property taxes, and, in the case of

their own refund and release procedures for the taxes and fees discussed in this chapter. The only exception to this rule is special assessments, which are governed by their own amendment procedures and can be modified only in cases of "irregularity, omission, error or lack of jurisdiction."[84]

For all other taxes and fees discussed in this chapter, a local government could choose to adopt the Machinery Act refund and release provisions or could adopt more flexible provisions that permit the consideration of a debtor's economic distress or other factors. Regardless of the policy that is chosen, local governments would be wise to adopt some type of formal refund and release policies for all of their taxes and fees before controversies arise. Such policies should be based on objective factors to avoid accusations of favoritism or discrimination.

Statutes of Limitation: Other Local Taxes

None of the provisions governing the taxes discussed in this chapter include a statute of limitations. However, certain remedies for these taxes are limited by provisions found elsewhere in the General Statutes.

Attachment and garnishment and levy and sale can be used for the collection of local taxes "under the rules and procedures proscribed by the Machinery Act."[85] It follows that the Machinery Act's ten-year limitation on the use of attachment and garnishment and levy and sale to collect property taxes also applies to the use of these remedies to collect all other local taxes.[86]

Criminal misdemeanor prosecutions of tax ordinance violations are subject to the general two-year limitation on all misdemeanor prosecutions.[87]

The two remaining remedies for the collection of other local taxes, civil lawsuits and set-off debt collection, are not subject to any statutes of limita-

---

nonpayment, may be collected in any manner by which delinquent personal or real property taxes can be collected." G.S. 153A-293 (counties); G.S. 160A-314.1(b). However, even this broader language does not implicate G.S. 105-381, which is neither a billing nor a payment nor a collection provision. This means that solid waste fees likely can be released or refunded without regard for G.S. 105-381.

84. G.S. 153A-198 (counties) and G.S. 160A-231 (municipalities). See "Special Assessments" section, above, for more details.

85. G.S. 153A-147 (counties) and 160A-207 (municipalities).

86. G.S. 105-378(a) prohibits the use of Machinery Act remedies unless the remedy is initiated within ten years of the date the taxes became due.

87. G.S. 15-1.

tion. Core governmental functions such as tax collection are exempt from the various general statutes of limitation found in Chapter 1 of the General Statutes.[88] Presumably this means that local governments can turn to civil lawsuits and the set-off debt collection process at any time, regardless of when the taxes in question were levied.

Statutes of Limitation: Fees and Costs

Public enterprise utility fees are subject to varying statutes of limitation:[89]

Sewer (Wastewater) Utility Fees:	Three years[90]
Stormwater Utility Fees:	Three years[91]
Water Utility Fees:	Four years[92]
Solid Waste Collection Fees:	Three years if billed as are other public utility fees[93] Ten years if billed with property taxes[94]
Ambulance Service Fees:	For foreclosure, earlier of ten years from date of services or three years from the death of the person who received the services[95] For attachment and garnishment, ten years[96]

---

88. *See* City of Greensboro v. Morse, 197 N.C. App. 624 (2009).

89. For more details on the collection of certain public enterprise fees, see Kara A. Millonzi, *A Guide to Billing and Collecting Public Enterprise Utility Fees for Water, Wastewater, and Solid Waste Service* (Chapel Hill: UNC School of Government, 2008).

90. G.S. 1-52(1), the general statute of limitations for actions based on contracts.

91. *Id.*

92. G.S. 25-2-725(1), part of the North Carolina version of the Uniform Commercial Code that governs the sale of goods.

93. *Id.*

94. G.S. 105-378(a). This limitation applies only if the local government includes its solid waste fees on its property tax bills and adopts an ordinance stating that the fees are payable and to be collected in the same manner as property taxes.

95. G.S. 44-51.1.

96. G.S. 44-51.4 states that Article 9B counties may "treat the amount due for such services as if it were a tax due to the county or municipality and may proceed to collect the amount through the use of attachment and garnishment proceedings

The three costs discussed in this chapter—special assessments, minimum housing standard enforcement costs, and public nuisance abatement costs—are all subject to ten-year limitations on collections.[97]

---

set out in G.S. 105-368." Presumably this reference to the Machinery Act attachment and garnishment process incorporates the Machinery Act's ten-year limitation found in G.S. 105-378(a).

97. For special assessments, see G.S. 153A-200(d) (counties) and 160A-233(d) (municipalities). Technically these provisions limit only foreclosures, but the author believes that a court would likely interpret them also to limit remedies against personal property, such as attachment and garnishment. Minimum housing standard enforcement costs for both counties and municipalities are collected as special assessments. G.S. 160A-443(6)(a). Nuisance abatement costs are collected as property taxes, meaning the Machinery Act's ten-year limitation applies. G.S. 153A-140 (counties) and 160A-193 (municipalities).

Property Taxes and Bankruptcy

Chapter 16

Property Taxes and Bankruptcy

Federal bankruptcy law is an immensely complex topic. Access to an experienced bankruptcy attorney can be crucial when a tax collector is faced with an unusually large or complicated bankruptcy case. But tax collectors need not become bankruptcy experts to protect their governments' interests in most cases. After learning some basic bankruptcy concepts, tax collectors should be able to navigate the process in most common bankruptcy situations to maximize the likelihood that their tax claims will be paid and, in more complex cases, be better positioned to work with bankruptcy counsel.

Bankruptcy law exists to give debtors a fresh start. The process provides debtors with relief from some of their financial obligations and gives creditors an orderly process for seeking payment of their claims. Bankruptcy is governed by federal law and federal courts, which means that a bankruptcy filing anywhere in the country can affect property tax obligations in North Carolina.

Before diving into the details, several key points about bankruptcy deserve mention.

First, *all* collection activities aimed at the taxpayer who filed for bankruptcy must stop while the proceeding is pending, else the tax collector risks being sanctioned by a federal judge for violating the automatic stay that arises immediately upon the filing of a bankruptcy petition.

Second, because property taxes generally receive preferential treatment in the bankruptcy process, the collection of many property taxes will be delayed but not eliminated by a bankruptcy filing. Bankruptcy proceedings can continue for years. Taxes that arise after the filing are always enforceable after the proceeding ends. The property taxes that most commonly become uncollectible after bankruptcy are those that predate the filing by more than a year and are not secured by a lien on real property.

Third, tax collectors should implement procedures to assure timely action on bankruptcy filings. Deadlines should be immediately noted and claims forms be completed and timely filed. It is crucial that the tax office have ready and prompt access to legal counsel, especially where large sums are involved. Legal assistance often will be provided by an attorney in the county or city attorney's office who has developed expertise in the area. In extremely complex cases, the local government may choose to retain outside counsel with extensive bankruptcy experience. The tax office should develop a one-page summary document to transmit concerns and important information (e.g., current statement of taxes owed, list of real property owned by taxpayer) to the attorney working on the case. When it appears that taxes may be in jeopardy, immediate communication with the attorney must take place. Sometimes responses or objections must be filed in distant courts in a matter of days. Failure to file a response or objection on time can (and has) cost local governments hundreds of thousands of dollars in taxes, regardless of the merits of the tax claim itself. An attorney will be necessary also for negotiations and court appearances required in unusually large or complex cases.

1. Some Basic Bankruptcy Terminology

Before diving into the details, tax collectors should first become familiar with some basic bankruptcy terms.

A *debtor* is an individual or corporate entity in financial distress that initiates a bankruptcy proceeding by filing a *petition* with a federal bankruptcy court. The filing of the petition immediately gives rise to an *automatic stay* that stops all litigation proceedings and collection actions, both formal and informal, against the debtor.[1]

The property of the debtor that comes under the control of the bankruptcy court as a result of the petition is the *bankruptcy estate*. All property in the estate is protected by the automatic stay. At least initially, tax collectors should assume that *all* of the debtor's property is part of the estate and therefore protected by the automatic stay. Property of the estate can be *abandoned* when it is deemed no longer valuable to the bankruptcy process.[2]

---

1. 11 U.S.C. § 362(a).

2. 11 U.S.C. § 554.

A *creditor* is an individual or entity to which the debtor owes money. Local governments are creditors for those who owe them taxes. Debtors are expected to list all known creditors on their petitions so that the court can provide formal notice of the bankruptcy filing to all parties with a potential interest in the debtor's property. Creditors not listed by a debtor are generally not bound by the results of the bankruptcy proceeding but are bound by the automatic stay.

A *claim* is the right to payment asserted by a creditor against a debtor. In other words, a claim is a debt owed to a creditor by the debtor.

A *proof of claim* is a document filed by a creditor with the bankruptcy court that formally requests payment of the claim as part of the proceeding. The tax collector's decision to file a proof of claim should be based on the type of claim and the type of bankruptcy involved. See Section 4 below for details. If a government creditor wishes to file a proof of claim, it must do so within six months (180 days) after the filing of the petition.[3] Proofs of claim are filed electronically in all three North Carolina federal court districts and must be accompanied by supporting documentation, such as a property tax bill. The tax collector should include reference to the Machinery Act interest provisions and request that interest be paid on all delinquent tax claims.[4]

A *secured claim* is a debt for which the creditor has a *lien* on the debtor's property. A lien is simply the right to collect a debt from a particular piece of property—in other words, the right to seize and/or sell that property to satisfy the debt. In North Carolina, the lien for taxes on real property arises as a matter of law on January 1 of each year without any action required by the taxing unit.[5] The statutory lien on real property also includes taxes on personal property other than registered motor vehicles (RMVs) owned by the same taxpayer in the same taxing unit.[6] Liens generally survive bankruptcy, meaning that after the conclusion of the proceeding the taxing unit will most likely retain the ability to foreclose on the property subject to the lien even if the property has been transferred by the debtor.

An *unsecured claim* is a debt for which the creditor does not have a lien on the debtor's property. Property taxes on personal property are unsecured

---

3. More accurately, the filing deadline is tied to the date of the "order for relief," which is issued immediately upon the filing of a petition. 11 U.S.C. § 502(b)(9).

4. 11 U.S.C. § 511.

5. See Chapter 5 for more details on property tax liens.

6. G.S. 105-355(a).

unless either (i) the taxing unit has actually seized and levied upon personal property to satisfy the taxes prior to the bankruptcy filing or (ii) the taxes are owed on personal property other than RMVs and the taxpayer also owns real property in the jurisdiction.[7] Unsecured claims may be discharged and therefore uncollectible after the successful conclusion of a bankruptcy proceeding.

An *administrative tax claim* is a debt that is incurred *after* the filing of the bankruptcy petition. Administrative claims are the second highest priority claims and are therefore paid before all claims except those for domestic support obligations.[8] Given that priority, it usually is in the tax collector's interest to have a tax obligation labeled as an administrative claim.

Property tax claims on real property and personal property other than RMVs are incurred for bankruptcy purposes on January 1 each year, despite the fact that the definite amount of tax obligation will not be determined until the tax rate is set later in the year.[9] Property taxes on an RMV are incurred on the date an existing registration is renewed or a new registration is applied for.[10]

For example, if a taxpayer files a bankruptcy petition on February 1, 2012, the 2012–2013 property taxes on the taxpayer's boat are not administrative expenses because they arose on January 1, 2012, prior to the filing of the petition. But if the taxpayer renews the registration on a motor vehicle in March 2012, then the 2012–2013 taxes on that motor vehicle will be considered an administrative claim because those taxes were incurred after the filing of the petition.

Unsecured property tax claims that are incurred *before* the filing of the petition but were last payable without interest or penalties within one year of the filing of the petition are considered *priority tax claims* and are paid before most other claims.[11] More technically, these taxes are called *eighth-priority* tax claims because they are ranked eighth in payment order.

---

7. G.S. 105-355(b). As mentioned above, if the taxpayer owns real property in the jurisdiction, then property taxes owed on all of the taxpayer's personal property other than RMVs are automatically secured by a lien on that real property.

8. 11 U.S.C. §§ 503(b)(1)(B)(i) and 507(a).

9. *In re* Members' Warehouse, 991 F.2d 116 (4th Cir. 1993).

10. G.S. 105-330.2.

11. 11 U.S.C. § 507(a)(8). Claims paid before eighth-priority tax claims include administrative tax claims discussed above, wages and employment contributions owed by a debtor corporation, and alimony and child support obligations.

Property taxes on real property and personal property other than RMVs become delinquent and begin accruing interest on January 6 following the year in which they are levied.[12] As a result, unsecured property taxes will be priority tax claims for a bankruptcy petition filed within one year of the January 6 delinquency date.

Consider the example from above, in which the debtor files the petition on February 1, 2012. Taxes on the debtor's boat for 2011–2012 became delinquent on January 6, 2012, which is within one year of the filing date. The 2012–2013 taxes will not become delinquent until January 6, 2013. As a result, both the 2011–2012 and the 2012–2013 taxes will be priority tax claims assuming they are not secured by liens on the debtor's real property.[13] However, taxes on the debtor's boat for 2010–2011 became delinquent on January 6, 2011, more than one year prior to the filing of the petition. As a result the 2010–2011 taxes are not priority tax claims and, assuming they are unsecured, likely will be discharged and uncollectible after a successful conclusion of the bankruptcy proceeding.

Taxes on RMVs normally become delinquent and accrue interest on the first day of the fifth month following the month in which an existing registration expires or a new registration is applied for.[14] Continuing with the above example, assume the debtor's motor vehicle registration expires in March of each year. If so, then the property on the debtor's RMV for 2011–2012 would have accrued interest on August 1, 2011, five months after the 2010–2011 registration expired in March 2011. As a result, the 2011–2012 taxes on the debtor's RMV would be a priority tax claim because they were last payable without interest within one year of February 1, 2012, the date on which the petition was filed.

Trustees are the individuals, usually attorneys with bankruptcy law experience, appointed by a bankruptcy court to oversee the administration of certain bankruptcy estates. The trustees, with the support of a judge when

---

12. G.S. 105-360(a).

13. If the taxes on the boat are secured by a lien on the debtor's real property, the bankruptcy court would not assign them priority status. But the taxing unit would still have a good chance of being paid eventually because the lien on the real property should survive bankruptcy and be enforceable through foreclosure once the proceeding ends. More on the enforcement of liens follows below.

14. G.S. 105-3330.4(b). The only exception to this rule is when the tax notice is prepared after the due date, in which case the taxes accrue interest beginning on the first day of the second month after the notice is prepared.

needed, are expected to ensure that debtors and creditors satisfy their obligations under bankruptcy law.

A *Section 363 sale* occurs when the trustee sells property of the debtor that is subject to a creditor's lien or security interest.[15] The property is sold free and clear of all liens and security interests, with the creditors' interests transferred to the proceeds. A tax collector holding a secured tax claim should be wary of a proposed Section 363 sale because the taxing unit's security will disappear if the sale does not produce sufficient proceeds. When the court accepts credit bids at such a sale, the likelihood that the proceeds will be insufficient to pay off tax claims increases dramatically. A *credit bid* allows a bidder to buy the property with its security interest in that property rather than with cash.[16] When a taxing unit receives notice of a proposed Section 363 sale, it should object to the sale unless the court makes clear that the tax lien will survive the sale or that the lien will be paid at closing regardless of possible credit bids.

For example, assume that the court proposes a Section 363 sale of Parcel A, which is subject to a $10,000 local property tax lien and a $100,000 mortgage lien held by Big Bank. If credit bids are permitted by the court, then Big Bank could offer its $100,000 mortgage lien as a bid on Parcel A. If that bid is the high bid, Parcel A would be sold to Big Bank free and clear of all liens with no cash proceeds available to satisfy the $10,000 tax claim.

To avoid similar results, tax collectors should consider objecting to proposed Section 363 sales of property on which they hold tax liens if those properties are subject to other liens and the court plans to accept credit bids. When the taxes owed are substantial, tax collectors should consult with their attorneys when they learn of proposed Section 363 sales.

A *preference* is a payment made by the debtor to a creditor shortly before the bankruptcy filing that can be "avoided"—in other words, reversed—by the trustee to prevent that creditor from receiving more of the debtor's assets than it would have under the bankruptcy proceeding.[17] Not every pre-petition payment is a preference, however, and even those payments that do qualify as preferences may not be avoided by the trustee. See Section 6 below for more details.

---

15. 11 U.S.C. § 363(f).
16. 11 U.S.C. § 363(k).
17. 11 U.S.C. § 547.

Bankruptcy proceedings can end in either dismissal or discharge. A *dismissal* occurs when a debtor fails to satisfy the requirements for continuing a bankruptcy case that are stipulated by federal law or the bankruptcy court judge. When a bankruptcy petition is dismissed, generally creditors can proceed as if the bankruptcy filing had never occurred.

A *discharge* occurs when the debtor satisfies all requirements to successfully conclude the bankruptcy case. Upon discharge, the debtor is relieved of responsibility for certain claims, usually those that are unsecured and were more than a year delinquent at the time the petition was filed. The court may retain control over some estate property after discharge, which could affect the creditors' ability to use that property to satisfy debts that were not discharged. See Section 9 below for more details on the consequences of a discharge.

2. How the Tax Collector Learns of a Bankruptcy Filing

Most often tax collectors learn of bankruptcy filings either directly from the taxpayers involved or through notices provided by bankruptcy courts to the creditors listed by debtors on their petitions. Notice from a bankruptcy court should put an immediate halt to all collection actions under way against the debtor. If the information of a bankruptcy filing comes from the taxpayer, the tax collector should confirm whether a bankruptcy proceeding is under way before continuing collection efforts. A tax collector who moves forward with collection efforts after being put on notice of a bankruptcy filing runs the risk of being sanctioned by the bankruptcy court. That said, knowledge that a taxpayer *might* soon file for bankruptcy is not sufficient grounds to stop collection efforts. In fact, knowledge of an impending insolvency gives the tax collector special authority to initiate collection actions *before* taxes become delinquent.[18]

The best method of confirming a bankruptcy filing is the online public access records system known as PACER, an acronym that stands for Public Access to Court Electronic Records. PACER registration is free, but

---

18. G.S. 105-366(c).

registered users are charged a small fee for each search.[19] Tax collectors can also call or visit their local bankruptcy courts to confirm that a taxpayer has filed a petition.[20]

3. Types of Bankruptcies

Bankruptcy proceedings are referred to using the relevant chapters of federal bankruptcy laws, all of which are found in Title 11 of the United States Code. Tax collectors are most likely to confront three types of bankruptcies: Chapter 7, Chapter 11, and Chapter 13.[21] A discussion of each type follows.

What is a Chapter 7 bankruptcy?

The majority of bankruptcy cases fall under Chapter 7, the liquidation provision.[22] Individuals, corporations, and partnerships can file Chapter 7 cases, but only an individual can obtain a discharge and therefore avoid personal liability for some tax obligations.[23]

In a Chapter 7 case a trustee is appointed to sell the debtor's nonexempt assets. A debtor is permitted to exempt certain property from the bankruptcy proceeding and thereby protect it from the reach of creditors. Federal bankruptcy law defers to state law on this issue, which means exemptions from bankruptcy can vary from state to state.[24] In North Carolina, exempt

---

19. See www.pacer.gov/reg_pacer.html (last visited Jan. 18, 2011). As of early 2011, the fee was $.08 per page.

20. Contact information for each of the bankruptcy courts in North Carolina's three federal court districts is found on the courts' webpages: www.nceb.uscourts.gov/ (Eastern District), www.ncmb.uscourts.gov/ (Middle District), and www.ncwb.uscourts.gov/ (Western District).

21. In addition to Chapter 7, Chapter 11, and Chapter 13 bankruptcies, two much more rare types of bankruptcies exist under Title 11. Chapter 9 covers bankruptcy petitions filed by municipalities, while Chapter 12 covers reorganization bankruptcies for family farmers and fishermen.

22. 11 U.S.C. § 701 *et seq.*

23. 11 U.S.C. §§ 109(b) and 727(a).

24. 11 U.S.C. § 522(b).

assets include a maximum $35,000 interest in the debtor's primary residence, a maximum $3,500 interest in a motor vehicle, individual retirement accounts, college savings accounts, and alimony and child support payments.[25] Property that is exempt cannot be sold by the trustee but remains subject to the automatic stay and therefore immune from collection actions by creditors.

Before the trustee can determine whether the debtor possesses any nonexempt assets appropriate for liquidation, the trustee will convene a Section 341 meeting of creditors. Due to their size and speed, these meetings rarely provide helpful information to creditors, such as local tax collectors. If a tax collector has specific questions for the trustee about a bankruptcy, it usually is more productive to attempt to contact the trustee beforehand rather than try to do so at the meeting.

In the typical Chapter 7 case the debtor owns no nonexempt assets, meaning there are no assets available for the trustee to liquidate (sell). In such a no-asset case, the tax collector need not file a proof of claim and likely will be instructed *not* to do so because there will be no funds available for distribution to creditors.

If the trustee determines that the debtor does in fact own nonexempt assets appropriate for liquidation, creditors will receive instructions on how and when to file proofs of claim. The trustee will then begin liquidating the debtor's nonexempt assets and paying claims according to the order of priority created by federal bankruptcy law.[26] Payment may take months or years depending on the type of assets being liquidated and the complexity of the case. If the trustee sells real property that is subject to a local property tax lien, the local government that holds the lien should be paid before all

---

25. G.S. 1C-1601. These exemptions are the same exemptions a debtor may use when creditors seek enforcement of claims in state court. Outside of the bankruptcy context, these exemptions do not apply to enforced collection efforts by state and local tax collectors. G.S. 1C-1601(e)(2). In other words, although this section provides protection for exempt assets when local tax collectors seek to enforce tax claims in bankruptcy proceedings, this section does *not* apply to collection efforts by local tax collectors against taxpayers who are not involved in a pending bankruptcy proceeding.

26. 11 U.S.C. § 507(a). The trustee will object to a tax claim if it relates to property that has been abandoned by the estate. 11 U.S.C. § 502. This objection does not discharge or invalidate the tax obligation; it simply means that the taxing unit can proceed with collections outside of the bankruptcy proceeding because the asset in question is not part of the estate.

other creditors.[27] But as mentioned above in Section 1, tax collectors should be concerned about proposed Section 363 sales that will allow credit bids.

Regardless of whether nonexempt assets exist, the court generally will discharge the Chapter 7 debtor within two to three months of the petition filing. After discharge, a Chapter 7 debtor is no longer personally responsible—and therefore immune from Machinery Act attachment and garnishment or sale and levy collection efforts—for the discharged debts.[28] The debtor remains personally responsible—and therefore subject to Machinery Act attachment and garnishment or levy and sale collection efforts—for (i) administrative tax claims, (ii) unsecured priority tax claims, and (iii) tax claims for which the taxing unit did not have the opportunity to file a timely proof of claim because the taxing unit was not listed as a creditor in the debtor's petition.[29] This last exception does not apply in no-asset cases because, regardless of whether they are listed, creditors do not have the opportunity to file proofs of claim if there are no assets to be liquidated.[30] Discharge does not affect property tax liens, which can still be enforced after discharge by foreclosure.[31]

------

27. 11 U.S.C. § 724(b). Prior to the major changes to bankruptcy law made by the federal Bankruptcy Abuse Prevention and Consumer Protection Act of 2005 (BAPCPA, Pub. L. 109-8, enacted Apr. 20, 2005), the sale proceeds of property subject to a tax lien were first distributed to higher priority bankruptcy creditors before being distributed to the holder of the tax lien. This is no longer the case for bankruptcy petitions filed on or after October 17, 2005, BAPCPA's effective date. Under current law, only creditors who hold liens on the property that are senior to the tax lien will be paid before the holder of the tax lien. Because the Machinery Act grants local property tax liens on real property super priority over all other liens except previously existing state income tax liens, local governments holding tax liens on liquidated real property are almost always paid first. See Chapter 5 for more details on property tax liens and their priority.

28. 11 U.S.C. §§ 525 and 727. A discharge also prohibits the use of set-off debt collection against the debtor for discharged taxes.

29. 11 U.S.C. § 523.

30. In a no-asset case the court does not accept proofs of claim from any creditors. A taxing unit therefore cannot show harm due to the debtor's failure to list it as a creditor and its failure to receive notice of the bankruptcy. *See In re* Bearden, 382 B.R. 911, 918 (Bankr. D.S.C. 2008). As a result, tax claims can be discharged in a no-asset Chapter 7 case even if the tax office receives no notice of the proceeding until after discharge.

31. Discharge affects personal liability, not *in rem* liability for liens. 11 U.S.C. § 524(a)(2). This distinction means that taxing units cannot use attachment and

See Section 9 below for more details on consequences of a Chapter 7 discharge.

What is a Chapter 11 bankruptcy?

Business entities seeking to reorganize their debts and continue operating must use the Chapter 11 provisions.[32] As part of the reorganization process, the debtor must submit a payment plan that indicates which claims will be paid in full and which will be "impaired" and therefore not paid in full.[33] Unlike Chapter 7 and Chapter 13 proceedings, no trustee is appointed in a Chapter 11 bankruptcy absent unusual circumstances.[34]

Tax collectors should carefully review all Chapter 11 plans for two important reasons. First, creditors whose claims are listed accurately by the debtor need not file proofs of claim.[35] But creditors who do not file proofs of claim will be bound by the amount and priorities listed by the debtor. Second, pre-petition liens on the debtor's property are eliminated after a Chapter 11 discharge unless the plan specifies otherwise.[36] This unique feature of Chapter 11 bankruptcies makes it imperative for tax collectors holding secured claims to file objections with the court if the plans do not protect pre-petition liens.

Similar to Chapter 13 proceedings, the Chapter 11 plan must provide for payment of both second-priority post-petition administrative tax claims and eighth-priority pre-petition tax claims.[37] Administrative claims must be paid in full as they come due, but pre-petition priority tax claims can be paid in installments over a five-year period.[38]

After discharge from Chapter 11 proceedings, corporations and other entities are no longer responsible for any pre-petition claims, even priority

---

garnishment to enforce tax liens after discharge, but they may foreclose on the property subject to the liens. *In re* Isom, 901 F.2d 744 (9th Cir. 1990) (tax lien remains enforceable *in rem* after Chapter 7 discharge).

32. 11 U.S.C. § 1101 *et seq.*
33. 11 U.S.C. § 1129.
34. 11 U.S.C. § 1104.
35. 11 U.S.C. § 1111.
36. 11 U.S.C. § 1141(c).
37. 11 U.S.C. § 1129(a)(9).
38. 11 U.S.C. § 1129(a)(9)(C).

claims.[39] Individual Chapter 11 debtors remain personally responsible for unpaid priority tax claims.[40] See Section 9 below for more details on the consequences of a Chapter 11 discharge.

What is a Chapter 13 bankruptcy?

Chapter 13 bankruptcies allow individuals to "reorganize" their financial obligations through court-approved, three- to five-year payment plans. Also known as the wage-earner provisions, Chapter 13 is available to individuals with regular income, secured debts of less than $360,475, and unsecured debts of less than $1,081,400.[41] A Chapter 13 debtor makes regular payments to the court-appointed trustee, who distributes those funds to creditors in accordance with the confirmed plan.[42]

A Chapter 13 payment plan must provide for full payment of all priority unsecured claims, including post-petition administrative claims, unless the creditor agrees to other terms.[43] The plan is not required to pay non-priority unsecured claims.[44] Generally, nonpriority unsecured claims, such as motor vehicle tax bills that are more than one year old, will not be paid in a Chapter 13 proceeding and will be uncollectible after discharge. Secured claims are not required to be covered by the plan either, but creditors holding secured claims will be able to enforce their liens on the property after discharge.[45] If the plan does cover secured claims it must ensure that the creditors' liens remain on the property.[46] That said, tax collectors holding secured claims should be wary of proposed Section 363 sales, discussed above in Section 1.

---

39. 11 U.S.C. § 1141(d)(1)(A).

40. 11 U.S.C. § 1141(d)(2).

41. 11 U.S.C. § 109(e). These debt ceilings are adjusted for inflation every three years. *Id.* § 104(a).

42. 11 U.S.C. § 1326(a)(2).

43. 11 U.S.C. § 1322(a)(2).

44. *Id.*

45. Regardless of the type of bankruptcy involved, preexisting liens on the debtor's property remain in effect after discharge or dismissal. Dewsnup v. Timm, 502 U.S. 410, 417 (1992); *In re* Hamlett, 322 F.3d 342, 347 (4th Cir. 2003).

46. 11 U.S.C. § 1325(a)(5).

Table 16.1.   Should the Tax Collector File a Proof of Claim in Chapter 13 Bankruptcy Proceedings?

Type of Claim	Should the Tax Collector File a Proof of Claim in a Chapter 13 Bankruptcy?
Nonpriority Unsecured Claim (pre-petition)	*Yes*, despite the fact that it is unlikely that such claims will be paid. Because the tax collector will lose all collection authority if the debtor successfully completes the plan and receives a discharge, the best course of action is to file a proof of claim to preserve at least a slight possibility of payment.
Priority Unsecured Claim	*Yes*. The plan should provide for full payment of these claims.
Secured Claims	*Not necessary*, unless the debtor or trustee files a proof of claim on behalf of the taxing unit that inaccurately describes the tax owed.[a] The tax collector can rely on its lien to enforce the claim after discharge or dismissal. But tax collectors must be careful of Section 363 sales, discussed above in Section I herein.
Administrative Claims (post-petition)	*Yes*. The plan should provide for full payment of these claims. If they are not paid, the claims will still be collectible after discharge or dismissal.

[a] *See In re* Tepper, 279 B.R. 859 (Bankr. M.D. Fla. 2002) (tax collector bound by proof of claim filed for him by debtor that incorrectly described the tax obligations as unsecured).

Unlike in Chapter 7 bankruptcies, the trustee will always accept proofs of claim in a Chapter 13 case. Table 16.1 provides guidance on whether a local tax collector should file a proof of claim depending on the type of claim held by the taxing unit.

If the debtor fails to satisfy the obligations of the payment plan, creditors can request that the court convert the bankruptcy into a Chapter 7 liquidation or dismiss it entirely.[47] If the proceedings are dismissed, the tax collector can resume collection efforts as if the petition had never been filed.

---

47. 11 U.S.C. § 1307.

If the debtor successfully completes the payment plan, the court will issue a discharge.[48] After a Chapter 13 discharge, the debtor is no longer responsible for all claims that were disallowed or provided for in the plan.[49] As a result, the tax collector will usually no longer be able to hold a Chapter 13 debtor personally responsible for unpaid pre-petition tax claims regardless of their priority. See Section 9 below for more details on consequences of a Chapter 13 discharge.

4. Filing Proofs of Claims

As the discussion of the different types of bankruptcies suggests, the decision whether to submit a proof of claim depends on the type of bankruptcy involved and the type of claim held by the tax collector. Figure 16A provides a framework for this decision in flowchart format.

If the tax collector chooses to file a proof of claim, he or she must do so within six months (180 days) after the petition is filed.[50] The bankruptcy court for the Western District of North Carolina requires proofs of claim to be filed electronically, while the Middle District and Eastern District courts encourage this method.[51] Tax collectors should include supporting documentation, such as a property tax bill, and make reference to the Machinery Act interest provisions while requesting that interest be paid on all delinquent tax claims.[52] See Section 8 below for more details on how and when interest accrues on tax claims.

---

48. 11 U.S.C. § 1328(a).

49. *Id.*

50. The deadline for filing proofs of claim technically is tied to the "order for relief," but that order is issued immediately upon the filing of the petition. 11 U.S.C. § 502(b)(9).

51. Western District: www.ncwb.uscourts.gov/credfiling/poc/main.html; Middle District: www.ncmb.uscourts.gov/info/efileclaims/; Eastern District: www.nceb.uscourts.gov/documents/proofofclaim/Fileproofofclaim.pdf (all sites last visited Feb. 7, 2011).

52. 11 U.S.C. § 511.

Figure 16A.   Should the Tax Collector File a Proof of Claim in a Bankruptcy Proceeding?

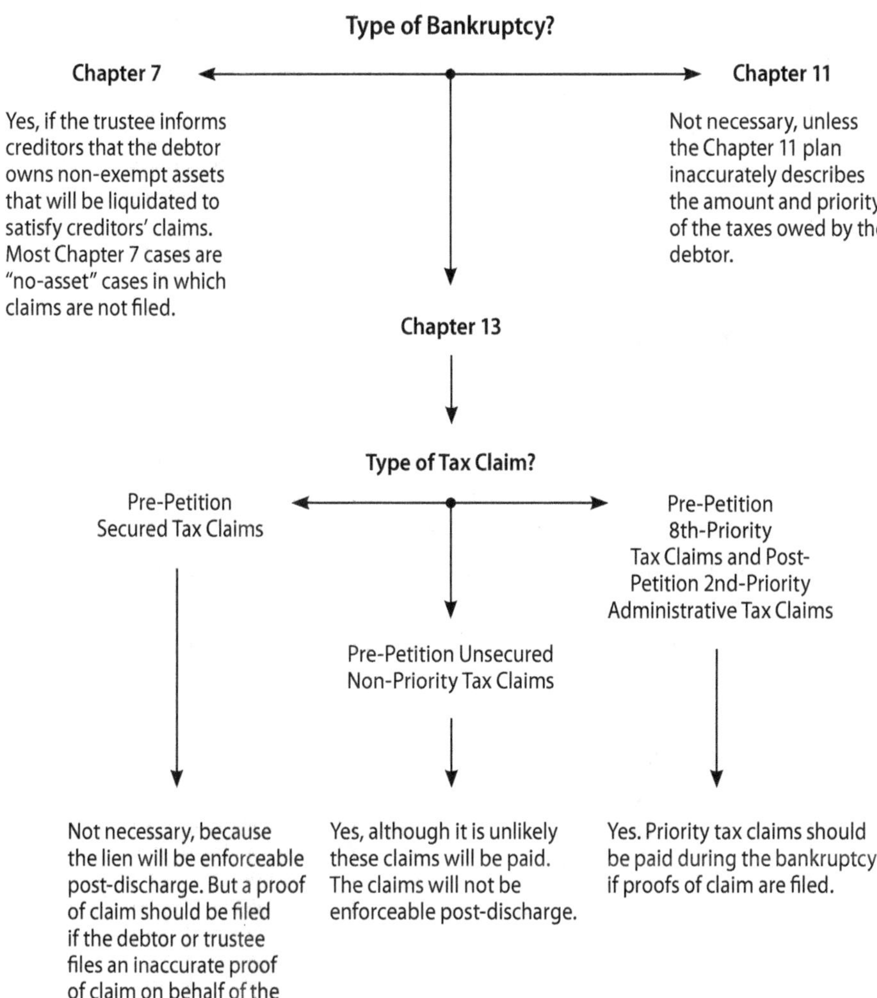

Source: Chris McLaughlin, UNC School of Government

5. The Automatic Stay

When a debtor files a petition with the bankruptcy court, an automatic stay immediately arises and prohibits litigation and collection efforts aimed at any property owned by the debtor.[53] The stay applies to all collection remedies for all claims, regardless of whether the claims arose before or after the filing of the petition.[54] The purpose of the stay is to prevent "disorderly, piecemeal dismemberment" of the debtor's assets and to permit the court to control how those assets are distributed among creditors.[55]

What does the stay prohibit?

After learning of a bankruptcy filing, tax collectors should stop all collection actions, including bank account attachments, wage garnishments, levies and sales of personal property, and foreclosures. It matters not what stage the collection action is in or when it began. If a wage garnishment is in place, the tax collector should contact the taxpayer's employer and ask that the garnishment be removed. If a foreclosure sale is scheduled, the tax collector should instruct the attorney or sheriff conducting the sale to postpone it until the bankruptcy concludes. If the tax collector inadvertently receives funds from a collection action after the stay takes effect, the funds should be returned to the court with a letter of explanation.

Even indirect collection actions should stop once the stay arises. For example, a tax collector should not ask the N.C. Division of Motor Vehicles to place a block on a debtor's RMV for failure to pay delinquent taxes on that

---

53. 11 U.S.C. § 362(a).

54. 11 U.S.C. § 362(a)(6) bars collection actions only for claims that arose before the petition was filed. But 11 U.S.C. § 362(a)(3) prohibits any action to obtain possession of any property of the bankruptcy estate, regardless of when the claim arose. Because (at least initially) all property of the debtor is considered part of the bankruptcy estate, collectively these two provisions bar all collection action aimed at the debtor for all claims.

55. Soares v. Brockton Credit Union, 107 F.3d 969, 975 (1st Cir. 1997) (automatic stay intended to provide debtors "breathing room" from credit harassment).

RMV.[56] Nor should tax collectors include debtors on the list of delinquent taxpayers advertised in the newspaper each spring.[57]

What does the stay permit?

Tax collectors are not prohibited from accepting voluntary tax payments from debtors while the automatic stay is effective. The stay concerns collection efforts by creditors, not payments by debtors. If the debtor offers payment of a tax obligation during the bankruptcy proceeding, the tax collector should accept the payment, apply it toward the appropriate tax accounts, and amend any proofs of claims for those accounts that the tax collector previously filed with the court.

An automatic stay protects only property owned by the debtor, not property owned by the debtor's relatives or property owned by corporations related to the debtor.[58] For example, if Tom Tarheel files a bankruptcy petition, the local tax collector may still take enforced collection actions against property owned solely by Tom's wife, Tina. Collection actions should cease for taxes on all jointly owned property, however. For example, assume Tom and Tina jointly own a 2006 Toyota Camry on which taxes are delinquent. If Tom files for bankruptcy, the tax collector may not collect those taxes by attaching a bank account owned jointly by Tom and Tina. But the tax

---

56. Tax collectors may request the N.C. Division of Motor Vehicles to block registrations for RMV taxes that are more than four months past due. G.S. 105-330.7. For more on this option and the collection of taxes on RMVs, see Chapter 14. If a registration block is already in place at the time a petition is filed, the debtor should work directly with the N.C. Division of Motor Vehicles to remove the block.

57. G.S. 105-369. See Chapter 9 for more details on this issue.

58. There is one exception to this rule, but it does not apply to property tax collection actions. In Chapter 13 cases, the automatic stay also prohibits actions to collect consumer debt from a person who is jointly liable on the debt with the debtor. For example, assume A and B jointly own a car and are jointly liable for the financing loan on the car. If A files for bankruptcy, the lender cannot seek to collect the car loan from B's property. Called the "co-debtor stay," this protection does not apply to property tax collections because property taxes are not considered consumer debt. *See In re Willie J. Stovall,* 209 B.R. 849 (E.D. Va 1997). Continuing with the same example, despite A's bankruptcy filing the local tax collector could attach B's bank account for taxes owed on the car that is owned jointly by A and B.

collector could attach Tina's wages to satisfy the taxes on the jointly owned Toyota.

Similar reasoning applies to corporations. If Tom Tarheel files a bankruptcy petition, the local tax collector may still take enforced collection actions for taxes on property owned solely by Tarheels R Us, Inc., a corporation owned entirely by Tom. Corporations are legal entities distinct from their shareholders, meaning that a corporation's property tax obligations are not affected by the bankruptcy filings of some or all of the corporation's shareholders. The reverse is also true: a bankruptcy filing by a corporation does not affect the property tax obligations of its shareholders, even if the entire corporation is owned by a single shareholder.[59]

In contrast, a sole proprietorship, also known as a doing business as or DBA, is not a separate legal entity from its owner. Any property listed in the name of a sole proprietorship is legally owned by the individual or entity that is operating the business. If that individual or entity were to file for bankruptcy, the automatic stay would protect all property listed in the name of the sole proprietorship from collection actions.

The stay also permits a tax collector to create a tax assessment, to send a bill for that assessment and, if the tax is not paid and becomes delinquent, to send a "notice of tax deficiency."[60] However, tax collectors should be careful not to threaten any collection actions in such notices, else they risk violating the stay. Another exception permits the tax lien on real property to arise as a matter of law each January 1.[61]

What constitutes a willful violation?

Creditors who "willfully" violate the automatic stay will be liable to the debtor for damages and attorneys' fees and can be punished with contempt of court sanctions.[62] Thankfully a collection action is considered a willful violation only when it is taken with knowledge that the debtor has filed a

---

59. For more on the enforced collection of property taxes from corporations, see Chapter 6.

60. 11 U.S.C. §§ 362(b)(9)(B) and (D).

61. *Id.*

62. 11 U.S.C. § 362(h).

bankruptcy petition.[63] Thus a tax collector is protected when he or she first learns of a bankruptcy filing after a collection action begins, as is often the case. So long as the collector immediately halts the collection action upon receiving notice that the taxpayer is in bankruptcy, the violation will not be considered willful and the tax collector will not be at risk of sanctions from the court. However, the tax collector should return to the bankruptcy court any funds received from such inadvertent violations of the stay. Whenever a court threatens sanctions for an alleged violation of the automatic stay, a tax collector should immediately seek assistance from the local government's attorney.

When is the automatic stay terminated?

The automatic stay remains in place until the bankruptcy case is dismissed, the debtor is discharged, or the property in question is no longer part of the estate. Property can be excluded from the estate and therefore not protected by the automatic stay through at least two different procedures. First, a trustee can abandon property because it is no longer valuable to the process. A tax collector may initiate collection actions against abandoned property after receiving permission from the court. Second, some courts conclude that confirmation of a Chapter 13 payment plan terminates the estate entirely or limits the estate to the debtor's postconfirmation earnings necessary to satisfy the plan.[64] Either of these approaches could permit tax collectors to use enforced collection remedies against the debtor for post-petition tax claims. But because the courts have yet to resolve this question, the safest approach for tax collectors is to refrain from *any* enforced collection actions in a Chapter 13 case until discharge or dismissal.

---

63. 11 U.S.C. § 362.11.

64. *See In re* Mullins, 2009 WL 3160361 (S.D. W. Va., Sept. 30, 2009) (discussing four approaches to the question of what is included in a Chapter 13 postconfirmation estate).

Are there exceptions to the automatic stay?

Major changes to bankruptcy law in 2005 created exceptions to the automatic stay for repeat bankruptcy filings by the same taxpayer.[65] These special rules include:

- no stay as to real property on which the stay was lifted in a bankruptcy filing by the same debtor within the past two years that the court held to be part of a scheme to defraud creditors;[66]
- no stay as to real property that was part of a bankruptcy filing by the same debtor in the past 180 days which resulted in a dismissal;[67]
- no stay as to real property if the bankruptcy court in a previous proceeding barred the debtor from filing another bankruptcy petition;[68] and
- no stay as to any of the debtor's property if the debtor had two or more bankruptcy filings pending in the preceding year and all were dismissed.[69]

If a tax collector believes that a debtor is a repeat filer, the best course of action is to consult with the taxing unit's attorney before moving forward with a collection action based on one of these special rules. Otherwise the tax collector risks sanctions for a willful violation of the automatic stay.

6. Avoidable Preferences

Under the preference provisions, a trustee can avoid—in other words, recover—certain payments made by a debtor to creditors shortly before the bankruptcy petition was filed.[70] The intent of these provisions is to level the playing field for all creditors by preventing one creditor from receiving more

---

65. See Bankruptcy Abuse Prevention and Consumer Protection Act of 2005, Pub. L. 109-8. These special rules apply to bankruptcy petitions filed on or after October 17, 2005, the effective date of the act.

66. 11 U.S.C. § 362(b)(20).

67. 11 U.S.C. § 362(b)(21)(A).

68. 11 U.S.C. § 362(b)(21)(B).

69. 11 U.S.C. § 362(c)(4).

70. 11 U.S.C. § 547.

favorable treatment from the debtor than similarly situated creditors would receive in the bankruptcy proceedings.

Not all pre-petition payments are preferences, however, and even those that are may not be avoidable by the trustee. Bankruptcy law creates three criteria for a pre-petition debt to qualify as a preference. The payment must have:

1. been for a tax that was an "antecedent debt," meaning a tax that was delinquent before the payment was made;[71]
2. been made while the debtor was insolvent and not more than ninety days before the bankruptcy petition;[72] and
3. enabled the taxing unit to receive more than it would have under a Chapter 7 liquidation.[73]

Tax payments made before a tax becomes delinquent can never be preferences because they are not antecedent debts. This is true whether the payment was voluntary or the result of an enforced collection action. For example, assume that a taxpayer pays a 2011 real property tax bill on December 15, 2011, and files for bankruptcy on January 30, 2012. The pre-petition tax payment could not be a preference because the tax at issue would not have become delinquent until January 6, 2012, and therefore was not an antecedent debt. The same would be true if the tax collector obtained involuntary payment of the 2011 taxes through attachment and garnishment on December 15, 2011, after learning that the taxpayer was about to become insolvent.[74]

A tax payment for a delinquent tax is for an antecedent debt. Nevertheless, the payment will not constitute a preference if it did not put the taxing unit in a better position than it would have been in a Chapter 7 liquidation. If the debtor owns nonexempt assets and the pre-petition payment was for a tax that would have qualified as a priority claim, there is a good chance

---

71. 11 U.S.C. §§ 547(a)(4) and (b)(2).

72. 11 U.S.C. §§ 547(b)(3) and (4). These provisions create a presumption that the debtor was insolvent during the ninety days preceding the bankruptcy petition. *Id.* § 547(f). A creditor can rebut this presumption with evidence that the debtor was solvent at the time of the payment.

73. 11 U.S.C. § 547(b)(5).

74. G.S. 105-366(c) permits the use of enforced collections against personal property before the delinquency date when the tax collector learns that the taxpayer is insolvent. See Chapter 6 for more details.

that the tax collector would have received the same payment in a Chapter 7 proceeding. If so, the payment is not a preference and cannot be avoided by the trustee.

If a tax payment does qualify as a preference, the tax collector still can prevent the trustee from avoiding the payment by raising one of two defenses. First, the tax collector can demonstrate that the payment was in return for new value provided by the taxing unit.[75] The release of some or all of a tax lien constitutes new value.[76] Accordingly, full or partial payments on secured tax claims can never be avoided as preferences because in return the taxing units release all or some of the related tax liens. Second, the tax collector can demonstrate that the debtor paid the tax "in the ordinary course of business or financial affairs of the debtor" and "according to ordinary business terms."[77] Essentially, the tax collector needs to prove that the taxpayer did not pay the tax in order to avoid paying other creditors and that the tax collector did not attempt to induce payment by offering the taxpayer an unusual incentive.

Consider again the example from above but assume that the tax collector obtained voluntary payment from the taxpayer on January 15, 2012, after sending a notice of delinquency on January 6. This payment would qualify as a preference because it occurred within ninety days of the bankruptcy filing on January 30, 2012, and after the tax had become delinquent (and therefore constituted an antecedent debt). However, the tax collector may be able to prove that the payment was in the ordinary course of business because the debtor made it in response to the notice of delinquency that was sent to all delinquent taxpayers.

The most important point for a tax collector to remember about preferences is that a pre-petition tax payment should not be returned simply because the trustee alleges that an avoidable preference occurred. The tax collector first should review the situation to see if the payment in question constitutes a preference. If so, the tax collector should then consider raising either the "new value" defense or the "ordinary business" defense. The

---

75. 11 U.S.C. § 547(c)(1).

76. 11 U.S.C. § 547(a)(2) defines new value to include "the release by a transferee of property previously transferred to the transferee." A lien on property is itself considered property, meaning the release of a tax lien by the taxing unit constitutes release of property back to the debtor and therefore satisfies the definition of new property.

77. 11 U.S.C. § 547(c)(2).

bankruptcy court, not the trustee, is the final arbiter on this issue, with the burden of proving that a payment was a preference falling on the trustee rather than the tax collector.[78]

7. Challenging a Property Tax Assessment in Bankruptcy Court

A debtor cannot challenge a property tax assessment in bankruptcy court unless the time for appealing that assessment under state law has yet to expire.[79] For real property, a North Carolina local property tax assessment must be appealed before the county board of equalization and review adjourns,[80] which usually is in April or early May. For personal property, including RMVs, a North Carolina local property tax assessment must be appealed within thirty days of the first notice of the assessment.[81] After these deadlines have passed, the bankruptcy court has no power to adjust a tax assessment made by a North Carolina local government.[82]

---

78. 11 U.S.C. § 547(g). However, the burden of proving the "ordinary course of business" defense rests with the tax collector.

79. 11 U.S.C. § 505(a).

80. G.S. 105-322(g)(2).

81. G.S. 105-317.1(c) (personal property other than RMVs) and G.S. 105-330.2(b) (RMVs).

82. Although a debtor may not challenge a tax assessment after the appeal deadline passes, presumably a debtor could ask the bankruptcy court to order a refund or release under G.S. 105-381 at any point during the proceedings so long as the deadlines in that statute have not yet run. G.S. 105-381 permit refunds and releases of illegal taxes and taxes levied due to clerical error. The statute places no time limit on releases but generally limits refunds to five years from the original due date of the tax in question. For more details on refunds and releases, see Chapter 12.

Table 16.2. Machinery Act Interest Accrual on Tax Claims during Bankruptcy

Relevant Chapter of Federal Bankruptcy Law	Secured Pre-Petition Tax Claims	Unsecured Pre-Petition Nonpriority Tax Claims	Unsecured Pre-Petition Eighth-Priority Tax Claims	Secured or Unsecured Post-Petition Second-Priority Administrative Tax Claims
Chapter 7	Accrues if claim is oversecured. 11 U.S.C. § 506(b)	Accrues but is paid after all other claims. 11 U.S.C. §§ 726(a)(5) and 511(a)	Accrues but is paid after all other claims. 11 U.S.C. § 726(a)(5)	Does accrue. 11 U.S.C. § 503
Chapter 11	Accrues if claim is oversecured.[a] 11 U.S.C. §§ 506(b), 511(a), and 1129(a)(7)(b)	Does not accrue.	Does accrue. 11 U.S.C. §§ 1129(a)(9)(c) and 511(b)	Does accrue. 11 U.S.C. § 503
Chapter 13	Accrues if claim is oversecured.[a] 11 U.S.C. §§ 506(b), 1325(a)(5)(B)(ii), and 511(a)	Does not accrue.	Does not accrue. 11 U.S.C. § 1322(a); *In re* Fowler, 394 F.3d 1208 (9th Cir. 2005)	Does accrue. 11 U.S.C. § 503(b); *In re* Fowler

[a] For petitions filed before October 17, 2005, the effective date of the Bankruptcy Abuse Prevention and Consumer Protection Act of 2005 (Publ. L. 109-8), postdischarge interest accrues at the legal rate set by the bankruptcy court. In these cases, Machinery Act interest accrues from the date the petition was filed until the discharge date.

8. Accrual of Interest on Tax Claims during a Bankruptcy Proceeding

Machinery Act interest accrues for most tax claims during and after bankruptcy. Table 16.2 summarizes the interest provisions for different claims and different types of bankruptcies.[83] Interest generally has the same bankruptcy priority as the underlying tax claim.

A secured tax claim accrues interest during any type of bankruptcy proceeding and after discharge, assuming that the claim is oversecured—in other words, that the property's value is greater than amount of the tax lien.

Post-petition second-priority administrative tax claims also accrue interest during any type of bankruptcy proceeding and after discharge, regardless of whether the tax claim is secured or unsecured.

Pre-petition eighth-priority tax claims accrue interest in Chapter 7 and Chapter 11 bankruptcies but not in Chapter 13 bankruptcies.

Pre-petition unsecured non-priority claims accrue interest only in Chapter 7 bankruptcies. But such interest is unlikely to be paid, as all other claims first must be satisfied in full.

9. Enforceability of Tax Claims after a Discharge

The bankruptcy court issues a discharge after the debtor successfully completes the bankruptcy process. Table 16.3 summarizes the consequences of a discharge under the three types of bankruptcies discussed in this chapter. The same information is presented in flowchart format in Figure 16B, which is designed to help tax collectors better navigate postdischarge enforcement issues.

Remember that second-priority administrative claims can be either secured or unsecured but must have been incurred *after* the bankruptcy

---

83. Note that Table 16.2 applies to bankruptcy petitions filed on or after October 17, 2005, the effective date of the federal Bankruptcy Abuse Prevention and Consumer Protection Act of 2005 (BAPCPA, Pub. L. 109-8, enacted Apr. 20, 2005). For earlier petitions, postdischarge interest on secured claims in Chapter 11 and Chapter 13 cases is at the legal rate set by the court rather than at the Machinery Act rate.

Table 16.3.   Tax Claim Enforcement after Discharge

Bankruptcy Chapter	Secured Pre-Petition Tax Claims	Unsecured Pre-Petition Nonpriority Tax Claims	Unsecured Pre-Petition Eighth-Priority Tax Claims	Secured or Unsecured Post-Petition Second-Priority Administrative Tax Claims
Chapter 7	Lien remains on property and is enforceable through foreclosure only. Debtor is not personally responsible for the taxes, meaning the tax collector may not use attachment and garnishment, levy and sale, or set-off debt collection.	Debtor is not personally responsible for the taxes, meaning the tax collector may not use attachment and garnishment, levy and sale, or set-off debt collection.	Debtor remains personally responsible for the taxes.	Debtor remains personally responsible for the taxes.
Chapter 11	If plan so provides, lien remains on property and is enforceable through foreclosure only. Debtor is not personally responsible for the taxes, meaning the tax collector may not use attachment and garnishment, levy and sale, or set-off debt collection.	Debtor is not personally responsible for the taxes, meaning the tax collector may not use attachment and garnishment, levy and sale, or set-off debt collection.	An individual debtor remains personally liable for the taxes. An entity debtor, such as a corporation, is not personally liable for the taxes, meaning the tax collector may not use attachment and garnishment, levy and sale, or set-off debt collection.	Debtor remains personally responsible for the taxes.

| Chapter 13 | Unless modified by plan, lien remains on property and is enforceable through foreclosure only. Debtor is not personally responsible for the taxes, meaning the tax collector may not use attachment and garnishment, levy and sale, or set-off debt collection. | Debtor is not personally responsible for the taxes, meaning the tax collector may not use attachment and garnishment, levy and sale, or set-off debt collection. | Priority tax claims should be paid in full during the bankruptcy. If the taxes are not paid, debtor is not personally responsible for the taxes, meaning the tax collector may not use attachment and garnishment, levy and sale, or set-off debt collection. | Priority tax claims should be paid in full during the bankruptcy. If the taxes are not paid, debtor remains personally responsible for the taxes. |

Note: This table assumes that the debtor appropriately lists the taxing unit as a creditor in the bankruptcy petition. If the debtor fails to do so and the taxing unit receives no notice of the proceeding, the taxing unit's claims against the debtor generally will be unaffected by the outcome of the bankruptcy. One exception to that general rule is a no-asset Chapter 7 case in which all pre-petition debts are discharged regardless of if or when notice of the bankruptcy proceeding is provided to creditors.

Figure 16B. Determining The Type of Tax Claim and Its Enforceability after a Bankruptcy Dishcharge

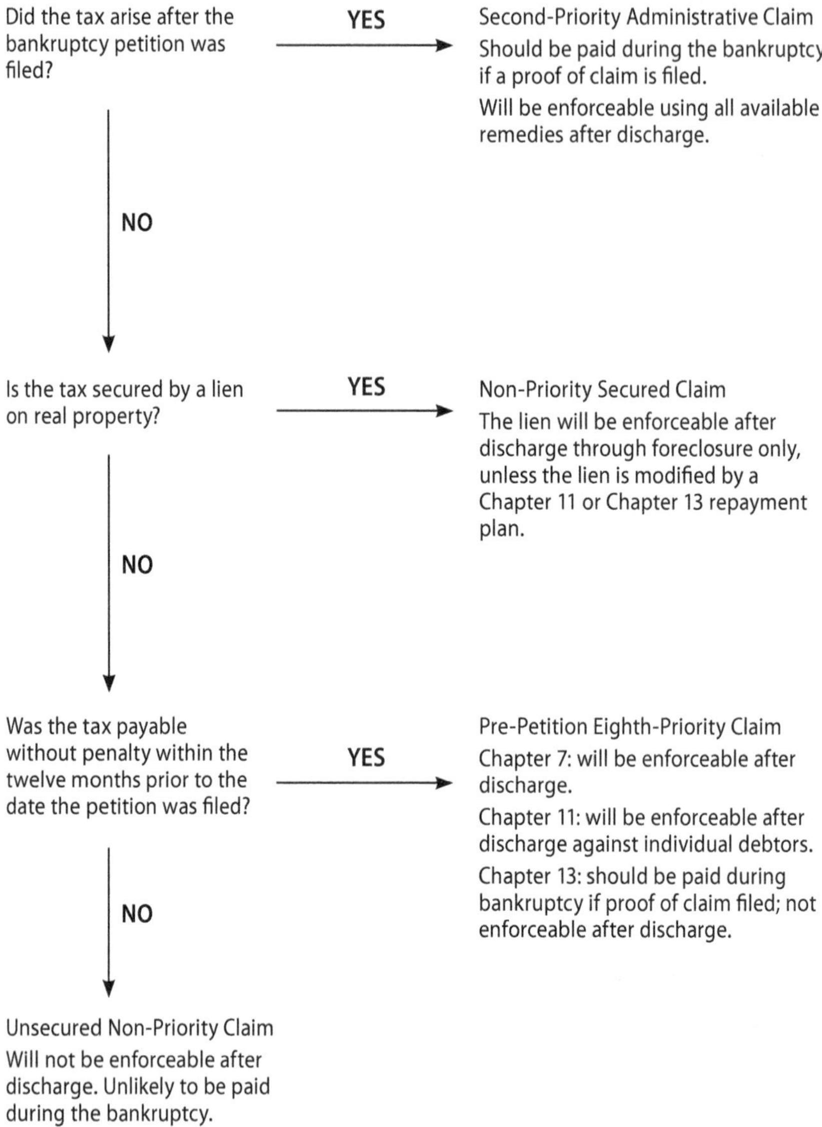

Source: Chris McLaughlin, UNC School of Government

petition was filed. Property taxes on real property and on personal property other than RMVs are incurred on January 1 preceding the fiscal year for which the taxes are levied. Property taxes on motor vehicles arise on the date an existing registration is renewed or a new registration is applied for. Eighth-priority tax claims are *unsecured* tax obligations that arose before the bankruptcy petition was filed and were last payable without interest or penalty within one year before the bankruptcy petition was filed.

If a debtor is no longer personally responsible for a tax claim, the tax collector may not target that debtor's personal property to satisfy the outstanding taxes. After a tax claim is discharged, the tax collector cannot turn to attachment of bank accounts, garnishment of wages, levy and sale of tangible personal property, or set-off debt collection from state income tax refunds.

If a tax lien on real property survives bankruptcy, as most do, that lien may be foreclosed upon to satisfy the outstanding taxes. But if the tax claim to which the lien relates has been discharged, foreclosure on the real property will be the only collection remedy available. The tax collector cannot enforce the lien by targeting the taxpayer's personal property.

For example, assume that a debtor files a Chapter 13 petition on February 1, 2011, and that the petition is discharged in February 2012. At the time the petition was filed, the debtor owed taxes on real property Parcel A for the years 2009 and 2010. After discharge, the taxing unit's lien on Parcel A will remain enforceable through foreclosure. But the debtor is no longer personally responsible for the 2009 and 2010 taxes because they did not qualify as eighth-priority tax claims due to the existence of the lien on Parcel A. As a result, the tax collector may not use attachment and garnishment or levy and sale or any collection remedy that affects the debtor's personal property to satisfy the 2009 and 2010 taxes. The same is true of the 2011 taxes, which do not qualify as second-priority administrative claims because they were incurred for bankruptcy purposes on January 1, 2011, before the petition was filed. However, the debtor would be personally responsible for the 2012 taxes on Parcel A if they are not paid during the proceeding because those taxes would be incurred after the petition was filed and therefore would qualify as an administrative claim.

Compare that situation to one in which the only taxable property owned by the debtor is an RMV. Again assume that the debtor files a Chapter 13 petition on February 1, 2011, and that the petition is discharged in February

2012. At the time of the petition, the debtor owed 2009 and 2010 taxes on the vehicle. The tax collector should file a proof of claim for both tax claims. The 2010 taxes qualify as an eighth-priority claim and should be paid during the proceeding. Not so for the 2009 taxes, which are more than one year old and therefore do not qualify as a priority claim and are unlikely to be paid during the proceeding. The tax collector should nonetheless file a proof of claim and hope for the best because, upon discharge, the 2009 taxes will no longer be collectible. Assuming the 2011 taxes on the vehicle are incurred after February 1, 2011, those taxes will be an administrative claim that should be paid during the proceeding if the tax collector files a proof of claim. If not, the administrative claim will still be enforceable postdischarge.

Chapter 17

Special Topics:
Annexations and Tax Districts

Special Topics: Annexations and Tax Districts

I. Municipal Annexations

1. How are municipal property taxes levied after an annexation?

Municipalities add territory to their jurisdictions through a process known as annexation.[1] Voluntary annexations require a petition signed by all real property owners that seek to become part of the municipality.[2] Involuntary annexations can be accomplished by the municipality without the consent of the affected real property owners.[3] In 2011 the General Assembly passed major changes to the annexation process, the most important of which is to require the termination of involuntary annexations if the owners of 60 percent of the tax parcels in the area to be annexed sign a petition in support of the termination.[4] The changes also affect the property tax implications of annexations.

---

1. G.S. Chapter 160A, Article 4A. For a complete discussion of the annexation process, see David M. Lawrence, *Annexation Law in North Carolina*, 2d ed. (Chapel Hill: UNC School of Government, 2006).

2. G.S. 160A-31 (contiguous areas); G.S. 160A-581. (noncontiguous areas).

3. G.S. 160A-33 through -54.

4. S.L. 2011-396, codified mostly in G.S. 160A, Part 7. For a detailed analysis of the law, see Frayda Bluestein, "Annexation Reform: A Summary of the New Law," *Coates' Canons N.C. Local Government Law Blog* (July 15, 2011), available at http://sogweb.sog.unc.edu/blogs/localgovt/?p=4494. These changes affect all annexations for which the ordinance was adopted on or after July 1, 2011.

The biggest change concerns the effective date of annexations. Under prior law, annexations could take effect at any point during the fiscal year. Now, involuntary annexations must take effect on June 30, the end of the fiscal year.[5] Voluntary annexations may still take effect in mid-fiscal year.[6] The effective date of an annexation controls how much, if any, municipal taxes will be levied on the newly annexed property in the year of annexation because those taxes are prorated based on the number of full months remaining in the fiscal year of annexation.[7] Proration will no longer apply to involuntary annexations because they will all take effect on the last day of the fiscal year, leaving no full months remaining in that fiscal year and therefore no municipal taxes to levy on the newly annexed territory for that fiscal year. For voluntary annexations that take effect mid-fiscal year, the effective date will also control the due date and the delinquency date of the prorated municipal taxes for that fiscal year: if the voluntary annexation occurs on or after September 1, then the prorated taxes become part of the tax levy for the *following* fiscal year.[8]

Here is how these rules work in practice. Assume that Blue Devil City voluntarily annexes Parcel A effective on August 1, 2010, when there are ten full months (September through June) remaining in the fiscal year. If city taxes on Parcel A for the entire 2010–2011 fiscal year would have been $1,200, then Blue Devil City will levy $1,000 in prorated taxes on the property for the annexation year. This amount represents ten-twelfths (or five-sixths) of the full city tax levy on the property. Because the annexation occurred prior to September 2, the prorated Blue Devil City taxes remain part of the 2010–2011 tax levy and are due on September 1, 2010, and are delinquent on January 6, 2011.

Assume instead that Blue Devil City's voluntary annexation is effective January 1, 2011. Because there are five full months remaining in the 2010–

---

5. G.S. 105-58.55(h).

6. Voluntary annexations may take effect immediately upon passage of the annexation ordinance by the municipality's governing board.

7. G.S. 105-58.10(b). Note this proration requirement applies only to real property and personal property other than registered motor vehicles, because tax years for registered motor vehicles are staggered throughout the calendar year based on their registration dates. The annexing municipality will not levy municipal taxes on a registered motor vehicle in the newly annexed territory until that vehicle begins a new tax year.

8. *Id.*

2011 fiscal year, Blue Devil City will levy $500 in city taxes for the annexation year, representing five-twelfths of the full $1,200 tax levy. Because the annexation occurred after September 1 of the fiscal year, the prorated municipal taxes for 2010–2011 become part of the 2011–2012 Blue Devil City tax levy and will not be due until September 1, 2011, and will not be delinquent until January 6, 2012.

Were Blue Devil City's annexation involuntary, it would be required to take effect at the end of a fiscal year and no proration would be required. An involuntary annexation must take effect on June 30 of the fiscal year in which the annexation ordinance is approved or on June 30 of the following fiscal year, depending on when the annexing municipality completes other procedures required for involuntary annexations.[9]

The proration and billing process for annexation-year taxes can produce much taxpayer consternation when the annexation takes effect in the middle of the fiscal year. This is especially true for home buyers and sellers because most residential real estate closings prorate the property taxes between the buyer and seller on a calendar-year basis despite the fact that property taxes are levied on a fiscal-year basis.[10] A related source of taxpayer angst can be the unusually large tax bills for annexed properties when the prorated taxes are shifted to the next fiscal year because the annexation occurred after September 1. Property owners can be handed bills for up to twenty-one months of city taxes: nine months from the year of annexation plus the full twelve months for the next tax year. Some municipalities will attempt to avoid this issue by billing the prorated taxes immediately after the annexation even if the prorated taxes are technically part of the subsequent year's tax levy and will not become due or delinquent for more than a year.

From a tax collector's perspective, the ideal date for an annexation is any day in June, as is now required for all involuntary annexations. Because no full months would remain in the fiscal year, neither proration nor shifting of taxes to the following year's levy would be required. But regardless of when an annexation occurs, taxpayer education is key to minimizing complaints and confusion.

---

9. G.S. 105-58.55(h) requires that before an involuntary annexation can take effect the annexing municipality must give the annexed property owners the opportunity to request water and sewer services, to petition for denial of the annexation, and to appeal decisions relating to those requests and petitions.

10. G.S. 39-60.

2. What are the special annexation rules for farmland?

Prior to the 2011 changes, involuntary annexations were not immediately effective for municipal tax purposes on land subject to present-use value taxation.[11] These provisions were not eliminated by the new involuntary annexation provisions. In their place, the legislature created an exception to the city's annexation authority for land used for bona fide farm purposes. In S.L. 2011-363 the legislature adopted G.S. 160A-58.54 (in the new Part 7 of the annexation laws), which provides, "Property that is being used for bona fide farm purposes on the date of the resolution of intent to consider annexation may not be annexed without the written consent of the owner or owners of the property." The term "bona fide farm purposes" includes a broad range of property, including property participating in the present-use value program, property for which the owner reports a profit or loss from farming for federal income tax purposes, and property for which the owner has received a farm sales tax exemption from the N.C. Department of Revenue.[12] The pertinent date is probably the date of the resolution of consideration. Taken together, these new provisions effectively exempt from annexation a significantly larger category of property than was covered by the prior "present use value" exception.

As a result, any land that is being used for bona fide farming purposes as of the date the involuntary annexation ordinance is adopted will not become part of the annexing municipality and therefore not subject to municipal tax *unless* the owner consents to the annexation in writing. And unlike under prior law, the annexation will remain ineffective against that property even if the owner stops using the land for farming purposes after the annexation takes effect. If the municipality wishes to involuntarily annex land that was previously used for farming purposes and therefore exempt from the original annexation ordinance, it must start the annexation process anew.

The 2011 changes do not affect present-use value property that was subject to an involuntary annexation that began prior to June 17, 2011, the effective date of S.L. 2011-363. Such annexations remain subject to the prior law that included present-use property in the annexation for limited municipal

---

11. G.S. 105-277.4 describes the present-use value deferred tax exclusion. For more details, see Shea Riggsbee Denning, *A Guide to the Listing, Assessment, and Taxation of Property in North Carolina* (Chapel Hill: UNC School of Government, 2009), chap. 7.7. For a discussion of deferred taxes in general, see Chapter 4.

12. G.S. 153A-340(b)(2).

purposes but prohibited the annexing municipality from taxing the present-use value property unless and until that property became ineligible for the present-use value exclusion.[13]

For example, assume Farmer Brown's property has been in the present-use value program for decades. In 2009, Blue Devil City involuntarily annexed territory that included Farmer Brown's land. The pre-2011 annexation provisions will continue to prevent Farmer Brown's property from being taxed by Blue Devil City until that land becomes ineligible for the present-use value exclusion. If Farmer Brown stops farming his property in 2015, Blue Devil City will then be able to begin taxing the property subject to the proration provisions described above.

II. Tax Districts

1. What are rural fire districts and special service districts?

Although created under different statutory provisions, both rural fire districts and special service districts have the same basic goal: to fund additional services for a specific unincorporated portion of the county beyond those provided to the rest of the county.[14] Taxes levied in these districts are the equivalent of general county property taxes levied by counties and therefore are governed by the Machinery Act's assessment and collection provisions.[15] Municipalities may also create special service districts; see Question 5 below.

Once levied, rural fire district taxes and special service district taxes apply equally to all taxable property within those districts, including real

---

13. G.S. 160A-37(f1) and G.S. 160A-49(f1), repealed by S.L. 2011-396.

14. County service districts can include incorporated areas with the consent of the municipality's governing board. G.S. 153A-302(a1).

15. G.S. 105-273(15) defines "taxes" as used in the Machinery Act to include "any property tax." Because rural fire district taxes and services district taxes are taxes on property, they fall within the scope of the Machinery Act and are subject to its assessment and collection provisions.

property, personal property, and registered motor vehicles.[16] Tax collectors have the same responsibility to collect these special district taxes as they do for general county property taxes. The district taxes may be collected using all Machinery Act remedies, including attachment and garnishment, levy and sale, and foreclosure, as well as set-off debt collection.

Rural fire districts, as the name implies, are created to fund fire protection services.[17] They must be initiated by a petition from resident property owners in the proposed district and approved by a majority of the voters in the proposed district.[18] The county commissioners are then authorized to levy additional taxes on property in the district of up to $.15 per $100 of property value.[19] All proceeds of this additional property tax must be used to provide fire protection or ambulance services within the district.[20]

Service districts can be created by a board of county commissioners to fund a variety of services, including fire protection, law enforcement, beach erosion control, water, sewer, and solid waste.[21] No petition or referendum of property owners is required.[22] Once a service district is created, the board of county commissioners may levy additional taxes on property in the district to fund the services for which the district was created at whatever rate the commissioners deem appropriate.[23]

---

16. The only exception is for electric-generating plants, which are excluded from rural fire districts created after May 1, 1971. G.S. 69-25.16.

17. G.S. Chapter 69, Article 3A.

18. G.S. 69-25.1. Of the resident property owners in the proposed district, 35 percent must sign the initial petition.

19. G.S. 69-25.4(a). Some rural fire districts created before 1959 are subject to a tax rate cap of $.10 per $100 of property value. G.S. 69-25.1.

20. The term "fire protection" is defined to include "emergency medical, rescue, and ambulance services to protect persons within the district from injury, or death." G.S. 69-25.4(b).

21. G.S. 153A-301. Counties can also create similar districts for scientific research and production facility services (G.S. Chapter 153A, Article 16, Part 2) and for economic development and training services (G.S. Chapter 153A, Article 16, Part 3).

22. G.S. 153A-302.

23. G.S. 153A-307. Absent voter approval, the combined service district tax rate and general county property tax used for most county services may not exceed $1.50 per $100 in assessed value. G.S. 153A-149(c). The same tax cap applies to municipalities. G.S. 160A-209(d). Not all governmental activities fall under these caps, however. For example, both counties and cities can levy property taxes to fund debt service on general obligation debt without regard for the $1.50 cap. In addition, counties may fund schools and social services without regard for the tax cap.

For more details on both rural fire districts and special service districts, see *Local Finance Bulletin* No. 43, authored by School of Government faculty member Kara Millonzi.[24]

2. What if territory is added to an existing rural fire district or special service district?

Territory can be added to rural fire districts at any time during the fiscal year if certain procedural requirements are met.[25] If the territory to be added is in the unincorporated portion of the county, approval from the property owners is required. If the territory to be added is part of an incorporated municipality, the governing board of that municipality must approve the change. Once added to a rural fire district, the affected taxpayers "shall pay taxes at the same rates as if said territory had originally been included in the said fire protection district."[26] In other words, those taxpayers will owe a full year of fire district taxes even if they are added to the district well after the fiscal year begins. For this reason, most additions to rural fire districts become effective on July 1, the start of the new fiscal year.

In contrast, territory may be added to a special service district only at the beginning of a fiscal year.[27] The governing board must first satisfy certain procedural requirements, albeit fewer than those required for changing the boundaries of a rural fire district.[28] The newly added territory will be subject to special service district taxes for that new fiscal year and all subsequent fiscal years for as long as the district exists.

---

24. Kara A. Millonzi, "County Funding for Fire Services in North Carolina," *Local Finance Bulletin* No. 43 (May 2011), available at www.sogpubs.unc.edu/electronicversions/pdfs/lfb43.pdf.

25. G.S. 69-25.11.

26. G.S. 69-25.12.

27. G.S. 153A-303.

28. *Id.*

3. How do annexations affect rural fire districts and county service districts?

Generally, the annexation of some or all of a county tax district does not affect the district's taxing authority over the annexed property.[29] The only exception to this general rule is for the annexation of property in a tax district that provides fire protection and law enforcement by a municipality that provides these same services. When such an annexation affects a rural fire district, the annexed territory immediately ceases to be part of that rural fire district.[30] When such an annexation affects a special service district, the annexed territory ceases to be part of the special service district unless the municipality's governing board agrees to allow the territory to remain in the special service district.[31] If the annexing municipality does not provide fire protection services, the annexed properties will remain in the rural fire district or county fire service district and be subject to district taxes unless and until that district is decreased in size or abolished.[32]

Whenever annexed territory is removed from a taxing district by a municipality that provides fire protection services, that municipality must pay prorated refunds of the current fiscal year's district taxes to the affected property owners.[33] The newly annexed areas are then excluded from the county tax districts for all subsequent tax years.[34] Otherwise, the annexed property owners would pay twice for fire protection or law enforcement,

---

29. Although G.S. 153A-302 states that incorporated areas may be included in a county service district only if the municipality's governing board consents, that provision appears to affect only the creation of new districts and not the continuation of an existing district after annexation.

30. G.S. 69-25.15.

31. G.S. 153A-304.1.

32. G.S. 69-25.11(2) (decreasing size of rural fire district); G.S. 153A-306 (abolishing service district).

33. G.S. 69-25.15(c) (rural fire districts); G.S. 153A-304.1(c) (county fire service districts). Prorated refunds are also required from municipalities that annex territory in county service districts organized to provide law enforcement. G.S. 153A-304.4. Note that if the annexing municipality contracts with the rural fire department to continue to provide services to the annexed area, the county must reimburse the municipality for the cost of those services. G.S. 69-25.15(d).

34. G.S. 69-25.15(a) (rural fire districts); G.S. 153A-304.1(a) (county fire service districts). G.S. 153A-304.4, concerning the annexation of law enforcement service district property, does not explicitly state that the annexed properties will be excluded from the district. But this result is strongly implied by the title of the provision ("Reduction

once to the county through the rural fire district tax or special service district tax and once to the municipality through its general property tax used to support municipal services.

The proration calculation is the same as for municipal taxes for a voluntary annexation that take effect in the middle of the fiscal year: take the number of full months remaining in the fiscal year, divide by twelve, and multiply by the full year rural fire district tax or service district tax. The resulting product is the refund that the municipality must provide directly to the affected property owners.

For example, assume that Tom Tarheel's property is voluntarily annexed by Blue Devil City in March 2010, with three full months remaining in the 2010–2011 fiscal year. Tom's property is part of Carolina County's rural fire district, for which his 2010–2011 taxes were $120. Blue Devil City provides fire protection services to its residents. Within ninety days of the annexation, Blue Devil City must pay Tom $30, representing three-twelfths (or one-fourth) of his rural fire district tax bill. This payment is required even if Tom has yet to pay his rural fire district tax bill; if he fails to pay that bill, the county retains enforced collection remedies against his property post annexation. For subsequent fiscal years, Tom's property will be subject to county and municipal general property taxes and will not be part of the Carolina County rural fire district.

4. How does an incorporation affect rural fire districts and county service districts?

A new city, village, or town is created when the N.C. General Assembly passes a bill that authorizes the incorporation of the municipality by creating its charter, the initial set of rules for the new local government.[35] The General Statutes offer no guidance on what, if anything, must occur when a newly incorporated municipality includes property in an existing county tax district. In theory, a district can continue to tax the newly incorporated areas regardless of whether the new municipality will be providing the same

---

in law enforcement service district after annexation") and by the use of identical refund provisions as for annexed county fire service districts.

35. See, e.g., S.L. 2009-431 (S.B. 539), "An Act to Incorporate the Village of Sneads Ferry."

services funded by the district taxes. In practice, the possibility of double taxation is usually eliminated by an agreement between the county and the new municipality concerning the provision of the services in question. This issue could also be addressed in the new municipality's charter.

5. What are municipal service districts?

Service districts are not limited to counties. A municipality also can create service districts within its borders to fund additional services beyond those provided to the rest of its residents. As is true for their county equivalents, municipal service districts can fund beach erosion control, flood and hurricane protection, sewer systems, and watershed improvement projects.[36] But municipal service districts may also fund downtown or urban area revitalization efforts commonly known as business improvement districts.[37] These tax districts can fund a variety of services and projects designed to improve the "economic well-being" of a municipality's core.[38]

Just like rural fire district taxes and county service district taxes, municipal service district taxes are additional property taxes levied on all property within the district and subject to all Machinery Act assessment and collection provisions, with one exception. Public service company property, all of which is assessed by the state and allocated to the local governments, is excluded from municipal service districts and is not subject to the additional taxes levied in such districts.[39]

---

36. G.S. 160A-536(a)(1), (3a), and (5).

37. G.S. 160A-536(a)(2) and (2a).

38. G.S. 160A-536(b) and (c).

39. G.S. 160A-544. The general provisions concerning the taxation of public service company property are in G.S. Chapter 105, Article 23.

Index

M